THE KAOBOYS
OF R&AW

DOWN MEMORY LANE

B. RAMAN

Lancer * New Delhi * Olympia Fields IL

www.lancerpublishers.com

Published in the United States

by Lancer Publishers,
a division of Lancer InterConsult, Inc.
19900 Governors Drive, Suite 104
Olympia Fields IL 60461

Published in India

by Lancer Publishers & Distributors
2/42 (B), Sarvapriya Vihar,
New Delhi-110016

Printed at Sona Printers, New Delhi.
Printed and bound in India.

ISBN: 0-9796174-3-x   978-0-9796174-3-0

Online Military Bookshop
www.lancerpublishers.com

Contents

Preface

This book would not have seen the light of the day but for Shakti Bhatt, a fascinating young girl, who was the daughter of Sheela Bhatt, the Executive Editor of Rediff.com, Delhi, and Kanti Bhatt, the Gujarati writer. She was the wife of Jeet Thayil, the poet.

I had met Shakti for the first time at a conference in New York in November,2002. She and Jeet were in the staff of "India Abroad", a well-known and well-circulated journal belonging to the Rediff.com group.

Shakti and Jeet returned to India in August,2004. After traveling around for a while, she joined the New Delhi office of a well-known international publishing house. A few months later, she quit the job. In September,2006, she was selected to head a new Indian publishing house.

In the first week of December,2006, I had been to Delhi for a conference. On coming to know of it, she invited me for lunch in the coffee shop of the Ambassador Hotel.

During the lunch, she told me about her job and her plans for the future. She said that she proposed publishing five titles in 2007— one non-fiction and four fiction. She wanted me to write a book on my years in the Research & Analysis Wing (R&AW).

I told her that previously some other publishers had also asked me to write on my years in the R&AW. I had said no to them since I did not like the idea.

She urged me to change my mind and accept her request as a special favour.

She was so infectious in her enthusiasm that I could not say no to her. I agreed.

After I returned to Chennai, I sat down to write the book. A few days later, I got a message from Shakti: "Mr. Raman, if you feel comfortable, may I have a look at a sample chapter?"

I sent her one. Within two hours, I got her reaction: "Fantastic. Makes compelling reading. You are very modern in your style of writing. Much beyond my expectations."

On March 24,2007, I informed her that I had completed the book and would meet her in Delhi on April 18 to hand over the manuscript after revision. She was excited and started drawing up plans for its editing, publication, marketing and launching.

But, fate was unkind. She passed away early in the morning of April 1,2007, after a sudden and brief illness. I was shattered. I lost interest in the book. I wrote it for her. I found it difficult to accept the idea of having it published when she was no more.

Ultimately, I decided that I owed it to Shakti to have it published.

What dreams for the future she had.

What a bundle of ideas she was.

How determined she was to make a name for herself in the world of publishing.

But, God willed otherwise. He called her to heaven before her dreams could be realised and her ideas could be carried to fruition.

She died young at the age of 26, but her memory, dreams and ideas should be kept alive. This book is my small contribution to doing so.

When you read this book, please do think of Shakti and pray to God that He should keep her happy in heaven.

I would not have written this book but for her powers of persuasion.

She had wanted this book to be my special gift to her. So it shall remain.

Chennai
18-5-07   B. Raman

CHAPTER I

Angry & Bitter

Throughout my 26 years in the Research and Analysis Wing (R&AW), India's external intelligence agency, I was known as a man with a poker face.

As someone, who showed no emotions or passion on his face or in his words.

As someone, who led a robot-like existence, working from 8 in the morning till 9-30 in the night—seven days a week, 365 days in a year.

As someone, who took life in its stride.

But, I was a different man that day—on August 31,1994, as I was driven home in the official car, after having attended a party hosted by the officers of the R&AW to bid farewell to another officer and me, who had retired that evening from service at the age of 58.

Anyone, who had seen me as I entered my flat that night, might not have recognized me.

All the pent-up emotions, all the anger and bitterness, which I had kept suppressed inside me for 26 years, burst out.

"BASTARDS", I shouted.

I was angry and bitter.

Not at my organization, which had always treated me with honour and generosity.

Not at my colleagues, who had always respected and admired me.

Not at Narasimha Rao, the then Prime Minister, and his predecessors, who were directly in charge of the R&AW, right from the day it was created on September 21,1968, by bifurcating the Intelligence Bureau (IB) on the orders of Indira Gandhi.

I was angry and bitter at the US State Department.

I have always loved the US.

I have always liked the American people.

But, there is one American species, which I could never bring myself to like during the 27 years I spent in the intelligence community — the officers of the US State Department.

During the one year I spent in the IB as in charge of Burma and South-East Asia before the R&AW was formed.

During the 26 years I spent in the R&AW.

My dislike for the US State Department went up even further during my last days in the R&AW.

A few days before my retirement, the chief of the R&AW told me that he had been called by Narasimha Rao for a discussion on a sensitive subject and that I should accompany him. I did so.

Narasimha Rao took out a personal message, which he had received from the Indian Embassy in Washington DC and gave it to my chief.

He went through it in silence and then passed it on to me.

As I read it , I felt like vomiting and spitting at the State Department officials. I might have done so had they been there.

The message said that the Ambassador had been called by a middle-level officer of the State Department and told that it was aware that the covert action division of the R&AW was meddling in the internal affairs of Pakistan and trying to destabilize it. The State Department officer, who had previously served in the US Embassy in New Delhi, asked the Ambassador to tell New Delhi that if the R&AW did not stop what the State Department described as its covert actions in Pakistan, the US might be constrained to act against Pakistan and India for indulging in acts of terrorism against each other.

According to the message, the State Department officer said: "You have been asking us for many years to declare Pakistan as a State-sponsor of terrorism. Yes, we will do so. But we will simultaneously act against India too if it did not stop meddling in Pakistan."

"What kind of covert actions you have in Pakistan?" Narasimha Rao asked.

"We have been actively interacting with different sections of Pakistani society, which are well disposed towards India and extending to them discreet political and moral support," I replied.

"Since when?" he asked.

"Since 1988, when Pakistan-sponsored terrorism in Punjab increased in its brutality and evidence came in from one of the Western intelligence agencies that they had received confirmation that Talwinder Singh Parmar, one of the terrorists of the Babbar Khalsa, Canada,who had participated in the blowing up of the Kanishka, the Air India aircraft, in June,1985, off the Irish coast, had been given sanctuary in Pakistan by its Inter-Services Intelligence (ISI) Directorate. Rajiv Gandhi asked us not to confine any longer our contacts to only the ruling circles of Pakistan, but to diversify them and start interacting with others too—particularly those who think and wish well of India," I said, and added: "We had also kept you informed of this when you took over as the Prime Minister in 1991 and subsequently."

"Yes. I know. But, why is the State Department talking of acts of terrorism? Can any of your actions be misinterpreted as acts of terrorism?"

"Definitely not, Sir."

Narasimha Rao thought for a while and said: "Let me have a draft reply to the Ambassador, directing him to strongly deny the allegations of the State Department. Don't discontinue your interactions. We have every right to maintain contacts with all sections of Pakistani society. We need not be worried if the Americans dislike this."

The draft of the reply to the Ambassador was the last paper I prepared before I retired. I gave it to my chief, who forwarded it to Narasimha Rao.

I do not know if Narasimha Rao sent it to the Ambassador and, if so, in what form and language.

The day after I retired, the late Rajesh Pilot, the then Minister of State for Internal Security, sent for me.

"What are your plans?" he asked.

"Sir, I am booked to return to Madras on September 20 to settle down there."

"There is no question of your returning to Madras. I have spoken to Rao about you. He has agreed that we should utilize your knowledge and experience in the North-East by appointing you as the Intelligence Co-Ordinator in that region. You have dealt with the North-East for many years in the 1970s and the 1980s. Your insights will be invaluable."

I told him I would prefer to go back to Madras. I added that any Intelligence Co-ordinator for the North-East has to be from one of the North-Eastern States and that an outsider would not be effective.

A few days later, Narasimha Rao sent for me.

"Pilot tells me you are returning to Madras for good on the 20th."

"Yes, Sir."

"But, why are you in a hurry? We want to utilize your services. If you don't like dealing with the North-East, we can find something else for you."

I expressed my regrets and requested him to permit me to return to Madras.

"If you insist. But do keep in touch with me."

As I was about to get up and leave, he mentioned the name of an official of the US State Department and asked me what I thought of her.

I told him that my impression was that she had a visceral dislike of India. I added: "Sir, she is behind much of our troubles in Jammu and Kashmir. She is the mentor of the anti-New Delhi Kashmiri leaders. She is a close personal friend of Benazir Bhutto. I had a suspicion that she had shared with Benazir the contents of some of our intelligence reports regarding the activities of the Khalistani terrorists in Pakistani territory, which we had shared with the US. We lost a couple of valuable sources."

Benazir Bhutto was then the Prime Minister of Pakistan.

Narasimha Rao said: "I know the State Department has never been well disposed towards India. Why this sudden increased dislike of India?"

"Sir, it is not sudden. If you recall, in 1992 they had threatened to impose economic sanctions against India by declaring it as non-cooperating with the US in the fight against narcotics."

"Yes. I remember vaguely. Why did they do so?"

"They alleged that there was large-scale illicit opium cultivation along the Sino-Indian border in certain areas and wanted the Directorate-General of Security (DGS) to take aerial photographs of the region with the help of an aircraft given by the US some years ago. We agreed to do so. They said that they wanted one of their intelligence officers to travel in the aircraft when it went on aerial photography missions along the Sino-Indian border. When we did not agree to this, they threatened to declare India as not co-operating in the fight against narcotics. With your approval, we stood firm in our refusal. They did not raise the issue again."

" We have to get along with them;at the same time, we have to be careful of them," he remarked and wished me farewell.

That was my last meeting with Narasimha Rao, but I kept writing to him from Madras from time to time expressing my thoughts on matters of national security. He never replied to them, but I had an impression that he did read them, because on a couple of occasions, serving officers of the intelligence community met me as desired by Rao to discuss some of the points made by me in my letters to him--particularly on the dangers of allowing foreign participation in our telecom services.

CHAPTER II

Bangladesh & The Kaoboys

Covert action capability is an indispensable tool for any State having external adversaries. Its purpose is not just collection of intelligence, but the protection of national interests and the safeguarding of national security through deniable actions of a political, economic, para-diplomatic or para-military nature. A State resorts to covert action if it finds that its national interests cannot be protected or its national security cannot be safeguarded through conventional political, economic, diplomatic or military means or if it concludes that such conventional means are not feasible.

Any intelligence agency worth its salt will have a covert action capability ready for use, when necessary. The Governments of some countries openly admit the availability of such a capability in their intelligence agencies, but not the details of their operations, which have to be secret and deniable. Others don't admit even its existence.

In India too, the IB, under the foresighted leadership of the late B.N.Mullik, its second Director, had a limited covert action capability for possible use. The covert action division of the IB played a notable role in the then East Pakistan to counter the activities of the ISI in India's North-East.

In India, one tends to think that Pakistan's use of terrorism against India started in 1989 in Jammu and Kashmir (J&K). It is not so. It started in 1956 in Nagaland. The ISI trained the followers of Phizo, the Naga hostile leader, in training camps set up in the Chittagong

Hill Tracts (CHT) of East Pakistan. It also provided them with safe sanctuaries in the CHT from which they could operate in the Indian territory through northern Myanmar.

In the 1960s, it started providing similar assistance and sanctuaries to the Mizo National Front (MNF) headed by Laldenga in the CHT. The ISI's set-up in East Pakistan also enabled the Naga and Mizo hostiles to establish contact with the Chinese intelligence. This paved the way for the training of the Naga and Mizo hostiles in training camps set up by the Chinese intelligence in the Yunnan province of China.

It was partly to put an end to the activities of the ISI in India's North-East from East Pakistan that Indira Gandhi decided to assist the Bengali-speaking people of East Pakistan in their efforts to separate from Pakistan and achieve an independent State to be called Bangladesh. This was in the wake of the widespread disturbances in East Pakistan in the beginning of 1971 following the refusal of the military regime of Pakistan headed by Gen. Mohammad Yahya Khan to honour the results of the December,1970,general elections in which the Awami League of Sheikh Mujibur Rahman won a majority in the Pakistani National Assembly.

When the people of East Pakistan rose in revolt in March,1971, the R&AW was two and a half years old. It was still in the process of finding its feet as a full-fledged external intelligence agency, with a hardcore of professional intelligence officers capable of operating under cover in foreign territory as well as across the border in the neighbouring countries.

The R&AW had inherited from the IB its intelligence collection and covert action capabilities relating to Pakistan and China. These were not up to the standards of the intelligence agencies of the Western countries and Israel. They had many inadequacies, which had become evident during the Chinese invasion of India in 1962, during the Indo-Pakistan war of 1965 and during the counter-insurgency operations in the North-East.

The late Rameshwar Nath Kao, who headed the external intelligence division of the IB, was appointed by Indira Gandhi as the head of the R&AW when it was formed on September 21,1968. In the first few months after its formation, he gave it two priority tasks— to strengthen its capability for the collection of intelligence about Pakistan and China and for covert action in East Pakistan.

A little over two years is too short a time to build up an effective covert action capability, but the R&AW managed to do so. It went into action the moment Indira Gandhi took the decision to help the people of East Pakistan achieve their independence from Pakistan.

The 1971 war against Pakistan was not a war won by India alone. It was a war jointly won by India and the people of East Pakistan. It would be wrong to project that India was the architect of an independent Bangladesh. India's role was more as a facilitator than as a creator.

Without the desire and the will of the people of East Pakistan to be independent, there would have been no Bangladesh. Their sacrifices for their cause were immense. How many of them were brutally killed by the Pakistan Army! How many of the Bengali intellectuals were massacred by the Pakistan Army and by terrorist organizations such as Al Badr and Al Shams created by the ISI! It is their sacrifice, which laid the foundation for an independent Bangladesh. What India did under the leadership of Indira Gandhi was to make sure that their sacrifices were not in vain.

The Indian Armed Forces under the leadership of Field-Marshal (then General) S.H.F.J. Manekshaw and the Border Security Force (BSF) headed by the late K.F.Rustomji overtly and the R&AW and the IB covertly ensured this. But, they would not have been able to succeed as well as they did without the political leadership provided by Indira Gandhi and the phenomenal work done by the civilian officials of West Bengal, Assam and Tripura in organizing humanitarian relief for the millions of refugees who crossed over into India from East Pakistan.

Indira Gandhi's dramatic decision to ban all Pakistani flights over India to East Pakistan in retaliation for the hijacking of an Indian Airlines flight by two members of the Jammu and Kashmir Liberation Front (JKLF) to Lahore in January,1971, paved the way for the ultimate victory in East Pakistan. When the Pakistani aircraft tried to fly round India over the sea by availing of re-fuelling facilities in Sri Lanka, Indira Gandhi pressurized the Government of Sri Lanka to stop providing the re-fuelling facilities. This greatly weakened the ability of the headquarters of the Pakistani Armed Forces in West Pakistan to send reinforcements to East Pakistan and to keep their garrisons in East Pakistan supplied.

The R&AW's role was five-fold: Provision of intelligence to the policy-makers and the armed forces; to train the Bengali freedom fighters in clandestine training camps; to network with Bengali public servants from East Pakistan posted in West Pakistan and in Pakistan's diplomatic missions abroad and persuade them to co-operate with the freedom-fighters and to help in the freedom struggle by providing intelligence; to mount a special operation in the CHT against the sanctuaries and training camps of the Naga and Mizo hostiles;and to organize a psychological warfare (PSYWAR) campaign against the Pakistani rulers by disseminating reports about the massacres of the Bengalis in East Pakistan and the exodus of refugees.

The flow of intelligence to the policy-makers from the R&AW and the IB was continuous and voluminous. This was facilitated by the co-operation of many Bengali public servants of East Pakistan and by the poor communications security of the Pakistani Armed Forces. One of the first acts of Kao after the coming into being of the R&AW was to set up a Monitoring Division headed by a distinguished retired officer of the Army Signal Corps to collect technical intelligence (TECHINT) from Pakistan and China and a Cryptography Division, headed by a cryptography expert from the IB. While the performance of the Monitoring and Cryptography Divisions in respect of China was unsatisfactory, they did excellent work in intercepting electronic communications within West Pakistan as well as between West and

East Pakistan and in repeatedly breaking the codes used by the
Pakistani authorities for their communications.

The poor sense of communications security in the Pakistani Armed
Forces was evident from the careless use of telephones by senior
officers, including Gen.Yahya Khan, for conveying instructions to
their officers in East Pakistan—without even taking basic precautions
such as the use of scrambling devices to make their conversations
unintelligible to anyone intercepting them. Almost every day, Indira
Gandhi and others entrusted with the conduct of the war had at
their disposal extracts from the telephonic conversations of Yahya
Khan and others with their officers in East Pakistan.

1971 in East Pakistan was a dream situation for professional
intelligence officers. Often, they did not have to go after intelligence.
It came after them. There was such a total alienation of the people of
East Pakistan that many were eager and willing to convey intelligence
to their own leaders as well as to the Indian intelligence agencies.
Co-operation with the Indian intelligence agencies was looked upon
by them as their patriotic duty in order to facilitate the liberation of
their country.

The IB before 1968 and the R&AW thereafter had built up a
network of relationships with many political leaders and Government
officials of East Pakistan. They were helped in this networking by
the sense of humiliation of the Bengali leaders and officials at the
hands of their West Pakistani rulers. This networking enabled the
R&AW and the leaders and officials of East Pakistan to quickly put
in position the required infrastructure for a liberation struggle
consisting of a parallel government with its own fighters trained by
the Indian security forces and its own bureaucracy. The only sections
of the local population, who were hostile to India and its agencies,
were the Muslim migrants from Bihar. These Bihari migrants were
loyal to their West Pakistani rulers and co-operated with them in
carrying out the brutal massacre of the Bengalis. However, since
their number was small, the Bihari migrants could not come in the
way of the liberation movement.

1971 also saw the coming into being of the R&AW's Psychological Warfare (PSYWAR) Division, euphemistically called the Information Division. Media professionals from the Ministry of Information and Broadcasting as well as from the Army were given by Kao the task of ensuring that international spotlight was kept focused on the brutalities being committed by the Pakistan Army in East Pakistan and the resulting exodus of millions of refugees into India.

They did excellent work, but if the international community became aware of the seriousness of the ground situation and of the compulsions on India to act, the real credit for it should go to Indira Gandhi. She was a born Psywarrior. Through her travels across the world to draw attention to the situation in East Pakistan and the bordering States of India, she managed to create an atmosphere, which would not have been hostile to the ultimate Indian intervention- —even if it was not supportive of it.

The main hostility to India was from the US and China. Neither of them wanted India to succeed in what they perceived as its designs to break up Pakistan. They had convinced themselves that what they saw as the Indian designs was not the immediate outcome of the disturbances in East Pakistan and the resulting exodus of refugees. Instead, they tended to agree with the military rulers of Pakistan that the disturbances and the refugee exodus were the outcome of the Indian designs. India's perceived closeness to Moscow under Indira Gandhi added to their hostility.

Those were the days of the first covert contacts between the administration of President Richard Nixon in Washington DC and the regime of Mao Zedong in Beijing. These contacts were facilitated by the military rulers of Pakistan. Yahya Khan earned the gratitude of both the US and China by making possible the first secret visit of Henry Kissinger, Nixon's National Security Adviser, to Beijing in July, 1971, for talks with Mao and his associates.

The developing Washington-Beijing understanding was mainly directed against Moscow, but India too, which was perceived by both the US and China as the USSR's surrogate, came under their scan.

There was an undeclared convergence of views between Washington DC and Beijing that Pakistan should be protected from India and that India should not be allowed to emerge as the dominating power of the South Asian region.

In view of the widespread revulsion across the world over the brutalities of the Pakistan Army in East Pakistan, both Nixon and Mao realized that there was not much they could do to help Pakistan retain its control over East Pakistan. Even while mentally reconciling themselves to the inevitability of Pakistan losing its eastern wing, they were determined to thwart any designs of Indira Gandhi to break up West Pakistan after helping the Bengali people of East Pakistan in the liberation of their homeland. They had convinced themselves that Indira Gandhi had such designs and that after Bangladesh, she would turn her attention to Balochistan on the Iranian border, where there were already signs of growing alienation of the people against what they perceived as the Punjabi domination of their homeland.

To counter the perceived Indian designs, the Chinese stepped up the supply of arms and ammunition to Pakistan. They also expedited the construction of the Karakoram Highway, which would link the road network of the Xinjiang region of China with that of Pakistan, and thereby enable the Chinese Armed Forces to intervene in support of Pakistan, if necessary, in future. However, this could be completed only in 1978. The Nixon Administration colluded with the Yahya regime by initiating a covert action plan for the destabilization of India. This plan envisaged the encouragement of a separatist movement among the Sikhs of India's Punjab for an independent State to be called Khalistan.

There was a Sikh Home Rule Movement headed by one Charan Singh Panchi in the UK even before 1971, but it had practically no support from the Sikh diaspora and was ignored by the international community and media. In 1971, one saw the beginning of a joint covert action operation by the US intelligence community and Pakistan's ISI to create difficulties for India in Punjab. US interest in this operation continued for a little more than a decade and tapered off after the assassination of Indira Gandhi by two of her Sikh security guards on October 31,1984.

In 1971, as Indira Gandhi and the R&AW's Psywar Division stepped up their campaign against Pakistan on the question of the violation of the human rights of the people of East Pakistan, one saw the beginning of an insidious Psywar campaign jointly mounted by the US intelligence and the ISI against the Indira Gandhi Government, with dissemination of stories about the alleged violations of the human rights of the Sikhs in Punjab.

Dr.Jagjit Singh Chauhan, a Sikh leader of Punjab with not much following, went to the UK, took over the leadership of the Sikh Home Rule movement and re-named it the Khalistan movement. The Yahya regime invited him to Pakistan, lionized him as the leader of the Sikh people and handed over him some Sikh holy relics kept in Pakistan. He took them with him to the UK and tried to use them in a bid to win a following in the Sikh diaspora in the UK. At a press conference at London in September,1971, he gave a call for the creation of an independent Khalistan.

He also went to New York, met officials of the United Nations and some American journalists and voiced allegations of the violation of the human rights of the Sikhs by the Indira Gandhi Government. These meetings were discreetly organized by officials of the US National Security Council Secretariat then headed by Kissinger.

With American and Pakistani encouragement, the activities of Chauhan continued till 1977. After the defeat of Indira Gandhi in the elections of 1977 and the coming into power of a Government headed by Morarji Desai, Chauhan abruptly called off his so-called Khalistan movement and returned to India.

After Indira Gandhi came back to power in the elections of 1980, the US suspected that India supported the presence of the Soviet troops in Afghanistan and that the Indian intelligence was collaborating with its Afghan counterpart. Chauhan went back to the UK and resumed the Khalistan movement.

In addition to stepping up the supply of arms and ammunition to the Pakistani Armed Forces and expediting the construction of the Karakoram Highway, the Chinese also wanted to destabilize India's North-East by helping the Naga and Mizo hostiles in their insurgencies against the Government of India. However, their interest in the North-East was not the outcome of the events of 1971 in East Pakistan. It began in 1968.

While the intelligence agencies of the US and Pakistan co-operated with each other in creating difficulties for India and Indira Gandhi in Punjab, the ISI and the Chinese intelligence co-operated with each other in creating difficulties for them in India's North-East. The Pakistani aim in destabilizing the North_East was to keep the Indian security forces preoccupied with counter-insurgency duties in the North-East, in the hope of thereby reducing any Indian threat to their position in East Pakistan. The Chinese aim was, in addition to helping Pakistan retain control over its Eastern wing, to weaken the Indian hold in this area in order to safeguard their own position in Tibet and to facilitate the eventual achievement of their objective of integrating India's Arunachal Pradesh with Tibet.

Even as the Indian Army—ably assisted by the Air Force and the Navy—was moving towards Dhaka , covert action units of the R&AW and the Directorate-General of Security (DGS), which also came under Kao, raided the CHT in order to put an end to the insurgency infrastructure of the Naga and the Mizo hostiles. They found that the Nagas, anticipating the raid, had already shifted their infrastructure to the Burma Naga Hills area. The Mizos had not shifted, but they managed to escape capture by the units of the R&AW and the DGS and crossed over into the Chin Hills and the Arakan Division areas of Burma. Laldenga, the head of the MNF, proceeded to Rangoon from where he was taken to Karachi by the ISI. Apart from destroying the physical infrastructure of the hostiles, the only other useful outcome of the raid was the capture of all the documents kept in the MNF headquarters, which gave a lot of valuable intelligence about the contacts of the MNF with the ISI and the Chinese intelligence. The Naga and the Mizo hostiles lost their safe sanctuaries, but their manpower remained intact. However, the loss of the sanctuaries and an important source of funds and arms and ammunition created doubts in the minds of their leadership about the continued viability of their insurgent movement. As will be discussed in a subsequent chapter, this ultimately led to peace in Mizoram and partial peace in Nagaland.

The 1971 war and our counter-insurgency operations against the Naga and the Mizo hostiles once again highlighted the importance of Northern Burma from the point of view of the security of India's North-East. To explain this, I have to go back to my entry into the intelligence community.

I joined the IB in July 1967. After my training, Kao, who then headed the external intelligence division of the IB, told me that I had been selected to head the Burma Branch. The branch was created after the Sino-Indian war of 1962 and he felt that it was as important as the branches dealing with Pakistan and China. He wanted me to acquire expertise not only on Burma, but also on the Yunnan province of China.

I continued to be in charge of the Burma branch for nearly five years – handling analysis as well as clandestine operations – and acquired such expertise that people used to refer to me as 'Burma Raman.'

After taking over, I thought I would familiarise myself with the background to the creation of the Branch, and sent for the relevant file. It was there that I saw a one para hand-written note by B.N. Mullik, who was the Director of the IB at the time of the Chinese invasion of India. The note had been recorded by him shortly after the war with China had come to an end.

The note said: "I have discussed with the Prime Minister and the Home Secretary. They have agreed that we must urgently create a Burma Branch. It should start functioning from today without waiting for a formal approval from Finance. Action for obtaining approval from Finance may be taken separately."

In order to understand why the Branch was created in such an urgency – almost in panic – I then requisitioned all Burma-related files of 1962 and the years before from the Record Room (Archives).

From the various notings in those files, I noticed that Mullik and others felt that the Indian Army was so badly taken by surprise in what today is called Arunachal Pradesh because some Chinese troops had entered Arunachal Pradesh not directly from the North, but from Yunnan in the East.

They had clandestinely moved across the Putao region of the Kachin state of Burma without being detected by the IB. The Kachin State and the Burma Naga Hills were a no-man's land in those days, with practically no Burmese administrative or military presence outside the towns of Myitkyina and Putao. The Chinese had taken advantage of this.

I then went through all the pre-1962 source files in order to understand how the IB's sources in North Burma had missed this. In those days, whatever roads were there in the Kachin State and the Burma Naga Hills had been blown up by the anti-Rangoon insurgents. The only way of moving about and carrying goods from one place to another was on the back of mules. North Burma had a large Chinese population of Yunanese origin. Many of them earned their living as muleteers.

In the year before the 1962 war, the IB's trans-border sources in the North-East were repeatedly reporting about a tremendous increase in the number of mules and Chinese muleteers in the Kachin State and the Burma Naga Hills.

The then officers of the IB had sent out a wake-up call by drawing the attention of the policy-makers to the national security implications of this development in the areas adjoining the Indian border in Nagaland and Arunachal Pradesh. But they were ridiculed and accused of nursing imaginary fears.

It was realised only belatedly that these muleteers were actually Chinese Army and intelligence officers based in Yunnan, who had taken up position across our border in Burmese territory in the months before the invasion. After the war was over, there was a steep drop in the number of mules and Chinese muleteers in North Burma.

In 1968, the Governments of India and Burma agreed to set up a Joint Commission for the Demarcation of the Indo-Burmese boundary except in the northern and southern trijunctions.

Kao spoke to the then Foreign Secretary and persuaded him to include me in the Commission under the cover of a Deputy Secretary of the Ministry of Home Affairs dealing with the North-East.

By that time, Indira Gandhi had decided to bifurcate the IB and create the R&AW under the charge of Kao. It was, therefore, decided that I, along with the Burma Branch, would stand transferred to the R&AW, but I would keep the late MML Hooja, the then Director, IB, in the picture regarding my work.

Kao, therefore, took Hooja's concurrence for my being the joint representative of the R&AW and the IB in the Commission. My membership of the Commission gave me an opportunity to travel frequently and widely in remote areas of North Burma.

The Commission used to meet alternately in India and Burma. Normally, joint aerial photography of the border areas is the starting point for the demarcation work. At a meeting of the Commission in Rangoon, the Indian delegation proposed that such aerial photography be undertaken. We added that since the Burmese Air Force might not have a plane capable of good aerial photography, we would be happy to request the Indian Air Force to do this job for the Commission and that we would not charge the Burmese Government for it. A Burmese officer could be attached to the IAF for guiding in the aerial photography mission, we said.

The Burmese replied that they already had aerial photographs of the Indo-Burma bordering areas, and that we could use them as the starting point.

The photographs were of excellent quality. Totally surprised, we asked them how they took them since their Air Force did not have a plane capable of taking such aerial photography. To our shock, they replied: "Our Chinese friends helped us. We sought their help. They sent a plane of their Air Force to fly over the Indo-Burmese border to take the photographs."

When we strongly protested against their allowing a Chinese Air Force plane to fly over our sensitive border areas and take photographs without our permission, the Burmese replied: "We will never let down our Indian friends. We did take your prior permission."

They then showed us a note from the then Indian Ambassador in Rangoon to their Foreign Office, stating that the Government of India would have no objection to their requesting the Chinese for assistance in the aerial photography.

On my return to Delhi, I briefed Kao about this, and suggested that he should advise the Prime Minister to order an enquiry into how a matter having serious national security implications was handled so casually, and fix responsibility.

Kao replied: "Raman, the R&AW has only recently got going. We will need the goodwill of the Ministry of External Affairs for functioning in the Indian embassies abroad. By raising this with the Prime Minister, we will unnecessarily be creating hostility to the R&AW in the MEA. I will mention this breach of security to the Foreign Secretary and let him decide what further needs to be done." Nothing further was done.

Towards the end of 1968 and throughout 1969, R&AW sources in the Kachin State of Burma started reporting that taking advantage of the absence of Burmese military presence in the areas of the Kachin State to the East and the South-East of Myitkyina and also in the Bhamo area—all adjoining the Yunnan border— a large number of Chinese troops from Yunnan had infiltrated into the Burmese territory in these areas and set up camps. The sources also reported that the Burmese Government had not taken any action against these intrusions.

One of my tasks as the head of the Burma branch was to closely monitor these intrusions should there be indications of these troops moving further Westwards towards the Indian border. Some of these troops went back into Yunnan in 1970, but others stayed put in Burmese territory till the 1971 war in East Pakistan was over.

Our concern was that the continued intrusions might be linked to the developments in East Pakistan and might have been intended to deter any Indian action in East Pakistan. But, further enquiries indicated that this was not so.

After the Chinese Communists extended their control over Yunnan post-1949, the surviving remnants of the anti-Communist Kuomintang (KMT) troops had crossed over into the Kachin and Shan States of Burma and set up bases there. Beijing was exercising pressure on Rangoon to expel them from Burmese territory. We assessed that the troop intrusions into the Burmese territory were meant to reinforce that pressure and had nothing to do with the developments in East Pakistan.

There was concern in the intelligence communities of India as well as the US that the Chinese might establish their control over North Burma by exploiting the weaknesses of the Burmese Government. This did not happen. The Chinese troops withdrew from the Burmese territory in the 1970s after the KMT remnants were airlifted to Taiwan.

This shared concern brought about a close working relationship between the R&AW and the US Central Intelligence Agency (CIA) in North Burma. Thus, one saw the curious spectacle of the US intelligence colluding with the ISI in assisting the Khalistan movement in Indian Punjab, with the Chinese intelligence for preventing a break-up of West Pakistan by India and with the Indian intelligence for preventing a possible Chinese take-over of North Burma. This may appear strange and incomprehensible, but such things are normal in the intelligence profession.

As the war in East Pakistan was reaching its climax, Nixon, reportedly as advised by Kissinger, ordered the USS Enterprise, a nuclear-powered aircraft carrier of the US Navy, to move into the Bay of Bengal. It reached there on December 11,1971. What was the purpose of the movement? The generally accepted assessment held that it was meant to convey a warning to India to stop the war after the liberation of Bangladesh and not to break up West Pakistan. Pressure from the policy-makers for more intelligence about the US intentions increased on the R&AW.

The R&AW felt handicapped in meeting the demands for intelligence about the movement of US ships and about the US intentions since it had very little capability for the collection of hard intelligence about countries other than India's neighbours and its capability for the collection of maritime intelligence was very weak. The follow-up action taken to remove these inadequacies will be discussed in a subsequent chapter.

Contrary to the fears of Pakistan, the US and China, Indira Gandhi had no intention of breaking up West Pakistan. She knew it would be counter-productive and antagonize large sections of the international community, which appreciated the compulsions on India to act in East Pakistan. Moreover, the only area of West Pakistan ripe for supportive action was Balochistan, but it did not have a contiguous border with India. Any Indian support could have been only by sea. This was not feasible. Moreover, any support to the Baloch nationalists would have sounded the alarm bells in Iran and antagonized the Shah of Iran. For these reasons, the idea of a possible break-up of West Pakistan was not even contemplated by her. Any intervention in West Pakistan would have added to the feelings of humiliation of the Pakistani Armed Forces and large sections of its people. This would not have been in the long-term interests of India.

Two questions often posed are: Indira Gandhi could have at least ordered the liberation of Pakistan-Occupied Kashmir (POK) and the Northern Areas (Gilgit and Baltistan), which India considers as an integral part of its territory under illegal Pakistani occupation. Why she did not do so?

India had taken 93,000 Pakistani military personnel prisoners
of war in East Pakistan. Why did she hand them over to Pakistan
under the Shimla Agreement of 1972, without insisting on a formal
recognition in writing by Pakistan that Jammu and Kashmir is an
integral part of India?

Nobody knows the definitive answers to these questions. My
assessment is that she wanted to be generous to Pakistan at the hour
of its greatest humiliation due to the misdeeds of its army and to
strengthen the political leadership of Pakistan and enable it to stand
up to the Army.

If this was her expectation, it was belied. Within five years of the
Shimla Agreement, the Pakistan Army headed by Gen. Muhammad
Zia-ul-Haq overthrew the elected Government of Zulfikar Ali Bhutto
and had him executed after a sham trial. Misplaced generosity should
have no place in our relations with Pakistan.

As the war ended, the R&AW and Kao were the toasts of the policy-
makers. During 1971, Kao emerged as one of the most trusted
advisers of Indira Gandhi. He enjoyed this trust till her assassination
on October 31,1984. During 1971, she did not take any important
decision regarding the crisis in East Pakistan and her conduct of the
war without consulting him.

The Armed Forces had nothing but the highest praise for the
performance of the R&AW in East Pakistan, but its performance on
the Western front, where the Army did not do as well as in the East,
came in for some criticism.

Despite this, everyone was agreed that 1971 was the R&AW's finest
hour. There were dozens of officers of different ages and different
ranks, who contributed to its brilliant performance under the
leadership of Kao and K.Sankaran Nair, his No.2.

Kao was 53 years old in 1971 and Nair 50. Nair was an Indian
Police officer from the undivided Madras cadre and succeeded Kao
as the head of the organization in 1977, but quit after a few months
due to reported differences with Morarji Desai, the then Prime

Minister. He was considered one of the outstanding operational officers produced by the Indian intelligence community since India became independent in 1947. He and Kao became legends in their time in the R&AW.

Kao and the officers, who contributed to the success of the R&AW in 1971, came to be known as the Kaoboys of the R&AW. No one knows for certain, who coined this title. Some say Indira Gandhi herself; others say Appa B.Pant, the former Indian High Commissioner to the UK and Ambassador to Italy; and some others say T.N.Kaul, former Foreign Secretary.

Whoever coined it, it fitted those magnificent officers, who participated in the operations of 1971. George H.W. Bush, the father of the present US President, held office as the Director of the CIA for a brief period under President Gerald Ford from November,1975 to January,1977. He became a close friend of Kao. He had heard from the CIA station chief in New Delhi about Kao and his officers being fondly called the Kaoboys of the R&AW by Indira Gandhi and others.

It is said that during a visit paid by Kao to the CIA headquarters in Washington DC, Bush gifted to him a small bronze statue of a cowboy. Kao always used to keep it on his table in his office.

He had a large replica of this statue made by Sadiq, a sculptor from Kolkata, and gifted it to the R&AW. If you happen to visit the headquarters of the R&AW, you will find this statue of the cowboy in the foyer as you enter the building. Kao, who was himself a good sculptor, was a student of Sadiq. Sadiq made the face of the cowboy resemble that of Kao.

It stands there as Kao's tribute to the magnificent, but unknown to the nation and unsung Kaoboys of 1971.

CHAPTER III

Meet Mr. Kao

The year 1996 marked the 25th anniversary of India's triumph over Pakistan in the 1971 war and the birth of Bangladesh. Many commemorative meetings were held in New Delhi attended by the dramatis personae, civilian as well as military, of 1971. They spoke of their role and tributes were paid to them.

At one of those meetings, a Bangladeshi national resident in New Delhi noticed a tall, handsome and elegant man sitting inconspicuously at the back of the audience, went up to him and said: "Sir, you should have been sitting in the centre of the dais. You are the man who made 1971 possible." The handsome and shy man replied: "I did nothing. They deserve all the praise." Embarrassed at being spotted and recognised, he stood up and quietly left the hall.

His name was Rameshwar Nath Kao – Ramjee to his relatives, friends and colleagues and "Sir" to his junior colleagues. He was the founding father of the R&AW. Indira Gandhi chose him for the honour because she as well as her father, Jawaharlal Nehru, knew him well and thought well of his professionalism. Also because he headed the IB's external intelligence division and had made a name for himself as one of the founding fathers of the Directorate-General of Security (DGS), which was created after the disastrous 1962 Sino-Indian War with American and British assistance to fill up deficiencies noticed in the capability and performance of the Indian intelligence community during the war. She made Kao the head of the R&AW as well as the DGS.

In 1982, Count Alexandre de Marenches, who headed the French external intelligence agency then called the Service For External Documentation And Counter-Intelligence or SDECE   under President Valery Giscard d'Estaing, was asked by an interlocutor to name the five great intelligence chiefs of the 1970s. Kao, whom he knew well and admired, was one of the five named by him. He praised the way Kao had built up the R&AW into a professional intelligence organisation and made it play within three years of its creation a formidable role in changing the face of South Asia in 1971. He remarked: "What a fascinating mix of physical and mental elegance! What accomplishments! What friendships! And, yet so shy of talking about himself, his accomplishments and his friends."

That was Kao in a nutshell. He gave credit to his colleagues and subordinates when things went well and took the blame when things went wrong. He was liked by the high and the mighty not only in India, but also in many other countries, but throughout his life never once did he drop or use their names. He carried the secrets of his friendships with them to his funeral pyre in January,2002 when he died 25 years after his retirement. He lived inconspicuously and left this world equally inconspicuously. Apart from his relatives, close personal friends such as Naresh Chandra, the former Cabinet Secretary and Indian Ambassador to the US, and serving and retired officers of the Indian intelligence community, hardly any serving government official, junior or senior, outside the intelligence community,attended the cremation to bow their heads before the remains of a man whose personal contribution to an exciting and significant chapter of independent India's history should have been written in letters of gold. Amends were made subsequently by holding a well-attended condolence meeting at which speakers vied with each other in praising his services to the nation.

Like any human being, Kao had his faults as well as his greatness. Like any leader of an organisation, he had failures as well as successes. His judgement of men, matters and events proved presciently right often and wrong on occasions. He was a complex mix of objectivity and subjectivity in matters concerning human relationships. He was a man of tremendous vision, but was not uniformly successful in choosing the right men and women to give shape to his vision. His humility and mental generosity occasionally rendered him blind to faults in those around him. He trusted men and women to a fault, little realising that some of those trusted by him were not worthy of it.

Despite all this, no knowledgeable person can dispute that he strode elegantly, effortlessly and scintillatingly in the intelligence world of his time. In the Indian intelligence world of yesteryears, Kao was first; the rest nowhere. He was a legend and deserved to be. The triumph of 1971, India's role in the Great Game in Afghanistan, India's assistance to newly independent African countries in building up their intelligence and security set-ups, India's covert assistance to the African National Congress's anti-apartheid struggle in South Africa and to the independence movement in Namibia, the happy denouement in Sikkim and Nagaland in the 1970s and in Mizoram in the early 1980s etc etc. Kao was there in the midst of it all – active, but unseen.

It is a pity that there is no well-researched and well-documented record of Kao's monumental role in the world of Indian intelligence. At a time, when intelligence chiefs in the rest of the world are coming out of their shell after retirement and sharing with their people their experience, insights and views, Indian intelligence chiefs continue to prefer to stay inside their purdah. Apart from the late Mullik, another towering figure, who wrote on some aspects of his days at the head of the IB ("My Years With Nehru"), no other retired Indian intelligence chief has chosen to write his memoirs. To Indian intelligence officers, the very thought of recording their memoirs seems indecent, something not done by a spook.

Serving intelligence officers do not always reduce to writing all their thoughts and actions. It is part of what is called restrictive security. The more you write, the greater the possibility of a leakage and embarrassment. So it is thought. So, they carry their memories and insights with them to the funeral pyre. History will be poorer by such an attitude.

A similar attitude prevailed in the US' Central Intelligence Agency in the 1950s. They then started a historical division to maintain on a continuous basis a complete record of the role of the agency and its officers to ensure that their memories, perceptions, insights and conclusions were available, at least to their future generations of intelligence officers, if not to the general public and the historians. Since the 1970s, many CIA officers, including former chiefs, have shed the inhibition about writing on their days in the agency. This inhibition continues to prevail in the British intelligence community though some of its recent chiefs such as Mrs.Stella Rimington, who was the chief of the MI-5 (Security Service) in the early 1990s, have managed to free themselves of it.

Kao liked the US idea of a historical division tremendously. He was worried that once those officers of the R&AW and the DGS, who had played a role in connection with the 1971 war, passed away, the nation would have no authentic and first person account. In 1983, when he was Senior Adviser to Mrs Indira Gandhi, he persuaded the R&AW to set up a similar historical division to prepare an authentic account of the R&AW's role in 1971 on the basis of the recollections of these officers before their memories faded. After Kao left office in November,1984, this division was wound up before it could complete its work. What a pity! How short-sighted intelligence officers can be! Hardly a dozen retired officers of the R&AW and the DGS, who had played an active role in connection with the 1971 war, are still alive. After they disappear, a valuable part of the history of Indian intelligence saved in their memory, but not reduced to writing would be lost.

After 1996, a great admirer of Kao in the Indian Foreign Service persuaded him to leave for future generations his first person account of some aspects of his association with the world of intelligence. In the months before his death, he spent a few hours every day transferring his memory into a tape-recorder. The tapes were transcribed and he personally corrected the transcripts. The tapes and the transcripts have been left by him in the custody of a prestigious non-governmental organisation of New Delhi to which he was close with the wish that they should be made public only some years after his death. It is hoped these are preserved carefully. It ought to be a precious part of the history of independent India.

We have no sense of history and can be shockingly negligent in preserving it. Before ordering the Indian Army into the Golden Temple at Amritsar in June 1984, Indira Gandhi, through intermediaries, had long hours of secret negotiations with Sikh leaders — some extremists, some not — to reach a negotiated solution to their grievances. The negotiations in India were held on her behalf by Rajiv Gandhi and two of his close associates and those abroad by Kao, who took me along with him. Indira Gandhi was keen that a record of those negotiations should be kept so that history would know how desperately and in vain she had tried for a negotiated solution, before she reluctantly sent the army inside the Golden Temple. This task was entrusted to me. I had all these negotiations secretly recorded and spent endless hours transcribing them. When I retired on August 31,1994, I had handed over these records for safe custody in the archives of the organization. Today, 23 years later, nobody knows where those records of historical importance are.

CHAPTER IV

India's North-East

Ever since 1956, the Naga hostiles under the leadership of the late Phizo were in touch with Pakistan's ISI.

The ISI supported their struggle for independence and provided them with funds, training and arms and ammunition. It allowed them to set up sanctuaries and training camps in the Chittagong Hill Tracts (CHT) of East Pakistan. Between 1956 and 1967, many gangs of Naga hostiles went to the CHT for being trained by the ISI and then returned with arms and ammunition. They used to cross over into the Somra Tract of the Burma Naga Hills, move down south via Burma's Upper Chindwin District and Chin Hills Special Division and then cross over into East Pakistan. They used to follow the same route for their return journey.

The Burmese Army had no effective presence in the Burma Naga Hills and hence was not in a position to prevent them from using the Somra Tract. However, it had a better control over the Upper Chindwin District and the Chin Hills Special Division and could have, therefore, prevented them from moving to East Pakistan and returning from there with arms and ammunition. But, it did not do so. In fact, there was collusion between the Burmese Army officers posted in these areas and the Naga hostiles. In return for cash payments made by the hostiles and other gifts, the local Burmese Army officers used to close their eyes to this to and fro traffic.

Indira Gandhi and her then Foreign Minister, the late M.C.Chagla, (November 1966 to September, 1967) had repeatedly taken this up with the Burmese authorities in Rangoon. The Burmese authorities denied knowledge of such traffic through their territory and promised to stop it if it was correct, but there was no follow-up action. Indira Gandhi even offered to send Indian troops into the Burmese territory to disrupt the Naga movements to and from East Pakistan, if the Burmese experienced difficulty in doing so. They did not agree to this. They were worried that if they agreed to let the Indian troops operate in their territory against the Naga hostiles, they might face pressure from Beijing to let the Chinese troops similarly act against the KMT remnants, which had crossed over from Yunnan into the Shan State of Burma and were posing a headache for the Chinese Army's border posts.

Till around 1967, the Indian Naga hostiles avoided any fraternization with the Burmese Nagas lest this create difficulties in their relations with the Burmese Army. The position changed in 1967 after the Indian Naga hostiles joined hands with sections of the Burmese Nagas and the two called for a Greater Nagaland, consisting of the Naga majority areas on both sides of the Indo-Burmese border. This created serious concern in Rangoon and the Burmese Army headquarters in Rangoon asked its field units to stop the use of the Burmese territory by the Indian Naga hostiles for going to East Pakistan. They did so effectively, killing a large number of Naga hostiles, who tried to use the Burmese territory.

This disrupted the training of the Indian Naga hostiles by the ISI in the CHT. However, the Naga hostiles continued to maintain their sanctuaries and administrative infrastructure in the CHT. Small groups of hostiles managed to go to the CHT through the Indian territory in Manipur and Mizoram for specialized training and for talks with the officers of the ISI.

The leaders of the Naga hostiles, who were already in contact with officials of the Chinese intelligence based in Dhaka, sought Chinese help for training and arms and ammunition. The Chinese agreed to train them in camps in Yunnan. From October, 1968, the Naga hostiles started going to Yunnan via the Burma Naga Hills and the Kachin State of Burma for training and the procurement of arms and ammunition. Their traffic through the Kachin State was facilitated by the fact that the Burmese Army had no control over this area except in big towns such as Putao and Myitkyina. Isaac Swu and Thuingaleng Muivah, the present Bangkok-based leaders of the National Socialist Council of Nagaland (NSCN), and self-styled Gen. Mowu Angami, who headed the so-called army of the "Naga Federal Government" (NFG) as the organization of the hostiles was known, traveled with the first gang. Thereafter, a number of other gangs went to Yunnan by the same route.

There was a delay in the commencement of the training by the Chinese. This was because the Chinese imposed a condition that the training syllabus would include classes in Marxism and Mao's Thoughts. The gangs were accompanied by Naga pastors for holding the Sunday prayers and for conducting Bible classes. The Chinese were opposed to this and insisted that the pastors should go back to Nagaland. They seized from the hostiles all the copies of the Bible held by them. The Naga hostiles were reluctant to accept these conditions. This stalemate lasted several weeks. While Isaac Swu and Muivah were inclined to accept the Chinese conditions, the other leaders were not. Some of the leaders were taken to Beijing for talks with senior officials of the Chinese intelligence. Ultimately, it was the Chinese who gave in and dropped their conditions. The training started.

The IB and the R&AW vied with one another in reporting about the departure of one gang after another to Yunnan for training. Many of their reports came from tribal sources in North Burma, who were not known for the accuracy of their observation and reporting. Some reports of the R&AW came from monitored intercepts of the Naga hostiles and the Burmese Army. Some American Baptist missionaries who were living in the Kachin State under the protection of the Kachin Independence Army (KIA) and the KMT remnants, added to the confusion by sending alarming reports to the IB and the R&AW through couriers.

The position was so confusing and even alarming that the Joint Intelligence Committee (JIC) of the Government of India, which was responsible for assessing the intelligence inputs, asked the IB and the R&AW to set up a joint team to reconcile the reporting of the two organizations and come out with an agreed assessment.

In 1969,after re-examining all their reports, the IB and the R&AW jointly assessed that a total of 12 gangs with about 2100 members had managed to go to Yunnan. When this joint assessment came up before the JIC for consideration, Field Marshal Sam Manekshaw (then a Lt.General in charge of the Eastern and the North-Eastern sector) and Brig. M.N. Batra, the then Director of Military Intelligence (DMI), appeared before the JIC and challenged the assessment of the two civilian agencies. They contended that not more than three or four Naga gangs with a total strength of not more than about 450 had gone to Yunnan. The representatives of the Ministry of Home Affairs, the Ministry of Defence, the Ministry of External Affairs, the Air Force and the Navy supported the assessment of the IB and the R&AW.

Manekshaw said that if such a large number had gone to Yunnan as claimed by the IB and the R&AW, the local villagers and the administration would have known, but they had no idea of such a large movement. Even after hearing his arguments, the JIC decided to stand by the IB and the R&AW and accept their assessment. On the advice of Manekshaw, the Army refused to accept the assessment and insisted on appending a minute of dissent, giving its assessment.

Some months later, these hostiles returned from Yunnan after completing their training. The Burmese Army and the Indian Army through co-ordinated action managed to kill or capture many of the hostiles trained by China. Among those captured was Mowu Angami. A joint team of interrogators, consisting of representatives of the IB, the R&AW and the Directorate of Military Intelligence, was set up to interrogate the captured hostiles. I was in this team. Their interrogation revealed that Manekshaw was right and that the IB and the R&AW were wrong.

Manekshaw used to contend that the civilian intelligence agencies tended to over-assess threats in order to protect themselves should something go wrong and that this often led to over-reaction by the security forces making a situation even more difficult to handle than it was. However, it must be said in defence of the IB and the R&AW that their over-assessment was not deliberate. It was due to a superficial examination of the source reports emanating from trans-border tribal sources. Many of them, while apparently referring to the movement of the same gangs across the Kachin State, had given different dates, different place names and different strengths. Each of these reports was mistakenly taken by the agencies as indicating the movement of a separate gang. This was not so.

The disruption of the Naga traffic to Yunnan by the Indian and Burmese armies acting in co-ordination in 1969-70 and the disruption of their sanctuaries and infrastructure in the CHT by the clandestine units of the R&AW and the DGS during the 1971 war made many sections of the Naga hostiles— particularly those who felt uncomfortable with the Chinese attempts to brainwash the Nagas in Yunnan— realize the futility of continued insurgency against the Government of India. They decided to end the insurgency by accepting the Shillong Agreement of 1975. Those sections, which let themselves be influenced by the Chinese indoctrination and who are now in the NSCN, have not yet given up the insurgency. However, they have been observing a cease-fire and negotiating with the Government of India.

The Mizo National Front (MNF) established contact with the ISI in East Pakistan in the 1960s. As it did in the case of the Naga hostiles, the ISI allowed the MNF too to establish sanctuaries in the CHT and provided it with funds, training and arms and ammunition. The MNF gangs used to cross over into East Pakistan either directly across Indian territory or through Burmese territory in the Chin Hills Special Division. The stepped up activities of the Burmese Army in the Chin Hills area to disrupt the Naga traffic did not create any difficulties for the MNF since it had the option of directly crossing over through Indian territory.

Like the Naga hostiles, the MNF too was in touch with Chinese intelligence officers based in Dhaka and Laldenga himself had visited

Beijing to seek Chinese training and arms assistance. The Chinese were prepared to help if the Mizos were able to reach Yunnan via North Burma. The Mizos faced difficulty in going across to Yunnan since they had to traverse the Chin Hills Special Division and the Upper Chindwin District, where the Burmese Army had a better presence than in the Burma Naga Hills and the Kachin State. As a result, the MNF had to remain satisfied with the training of its cadres by the ISI in the CHT.

The raids by the clandestine units of the R&AW and the DGS in the CHT during the 1971 war destroyed the MNF sanctuaries there, but did not result in many captures or killings. The survivors crossed over into Burma or Mizoram and went underground. Laldenga himself fled to West Pakistan via Rangoon.

The liberation of Bangladesh deprived the MNF of its traditional sanctuaries. Laldenga was very uncomfortable in Pakistan and developed a dislike for the ISI officers, who were handling him. He realized the futility of continuing the insurgency against the Government of India and expressed his desire for talks if he was helped to get out of Pakistan. He was worried that if the ISI came to know of his intention to talk to the Indian authorities, it might prevent him from leaving Pakistan. He was advised to cross over into Afghanistan and reach Geneva. He claimed that he had a large bank balance in Pakistan and was worried that if he withdrew the amount, that might alert the ISI about his plans to leave. He, therefore, said that he would leave without this money and wanted an assurance that this amount would be later re-imbursed to him. That assurance was given.

He ultimately managed to reach Geneva in 1975. A joint team of the R&AW and the IB started talking to him in Geneva in order to pave the way for formal negotiations. The talks were proceeding slowly, but satisfactorily. Despite her preoccupation with the enforcement of the State of Emergency proclaimed by her in June,1975, Indira Gandhi managed to find the time to keep track of the talks and guide the IB and the R&AW.

The defeat of Indira Gandhi in the elections of 1977and the coming into power of a coalition Government headed by Morarji Desai as the Prime Minister practically brought the talks to an end. Laldenga was annoyed by the attitude of Charan Singh, the then Home Minister, to him and the MNF. Charan Singh reportedly doubted the wisdom of holding talks with Laldenga, who, according to Charan Singh, had been waging a war against India. The talks were discontinued. Laldenga took up residence in the UK. Since the Government of India had impounded his Indian passport,he found himself without any travel document. Some Baptist missionaries living in the UK persuaded the British authorities to issue British travel documents to him and his wife to enable them to travel to other countries to seek support for the Mizo cause. They also gave him money to meet the expenditure on their stay in the UK and their travel to other countries.

After Indira Gandhi came back to power following the elections of 1980, she initially did not have time to pick up the threads of the Mizo problem. She was preoccupied with the developments in Bangladesh and Afghanistan.The outbreak of terrorism in Punjab also took away a lot of her time. In 1983, she got herself briefed on the developments relating to Mizoram when she was out of power. She requested Kao, who had come out of retirement and re-joined the Cabinet Secretariat as her Senior Adviser, to re-establish contact with Laldenga in the UK and persuade him to shift to New Delhi and hold talks with the late G.Parthasarathi, whom she designated as her special representative for holding talks with him

At a meeting convened by her at which the decision to resume talks with him was taken, there was opposition to the proposal from some of the senior officials of the Government of India. They pointed out that Laldenga and his wife had become holders of British travel documents, which, for all practical purposes, made them into British citizens and asked how could the Government of India hold talks with someone holding a foreign travel document on the future of a portion of Indian territory.

Indira Gandhi rejected their reservations and pointed out that it was the Government of India, which had impounded their Indian passports and thereby forced them to seek British travel documents. They did not renounce their Indian citizenship. She added: "Without talks with Laldenga, there cannot be peace and a political solution in Mizoram. We have to talk to him, whatever be the travel document held by him."

A similar situation arose in 1990 when an Indian Kashmiri leader living in Europe, but holding a foreign travel document sought talks with the Government of India. George Fernandes, who was dealing with the Kashmir issue in the Cabinet of V.P.Singh, convened a meeting to discuss whether a representative of the Government of India should meet him. There was opposition from some of the senior officials on the ground that the Kashmiri leader held a foreign travel document. I narrated to Fernandes how Indira Gandhi had reacted in 1983 to similar objections in the case of Laldenga. He immediately gave instructions that someone should meet the Kashmiri leader without worrying about what travel document he held. However, nothing useful came out of this meeting, whereas Indira Gandhi's decision to resume talks with Laldenga paid rich dividends and led to peace in Mizoram.

At the request of Kao, the R&AW, then headed by G.C.Saxena, re-established contact with Laldenga and after three meetings persuaded him to shift to New Delhi and hold negotiations with G.Parthasarathi. After he shifted, Indira Gandhi again got pre-occupied with dealing with the problem posed by terrorism in Punjab and with the sequel to the raid of the Indian Army in the Golden Temple at Amritsar, which came to be called Operation Blue Star. This operation tragically led to her assassination on October 31,1984. As a result, she did not have much time for Laldenga and the Mizo problem. Rajiv Gandhi, who succeeded Indira Gandhi as the Prime Minister, too had other preoccupations.The Mizo problem and talking to Laldenga were not his first priority.

Laldenga started getting impatient and feeling ignored. He wanted to go back to London. He was persuaded to stay on and be patient.

His negotiations with G.Parthasarathi ultimately led to a solution of
the Mizo problem. He gave up the demand for Mizo independence
and accepted a solution within the Indian Constitution. Laldenga
became the Chief Minister of the State of Mizoram. He was keen that
a retired Army Brigadier in the R&AW, who had initially established
contact with him and helped him to escape to Geneva from Pakistan,
should be appointed the Lt.Governor of Mizoram by Rajiv Gandhi.
This officer and an officer of the IB had also held most of the initial
talks with Laldenga after he had escaped to Geneva in 1975. The
retired Brigadier was not interested. He ultimately rose to be the
No.2 in the R&AW and retired in 1979.

Thus, the 1971 war and the exit of Pakistan from its eastern
wing brought about a partial peace in Nagaland and total peace in
Mizoram. One thought one saw the beginning of an era of peace
and development in our North-East. Our hopes were belied. The ISI
managed to stage a come-back in Bangladesh after the assassination
of Sheikh Mujibur Rahman in August 1975 and the capture of power
by a group of Bangladeshi Army officers and their political supporters
not well disposed towards India. Bangladesh became a hub of anti-
Indian activities as East Pakistan was before 1971. The post-1980
insurgencies of sections of the tribals of Tripura and separatist groups
in Assam such as the United Liberation Front of Assam (ULFA) were
exploited by anti-Indian elements in the Bangladesh leadership and
administration and their Pakistani supporters to make India bleed
once again in the North-East.

We were back to where we were before 1971. In the place of the
Naga and Mizo organizations, insurgent organizations from Tripura
and Assam started operating from sanctuaries in the CHT with
financial, training and arms assistance provided by the Bangladesh
intelligence and its ISI collaborators. The CIA and the ISI sponsored
jihad against the Soviet troops in Afghanistan in the 1980s did not
leave Bangladesh untouched. The 1980s and the 1990s saw the
beginning of the revival of Islamic fundamentalist organizations
such as the Jamaat-e-Islami and others and the coming into being
of pan-Islamic jihadi terrorist organizations such as the Harkat-ul-

Jihad-al-Islami (HUJI) in Bangladesh territory. Bangladesh became as serious a source of worry to India's national security managers after 1975 as East Pakistan was before 1971.

A nuclear-armed Pakistan and a Bangladesh ill-disposed towards India became the ultimate outcome of the war of 1971. What contributed to the decline of the Indian influence and the goodwill towards India in Bangladesh? Mishandling by the political leadership? A sense of self-complacency in the national security bureaucracy? Misreading of the situation in Bangladesh and its people by the Indian intelligence, particularly the R&AW? A certain arrogance in the attitude of Indian officials towards their counterparts in Bangladesh? A lack of attention to the sensitivities of the Bangladesh leaders and people? The image of the Ugly Indian arising therefrom? Probably, a mix of all of them.

Indira Gandhi realized the importance of withdrawing from Bangladesh as quickly as we could after its liberation and refraining from playing up the role of the Indian Armed Forces in the liberation of Bangladesh. She knew that any attempt to create an impression that Bangladesh owed its independence to India would prove counter-productive and create resentment in Bangladesh. But, one cannot say the same thing about our armed forces and bureaucracy. Even today, 36 years later, we tend to play up our role and hardly highlight the role of the people of Bangladesh and the sacrifices made by them.

CHAPTER V

The Foreign Hand

The 1971 war highlighted two major deficiencies of the R&AW. The first was its poor capability for the collection of maritime intelligence in the Indian Ocean region. The second was its lack of capability for the collection of human (HUMINT) and technical intelligence (TECHINT) about the US and its activities directed against India.

The hostile attitude of the then US President Richard Nixon and his National Security Adviser Henry Kissinger to India, their ill-concealed attempts to prevent an Indian victory, their perceived collusion with China and their exploitation of Dr. Jagjit Singh Chauhan and other Khalistani elements to create embarrassment for India convinced Indira Gandhi that after Pakistan and China, the US should receive the priority attention of the R&AW.

Despite the resignation of Nixon in 1974 in the wake of the Watergate scandal, she felt that there was no change in the US hostility to India. She was further convinced that the US hostility was not only to India, but also to her as the Indian leader. She feared that the US intelligence was trying to destabilize her Government as a punishment for her action in East Pakistan. She started seeing the hand of the Central Intelligence Agency (CIA) everywhere— in the setting aside of her election to the Lok Sabha, in the mass movement against her started by Jai Prakash Narain, in her defeat in the elections of 1977, in the allegations made by the Government of Morarji Desai that her party had accepted money from a French oil company, in the various enquiries ordered by the Morarji Desai

Government against her and Sanjay Gandhi, her son, and in the outbreak of terrorism in Punjab.

Her fears were not totally imaginary. Between 1971 and her assassination in October,1984, the PSYWAR Division of the CIA mounted a vicious disinformation campaign against her projecting her as a Soviet surrogate. All sorts of false stories regarding her were disseminated through compliant foreign journalists. These stories alleged that she had agreed to give base facilities to the Soviet Navy in the Andaman and Nicobar Islands and in Vizag, that a large number of Soviet military officers were attached to the Indian Armed Forces in various capacities, that experts from the KGB, the Soviet intelligence agency, had played a role during Operation Blue Star in June 1984, when the Indian Army raided the Golden Temple in Amritsar to flush out the terrorists etc.

The CIA's disinformation campaign against Indira Gandhi was at its height between 1971 and 1977. It was discontinued between 1977 and 1980 when she was out of power, but even during this period, the CIA had a piece of disinformation about the Congress party accepting money from a French oil company during the Emergency planted on the Morarji Desai Government through a retired Indian military officer living in Europe. An enquiry by the Central Bureau of Investigation (CBI) into this allegation ordered by the Morarji Desai Government could not prove it.

After Indira Gandhi returned to power in 1980, the disinformation campaign against her was revived. Whereas before 1977, the disinformation campaign was triggered off by her actions in Bangladesh and by the Pokhran I nuclear test of 1974, the post-1980 disinformation campaign was caused by what the US perceived as the Indian support to Moscow on the Afghanistan issue and by US suspicion that the R&AW was collaborating with the Khad, the Afghan intelligence agency, and the KGB against US interests.

Dr.Chauhan, who had practically suspended his Khalistan movement after Indira Gandhi was defeated in the elections of 1977 and returned to India, went back to London and revived the

movement in 1980. Starting from 1981, there was a mushrooming
of Khalistani organizations—many of them operating from the UK,
the US and Canada. Dr.Chauhan had easy access to Congressional
committees and members and made allegations of violations of the
human rights of the Sikhs. He also carried on propaganda regarding
alleged military links between India and the USSR.

Worried by the increasing fraternization of elements close to the
Ronald Reagan administration with the Khalistani and other anti-
Indian elements, Kao, in his new post-retirement capacity as the
Senior Adviser to Indira Gandhi in the Cabinet Secretariat, visited
Washington DC and met George Bush, the father of the present
President, who was the Vice-President under Reagan. Kao had
known Bush when the latter headed the CIA in the 1970s. He tried
to remove US misapprehensions about India's policy on Afghanistan
and expressed his concern to Bush about the attention given in
Washington DC to the Khalistani elements. This meeting led to an
improvement in the atmosphere and the Khalistani elements found
that they were no longer as welcome in Washington DC as they were
before. Indira Gandhi's warm meetings with Reagan at Cancun in
Mexico in October,1981, and at Washington DC in July,1982, also
contributed to the improvement in the atmosphere.

Despite this, suspicion persisted in the Congress Party that the
CIA's malevolence towards Indira Gandhi had not ceased. There was
even suspicion of a possible CIA hand in her assassination by two of
her Sikh security guards in October 1984. After her assassination,
it came to notice that before her death an American academic had
undertaken a study of what could happen in India after her death.
Rumour-mongers tried to project this study as an indicator of a CIA
involvement in her assassination. An enquiry into their allegation
could not prove this suspicion.

The post-1971 disinformation campaign of the CIA against Indira
Gandhi led to a peculiar situation for the R&AW. The operational
and analysis divisions of the CIA were cordially co-operating with
the R&AW in the coverage of China. At the same time, its PSYWAR
Division was trying to undermine the authority of Indira Gandhi.

These things may seem strange to those outside the intelligence profession, but intelligence professionals take them in their stride as normal occupational hazards. The excellent relations of the French Government headed by President Francois Mitterrand with the Governments of Indira Gandhi and Rajiv Gandhi did not prevent their external intelligence agency from penetrating the office of our Prime Minister and stealing volumes and volumes of sensitive documents relating to the clandestine operations of the R&AW and the IB. The cordial relations of the Ronald Reagan administration with the Rajiv Gandhi Government did not prevent the CIA from penetrating the R&AW office in Chennai and stealing many of its files. During the Clinton Administration, the CIA did not hesitate to penetrate the Intelligence Bureau at a very senior level. During the present administration of George Bush, who never tires of expressing his admiration for India and its leaders, the CIA did not hesitate to penetrate the R&AW and the National Security Council Secretariat (NSCS), which is a part of the Prime Minister's Office. The CIA not only penetrated the R&AW through Rabinder Singh, but also took him out of the country reportedly with a US passport under an assumed name when he was about to be arrested. The Government managed to suppress the seriousness of the penetration of the NSCS by the CIA. Benevolence and malevolence go side by side in the relations between intelligence agencies.

The post-World War II period saw an increase in co-operation amongst the intelligence agencies of friendly countries for mutual assistance in matters relating to counter-subversion, counter-insurgency and counter-terrorism. India has had a long history of intelligence co-operation not only with the other member-countries of the Commonwealth excepting Pakistan, but also with the erstwhile USSR and other Communist countries of East Europe and, more importantly, with the US.

Active and fruitful intelligence co-operation with the US dates back to the early 1950s during Jawaharlal Nehru's Prime Ministership. This picked up momentum after the Sino-Indian War of 1962. The momentum was maintained even during the troubled days of Indo-

US relations after the Indo-Pakistan War of 1971, under Indira Gandhi. Many senior Indian intelligence officers of the pre-1990s had undergone some intelligence training or the other in the UK or the US. The Directorate-General of Security (DGS), which came into being after the 1962 disaster, was set up with American and British assistance.

India had considerably benefited from the co-operation of the R&AW with the CIA and the Secret Intelligence Service (SIS) of the UK, popularly known as the MI 6. The CIA played an important role in helping the IB initially and then the R&AW to strengthen their operational capability with regard to China. While the CIA and other agencies of the US intelligence community were not prepared to give any assistance to the R&AW in relation to Pakistan, they were always positive in their response to requests relating to China.

It was, therefore, felt that the positive side of this co-operation must be maintained and should not be allowed to be affected by the PSYWAR campaign against Indira Gandhi. At the same time, Indira Gandhi and Kao felt the urgency of giving the R&AW a capability for the collection of intelligence about the USA—particularly about the movements and activities of the US naval ships in the Indian Ocean region.

A number of steps was initiated in this regard such as opening new monitoring stations in India's island territories and opening new R&AW stations in countries in the Indian Ocean region. The possibility of tapping the R&AW's liaison network for the collection of intelligence about the US was also explored. The liaison with the KGB, the Soviet intelligence agency, brought in some inputs, but those were not sufficient enough. The other countries with which the R&AW had a liaison relationship such as the UK, Canada, West Germany, Israel and Japan were close to the US and, hence, could not have been expected to help India in this regard.

After a careful examination of the various options, Kao decided to explore the possibility of approaching the SDECE, as the French external intelligence agency was then known (it is now known as

DGSE), for assistance in improving the R&AW's capability for the collection of maritime intelligence in the Indian Ocean region and for intelligence and assessment sharing regarding the US. In the French language, SDECE stands for Service For External Documentation and Counter-Espionage. DGSE stands for Directorate-General for External Security.

After the exit of the French President Gen.Charles de Gaulle and the death of his successor Georges Pompidou, the relations between the US and France had improved under President Valery Giscard d'Estaing (1974 to 81). Paris had started once again to participate actively in the activities of the NATO. However, despite this, the French continued to nurse misgivings and reservations regarding the US. It was, therefore, felt by Kao that they might be more positive to India's request for assistance.

The SDECE was then headed by Le Comte Alexandre de Marenches, an officer with a military background, who was half French, half Scottish. The then Indian Ambassador to France was a Bengali, who had come to the Indian Foreign Service from the Armed Forces. He had a French-speaking wife from Luxembourg. He was a close personal friend of Michel Poniatowski, who was the French Interior Minister. At the request of Kao, the Ambassador conveyed to Poniatowski the R&AW's interest in a liaison relationship with the SDECE.

Alexandre de Marenches immediately responded positively and invited Kao to visit Paris for a discussion on this subject. Kao did so and was warmly received. The visit led to an agreement on the setting up of a liaison relationship for the collection and sharing of intelligence regarding the movements and activities of the US and Soviet naval fleets in the Indian Ocean region. Kao wanted it to be a bilateral project between the R&AW and the SDECE. Alexandre de Marenches proposed a trilateral network by also bringing in the SAVAK, the Iranian intelligence agency under the late Shah of Iran. Kao knew the Shah well. He liked the idea and accepted it. The Shah of Iran was amongst the closest allies of the US. He owed his continuance in power to the CIA and had reasons to be grateful to it. However, despite these factors, he felt the need for keeping a wary eye on the US. Difficult to believe, but true! Indira Gandhi was not the only leader, who did not feel comfortable with the US. Many supposedly close allies of the US did not either.

The idea was that the French would provide the required technology, equipment and technical advice, the SAVAK would provide the funds to the French and the R&AW would provide the skilled manpower to man the TECHINT stations to be set up for this purpose. The produce of these stations would be shared by the three services. The head of the Monitoring Division of the R&AW, a retired military officer from the Army Signals Corps, who had distinguished himself during the 1971 war, was put in charge of this project in the R&AW.

Kao decided that I would be posted in Paris to liaise with the headquarters of the SDECE on behalf of the R&AW. He also decided that I would be based in Paris under the cover of a journalist for an Indian newspaper and not as a diplomat working in the Indian Embassy there. Till then, the practice had been for all overseas field officers of the R&AW to work under the cover of diplomats. Foreign intelligence agencies use both diplomatic and non-diplomatic covers for their officers posted abroad, but the R&AW had not experimented with a non-diplomatic cover till then.

I was selected for two reasons. I had done a course in journalism in the University of Madras in 1956 and worked in the Southern editions of the "Indian Express" for four years before joining the Indian Police Service in 1961. I had studied French for four years in the Alliance Francaise of New Delhi between 1970 and 1974 and acquired a fairly good working knowledge of the language.

Kao sought the assistance of the late G.Parthasarathi for persuading "The Hindu", the well-known national daily of Chennai, to give me accreditation as their correspondent in Paris. The idea was that all the expenses towards my emoluments, office and travel as a journalist would be met by "The Hindu" and the expenditure thus incurred by them would be re-imbursed to them by the R&AW.

After discussing this idea with the person concerned in "The Hindu", Parthasarathi informed Kao that the newspaper owners were agreeable in principle, but before giving their final approval, they wanted to interview me. Kao said that he would take the clearance in principle of Indira Gandhi before I went to Chennai for the interview.

A couple of days later, Kao called me to his office and said: "The Prime Minister does not like the idea of your working there as a journalist. You better go as a diplomat."

After undergoing the required training in the training school of the R&AW, I arrived in Paris in April,1975, and took over as First Secretary in charge of UNESCO. Subsequently, the Ambassador changed my cover job as Consular Affairs instead of UNESCO. Thus, I worked in the Indian Embassy in Paris till September 1979 as the First Secretary in charge of Consular Affairs (passports and visas).

Some weeks after I had joined the Embassy, Kao came to Paris and introduced me to Alexandre de Marenches as his representative to liaise with the SDECE. The two agreed that my charter would be assisting in the implementation of the project for the collection of maritime intelligence regarding developments in the Indian Ocean region, and sharing of intelligence and assessments regarding developments in Indo-China, China, West Asia, the Gulf countries, North Africa and the US.

There is an unwritten code of conduct in liaison relationships under which officers posted in a country for liaison purposes cannot undertake clandestine espionage operations directed against the host country. Thus, I was debarred from collecting any intelligence from French nationals—whether working in the Government or the private sector. Before leaving Paris, Kao briefed me that while I should follow this strictly and refrain from raising any French national as a source for the collection of intelligence, I could undertake clandestine espionage operations directed against Pakistan, China and other countries through non-French sources. Subsequently, in 1978, as the Islamic movement against the Shah of Iran gained momentum in Iran, coverage of Iran through Iranians living in France became one of my priority espionage tasks.

So far as the implementation of the joint project for the collection of maritime intelligence in the Indian Ocean region was concerned, my job was merely to act as a facilitator for meetings involving the Monitoring Division of the R&AW and its counterparts in the SDECE and the SAVAK. A number of meetings were held in Paris, Teheran and New Delhi in 1975 and 1976 and a detailed project report was drawn up. The project report called for the setting up of two big monitoring stations in India—one each on the East and the West coast and two stations abroad.

The French started supplying the equipment and, with the help of their experts, the two monitoring stations in Indian territory were set up without any difficulty. Problems arose with regard to the overseas monitoring stations. At the request of Kao, who personally knew the leaders of many countries in the region, two well-located countries agreed to the R&AW setting up the monitoring stations in their territory, provided they functioned from the local Indian Embassy premises. The heads of the Indian diplomatic missions in those countries were opposed to a clandestine monitoring station of the R&AW functioning from within the premises of their mission. They were worried that if the information about it leaked out, there could be an embarrassing political controversy, which, they felt, could damage India's relations with that country.

As a result of this, the two overseas monitoring stations as envisaged in the joint project report could not be set up. The overthrow of the Shah of Iran and the triumph of the Islamic Revolution in Iran in 1979 led to the exclusion of the SAVAK from this project. The flow of funds from Iran dried up. The SDECE was interested in continuing with this project only if it meant no expenditure from their budget. The project ultimately petered out. The only benefit to the R&AW was that it got some modern monitoring equipment from France. The project did not produce much intelligence on developments in the Indian Ocean.

The liaison relationship with the French did not develop as satisfactorily as Kao thought it would for various reasons. The most important was the defeat of Indira Gandhi in the elections of 1977. Her successor Morarji Desai came to office as Prime Minister with a lot of reservations regarding the R&AW. He wanted to drastically reduce its strength and budget. The full implementation of the joint project with the French and the Iranians would have required the recruitment of a large number of technical personnel. This became out of question under Morarji Desai.

The second reason was that the successors to Kao as the chiefs of the R&AW did not evince the same interest as Kao did in operational co-operation with the French service. The project was not totally abandoned, but it lost its importance as the core element of the Indo-French intelligence co-operation. The liaison relationship continued in full steam even under the successors to Kao, but it was largely confined to intelligence and assessment sharing.

When Kao returned to office as Senior Adviser to Indira Gandhi in 1981, he tried to revive interest in the project and in operational co-operation with the French service. But in the French presidential elections of 1981, Francois Mitterrand, the leader of the Socialist Party, was elected. Alexandre de Marenches resigned as the chief of the French external intelligence agency and was replaced by Pierre Marion, the then Chief Executive Officer of Air France. He did not give to the project the same importance as Alexandre de Marenches did.

To sum up in one sentence the outcome of the Indo-French intelligence co-operation: High expectations, poor results.

Despite some improvement since 1971, the R&AW's capability for the collection of intelligence about the US and about naval developments in the Indian Ocean region remains weak. The present Government headed by Dr.Manmohan Singh, which seems to feel itself more comfortable with the US than Indira Gandhi did, does not seem to be unduly concerned about it.

CHAPTER VI

The Emergency

When Kao had come to Paris to introduce me to Alexandre de Marenches, he was in receipt of a top secret coded message from a senior leader of the Congress (I), a Kashmiri, who was known to be close to Indira Gandhi. It was about the worrisome situation in India as a result of the agitation against Indira Gandhi carried on by Jai Prakash Narain and others. The Congress (I) leader felt that there was a concerted attempt, allegedly funded by the CIA, to destabilize the country and teach a lesson to her for her independent policies. He also said that he and some others had advised her to impose a State of Emergency and ban all political activities and agitations for a while, but she was hesitant to do so. The message added that since she greatly valued the advice of Kao, he should also advise her on similar lines.

Kao sent a coded reply to the Congress (I) leader disagreeing with his views. He cautioned against taking any hasty step such as proclaiming a State of Emergency as it might prove unwise and counter-productive. He also repeated to Indira Gandhi the message, which he had received from the Congress (I) leader and his reply to it. Thereafter, Kao returned to India after his talks with Alexandre de Marenches were over.

On June 27,1975, early in the morning, I heard over the French radio that Indira Gandhi had imposed a State of Emergency, banned all agitations and other political activities and ordered the arrests of her critics and opponents. Did she reject Kao's advice against it? Or, did Kao change his mind and support it after he returned to New Delhi from his foreign tour? I could never find the answers to these questions. I never posed these questions to Kao. He never on his own talked about them.

Even before the proclamation of the Emergency—in fact, almost since 1972— there were indications of unease mixed with jealousy in some senior bureaucratic circles over the emergence of Kao as a highly trusted adviser of Indira Gandhi. These indicators were evident in matters such as instances of expression of unhappiness in the Joint Intelligence Committee over the habit of the R&AW and the IB sending their assessments directly to Indira Gandhi without having them vetted by the JIC; not sharing with other senior bureaucrats such as the Home, Defence and Foreign Secretaries the advice directly given by Kao to Indira Gandhi so that they could express their views on the advice; the rapid expansion of the R&AW's presence abroad, which was suspiciously viewed by some officers of the Ministry of External Affairs as an attempt by Kao to create a parallel Foreign Service by taking advantage of Indira Gandhi's trust in him etc.

This unease, now mixed with distrust, spread to political circles opposed to Indira Gandhi too after the proclamation of the Emergency. Just as Indira Gandhi and her political associates saw the hand of the CIA in every development adverse to her, her opponents saw the hand of Kao and the R&AW in every action taken by her against them. Some accused him unfairly of being the brain behind the Emergency. Others asked why the R&AW, which was an external intelligence agency, required so many offices inside the country in places such as Chennai, Mumbai, Kolkata, Lucknow, Patna, Cochin, Bangalore etc. They did not realize that these offices were set up not for keeping a watch on Indian political leaders and others as they suspected, but for looking for possible sources among those visiting India from abroad.

It was a fact that there was a needless expansion of the R&AW after 1971, which picked up further momentum after 1975. The expansion was in the R&AW's presence abroad as well as in the strength of its staff in its headquarters at New Delhi. This rapid expansion led to the induction into the organization of a large number of officers from other services and direct recruits from the market, many of whom subsequently proved themselves to be ill-suited to the intelligence profession. The result: a dilution in the quality and motivation of the officers at the middle and higher levels and of supervision. This, in turn, led to a dilution in the quality of the produce. This rapid expansion also led to allegations of nepotism and favouritism in the recruitment of officers, arising from the fact that some of the new recruits were related to some serving officer or the other in different Government departments and the Armed Forces.

This rapid expansion tarnished the image of the organization to some extent. However, it had no sinister motive as was alleged by the opponents of Indira Gandhi. Unfortunately, her opponents had convinced themselves, without justification, that this expansion was intended to enable the R&AW to keep a watch on her opponents and critics.

Their suspicions were further aggravated by the action of Vidya Charan Shukla, the then Minister for Information and Broadcasting, in inducting two officers from the R&AW and the IB into his Ministry to work as Joint Secretaries. This was a totally unwise move and the IB and the R&AW should not have agreed to send their officers to the Ministry. Rightly or wrongly, many suspected that the task of these officers was to make the media behave . Many critics of Indira Gandhi started alleging that after the proclamation of the Emergency, the R&AW had been converted into the KGB of India.

It is not correct as was alleged during the Emergency and immediately thereafter that the R&AW let itself be misused by Indira Gandhi to harass her opponents and to spy on her critics. Kao, who never got along well with the late Sanjay Gandhi, maintained a distance from him and ensured that the R&AW was not associated with any of the excesses allegedly orchestrated by Sanjay Gandhi. Indira Gandhi had such high esteem and affection for Kao that the fact that Kao and Sanjay Gandhi did not get along well had no influence on the trust reposed by her in Kao. During the entire

Emergency, I remained posted in Paris. During this period, the only instruction from the headquarters, which made me feel uncomfortable, was to make enquiries regarding the whereabouts of Leila Fernandes, the wife of George Fernandes. The Government of India suspected that she had been given shelter in France by the French Socialist Party. I did make enquiries about her, but could not locate her. Apart from this, there was no circular of a questionable nature from the headquarters. Despite this, there was a widespread perception that the R&AW was associated with many wrong-doings during the Emergency. This perception prevailed even in sections of the bureaucracy, including in the Foreign Service.

The R&AW also lost some of its shine as an intelligence collection agency because of the assassination of Sheikh Mujibur Rahman in August, 1975, and the subsequent developments in Bangladesh, which resulted in an erosion of the Indian influence there. This was projected by the critics of the R&AW as an instance of a serious failure of intelligence. The Indian Ambassador in Paris, who was a close personal friend of Kao, was very critical of the R&AW after this incident. He used to ask me: "How did the R&AW remain totally oblivious of the anti-Mujibur plot?"

I had written a personal letter to Kao about the criticism of the R&AW, which was prevalent not only in the Embassy, but also among senior officers visiting Paris from New Delhi. Some weeks after the assassination, Kao had come to Geneva on an official visit. He called me to Geneva for a discussion on my letter. He said that there was no failure of the R&AW in Bangladesh. According to him, it was aware of the growing unpopularity of Mujib, particularly in the Bangladeshi Armed Forces, and of the plots being hatched against him. Indira Gandhi had been kept informed by Kao of these developments. She had also been told that there was a threat to Mujib's life. Indira Gandhi had these reports and warnings conveyed to Mujib through an intermediary, but he dismissed them derisively. He had convinced himself that he continued to be as popular as he was in 1971 and that there was no threat to his life. Kao asked: "How can the R&AW be held responsible if Mujib won't take our warnings seriously?" He added that there was no need for me to be defensive and asked me to convey to the Ambassador whatever he had told me. I did.

Despite this, an impression persisted even in the R&AW that it had lost touch with Bangladesh and that it was no longer as well-informed about Bangladesh as it was about East Pakistan. Its analysts had a better feel for Pakistan than for Bangladesh. Over the years since then, the R&AW's assessments on Pakistan had proved correct more often than its assessments about Bangladesh. One remembers how in 1991, an assessment prepared by the Bangladesh analysis branch in the R&AW about the likely outcome of the elections there proved to be wrong. Fortunately, the then chief of the R&AW, who had some reservations in his mind about the objectivity of the branch, did not forward it to the Prime Minister. This saved the organization from embarrassment.

Failure to diversify contacts in Bangladesh, pockets of hostility in its security forces and intelligence community towards India and the R&AW, suspicion and resentment in the non-Awami League political circles over what was perceived as Indian favouritism towards certain sections of the political spectrum and a lack of objectivity in the Bangladesh analysis branch contributed to the decline in the R&AW's performance in Bangladesh during the Emergency. This has continued since then.

CHAPTER VII

Under A Cloud

On January 23,1977, Indira Gandhi called for elections to a new Lok Sabha. The elections were held in March,1977. The State of Emergency was lifted on March 23,1977. The Congress (I) was badly defeated in the elections, indicating the extent of the unpopularity of Indira Gandhi and Sanjay Gandhi and the public anger over the perceived excesses during the Emergency. She and Sanjay Gandhi suffered a humiliating defeat. The Janata Party, which won the elections, came to power with Morarji Desai, a former senior Congress leader, as the Prime Minister. Charan Singh became the Home Minister and Atal Behari Vajpayee the Foreign Minister. Through an intermediary, the then King of Nepal sent a message to her advising her to shift to Nepal with her family. While she did not want to shift herself, she was inclined to ask Sanjay Gandhi and Rajiv Gandhi to shift to Nepal with their families. She consulted Kao. He advised her against it. He felt this could damage her political career beyond repair. She gave up the idea.

The election campaign was marked, inter alia, by a strong criticism by the opposition parties of the role of the IB, the R&AW and the Central Bureau of Investigation (CBI) during the Emergency. Their chiefs were accused of letting themselves and their organizations be misused by Indira Gandhi and Sanjay Gandhi for suppressing the opposition and the other critics of Indira Gandhi. All of them were replaced by the new Government.

Kao, who had only a few months of his extended service left, himself chose to quit following a humiliation by Morarji Desai when he called on him after the latter had assumed office as the Prime Minister. He was replaced by K.Sankaran Nair, his No.2. Nair resigned within three months in protest against the new Government's decision to re-designate the chief of the R&AW as Director—on par with Director, IB— instead of Secretary as it was till then. Nair reportedly felt that this could reduce the importance of the position of the chief of the R&AW and decided to leave. Some senior officials, who were close to Morarji Desai, tried to persuade him not to quit in a huff. They reportedly assured him that there would be a change only in the designation, but he would have the same powers and status as enjoyed by Kao. They could not succeed.

The entire officer class of the R&AW was saddened by the departure of Sankaran Nair. He was a legendary operational officer— totally professional and apolitical, who kept away from all politicians. He was nobody's man. Before the proclamation of the Emergency, Indira Gandhi had selected him for appointment as the DIB. Sanjay Gandhi sent word to him through R.K.Dhawan that he should meet him at his residence before he took over as the DIB. Nair declined. Sanjay Gandhi got his mother's orders posting him as the DIB cancelled. He also wanted him to be moved out of the R&AW and sent back to his State cadre. Kao refused to oblige and expressed to Indira Gandhi his unhappiness over Sanjay Gandhi's interference. She reportedly asked Sanjay Gandhi to keep off the R&AW.

Nair was the leading expert of the intelligence community on Pakistan and the rest of the Islamic world. He was dealing with Pakistan even in the IB before the R&AW was formed . He had built up a network of sources in Pakistan at various levels—particularly in the Armed Forces. A mole of his in the office of Gen.Yahya Khan reported in the last week of November,1971, that the Pakistan Air Force (PAF) intended making a pre-emptive strike on the forward air bases of the Indian Air Force (IAF) in the Western sector on the evening of December 1. The IAF was immediately alerted by Nair and Indira Gandhi was informed by Kao. The IAF ordered a high alert and took necessary precautionary measures to thwart the planned pre-emptive strike. Nothing happened on December 1 and 2. On the morning of December 3, the IAF headquarters told Nair that they could not continue to keep their pilots in a state of high alert any longer. He requested them to continue it for another 24 hours and downgrade it on the morning of December 4, if nothing happened. He assured the IAF headquarters that his source was very reliable and generally accurate in his intelligence. The IAF headquarters agreed to continue the high alert. On the evening of December 3, the PAF launched its pre-emptive strike, which was a total failure because the IAF had an advance warning of it from the mole of Nair. Nair checked up as to how, his source, who was generally accurate, gave the date of the planned strike as December 1. It was found that in his coded message the source had given the date correctly as December 3, but the decoders in the R&AW headquarters had incorrectly decoded it as December 1.

Nair was a very close personal friend of Kao. Their friendship and loyalty to each other was legendary. Kao never did anything without consulting Nair and the latter never misused Kao's trust in him by doing anything without Kao's approval. Nair was as much the founding father of the R&AW as Kao was. In fact, when Kao was informed of the decision of Indira Gandhi to bifurcate the IB and create the R&AW and make him the chief, it was to Nair that he turned for helping him in creating the new organization.

The R&AW's success in East Pakistan, which led to the birth of Bangladesh, would not have been possible without the leadership of Kao and the ideas of Nair. The vision was of Kao and the ideas to give shape to the vision were largely of Nair. Like Kao, Nair too was held in high esteem in the community of international intelligence professionals.

When the Morarji Desai-led Government came to power, it had all the records of the R&AW scrutinized in the hope of finding instances of the misuse of the organization by Indira Gandhi and Sanjay Gandhi. It could not find any. However, it came across a curious case in the files of the Ministry of Finance and the Reserve Bank of India, which it thought it could use to fix the R&AW, Kao and Nair. This related to Nair being sent to Geneva during the Emergency to deposit a cheque for US Dollars six million in a numbered account of a bank in Geneva. Morarji Desai suspected that this account belonged to Sanjay Gandhi.

However, enquiries revealed that this account actually belonged to one Rashidyan, an Iranian middleman, who was a close personal friend of Ashraf Pehlawi, the sister of the Shah of Iran. On the recommendation of the Hindujas, the well-known business family, the Ministry of Finance of the Government of India had used the services of this man to request Ashraf Pehlawi to persuade the Shah to grant two soft loans to India— one for the implementation of the Kundremukh iron ore project and the other to pay the import bill of India. In view of the action taken by the US Government against India after the Pokhran I nuclear test in 1974, the Government of India was facing serious financial difficulties and had requested the Shah of Iran for a soft loan of US Dollars 250 million. At the urging of Ashraf Pehlawi, the Shah agreed to help India out. The Finance Ministry accepted a recommendation of the Hindujas that a commission of US dollars six million should be paid to Rashidyan for getting this loan through the sister of the Shah of Iran. The Reserve Bank of India sent a telex to a bank in Geneva, asking it to hand over a draft for this amount to Nair. The Finance Ministry had requested Kao to depute Nair to Geneva to collect this draft and deposit it in the numbered account of Rashidyan. Kao obliged. When these facts were ascertained, Morarji Desai did not pursue the case further and ordered it closed without any further action. Moreover,the Hindujas were even closer to Morarji Desai, Vajpayee and L.K.Advani than they were to Sanjay Gandhi. When they found that the commission had been paid by the Finance Ministry on the alleged recommendation of the Hindujas, they had apparently no desire to pursue the matter further.

Nair's decision to quit the R&AW was a blow not only to the organization and the intelligence community, but also to the large number of friends and admirers which he had in the administration as a whole. Fortunately, the effect of this blow was mitigated by the wise decision of Morarji Desai to appoint N.F.Suntook, the then Chairman of the Joint Intelligence Committee (JIC) of the Government of India, as the head of the R&AW with the new designation of Director, R&AW. During the Prime Ministership of Indira Gandhi, he had gone on deputation to the JIC.In the R&AW, he ranked No.3 after Nair.

Suntook started his career as an emergency commissioned officer of the Indian Navy. From there, he got into the Indian Police Service and then joined the Indian Frontier Administration Service (IFAS),when it was constituted by Jawaharlal Nehru to look after the administration of the tribal areas of India's North-East and the Andaman and Nicobar Islands. Suntook distinguished himself in the North-East and the Andaman and Nicobar Islands, where many old tribals, who had known him, remember him with affection even today. Suntook and Wing Commander Murkot Ramunny are considered the best among the officers produced by the IFAS and their contribution to the administration of the tribal areas was immense.

A few months after the formation of the R&AW, Kao, who had known Suntook, persuaded him to join the R&AW and made him in charge of administration and the Africa Division. Like Nair, Suntook was highly professional and apolitical, but unlike Nair, he had very little exposure to operational work and only limited knowledge of the intelligence tradecraft. However, this did not stand in the way of his success as the chief of the R&AW. He chose four outstanding officers as his No.2 in succession. Initially, Brig. I.S.Hassanwalia, a retired officer of the Army, who was No.2 to Nair in the Pakistan operations division of the IB and then the R&AW, functioned as Suntook's No.2. After his retirement, S.P.Karnik, an IPS officer from Maharashtra, who had served in the China Division of the IB and then of the R&AW, took over as No.2. Karnik was succeeded by Shiv Raj Bahadur, another IPS officer of IB vintage from the Orissa cadre. Bahadur was succeeded by G.C.Saxena, an IPS officer of Uttar Pradesh, as Suntook's No.2. Saxena succeeded Suntook as the head of the organization in April,1983. Hassanwalia and Karnik retired as the No.2. Bahadur was removed from the organization by Indira Gandhi when she returned to power in 1980.These officers saw to it

that the operational capability of the R&AW did not suffer as a result
of the changes made by Morarji Desai in 1977.

Whereas Kao had a tenure of nearly nine years as the head of
the R&AW— the longest tenure anyone has had in the intelligence
community after Mullik, who had a tenure of nearly 16 years as
the DIB—Suntook had a continuous tenure of nearly six years, the
third longest. M.K.Narayanan, the present National Security Adviser,
almost shared Suntook's record as the DIB, but his long tenure was
in two spells. Mullik and Kao served as the chiefs under one Prime
Minister—Mullik under Jawaharlal Nehru and Kao under Indira
Gandhi, but Suntook had the distinction of serving as the chief
under three Prime Ministers of widely differing temperaments and
belonging to different poles of the political spectrum—Morarji Desai,
Charan Singh and Indira Gandhi. The fact that he was chosen by
Morarji Desai, did not stand in the way of his continuing as the chief
when Indira Gandhi, a sworn adversary of Morarji Desai, returned
to power as the Prime Minister in the elections of 1980. This speaks
highly of the manner in which Suntook managed to win the trust of
all the three Prime Ministers. The fact that he was close to Kao and
enjoyed his total confidence also helped in his continuing under
Indira Gandhi.

Suntook was a man of many endearing qualities. He never bragged
about himself. He was discretion personified. He never talked ill of
his predecessors. He was not one of those who try to shine, not on
their own merits, but by projecting their predecessors in negative
colours. There was nothing mean about him.

He could have ingratiated himself with Morarji Desai by carrying
tales about Kao and Indira Gandhi to him or by letting himself be
used by the new Government to witch-hunt Kao or Indira Gandhi or
both. He never stooped to this. He maintained his personal loyalty to
Kao and protected him from possible acts of humiliation.

Morarji Desai, Charan Singh and Vajpayee came to office with the
impression that Kao played an important role in the proclamation
of the Emergency and that he let Indira Gandhi and Sanjay Gandhi

misuse the R&AW for partisan political purposes. Morarji Desai was so distrustful of Kao that he sent the Cabinet Secretary to Kao's office to make sure he did not destroy any papers before handing over to Nair.

After spending hardly some weeks in office, they realized that their impression was not justified. Charan Singh took the initiative in telling Kao that enquiries got made by him after assuming office as the Home Minister had convinced him that he (Kao) had conducted himself honourably and that the allegations made against him were wrong. Years later, Kao recounted this to me and said that he was greatly touched by Charan Singh's gesture.

Fears in the R&AW that there could be a witch-hunt in the organization by the new Government were belied. Barring Kao, no one had to go for political reasons. One cannot say the same thing about Indira Gandhi. When she returned to power in 1980, there was a witch-hunt in the organization and four Indian Police Service officers, including Bahadur, the No.2 to Suntook, were unceremoniously thrown out by her due to suspicions of their links with Morarji Desai and Charan Singh. There were no such links, excepting the fact that one of the shifted officers was related to Charan Singh.

A large part of the credit should go to Suntook for ensuring that there was no witch-hunt in the R&AW under Morarji Desai. But neither he nor Kao could prevent a witch-hunt when Indira Gandhi returned to power in 1980.

Suntook was thus able to save the honour of the R&AW as a professional, apolitical organization with no involvement in politics, but he was unable to protect the structure of the organization from the onslaught of the Morarji Desai Government. It came to office with the impression that taking advantage of his closeness to Indira Gandhi, Kao had indulged in empire-building and that the organization had bloated unnecessarily. The Ministry of External Affairs, which had watched with concern and jealousy the rapid expansion of the R&AW under Kao, started pressing for a re-look at the performance of the organization and its size.

While the Morarji Desai Government was convinced quickly that the R&AW was not involved in domestic politics, it continued to have a strong suspicion that the R&AW was being misused by Indira Gandhi to harass members of the overseas Indian community, who were critical of the Emergency. This suspicion was strengthened when some members of the overseas Indian community and former members of the staff of the R&AW, who had settled down in the West without returning to India after completing their posting, carried to Morarji Desai and other members of the new Government tales regarding alleged harassment by some R&AW officers posted abroad.

As a result of all this, Morarji Desai remained firm that the organization should be pruned drastically. Initially, he imposed a 50 per cent cut in the budget of the organization, thereby seeking to force it to cut its staff strength correspondingly. Subsequently, he did not insist on a 50 per cent cut, but wanted a major cut without specifying any percentage.

Suntook carried out his instructions by stopping all new recruitment, abolishing posts which had become vacant as well as many stations abroad and winding up some of the divisions in the headquarters set up by Kao. For example, he wound up the Political Division set up by Kao to make long-term assessments of developments in the neighbouring countries on the basis of open source information and the Information Division, which had been set up to monitor reporting in the Indian media on developments of concern to national security, for interacting with journalists and for PSYWAR purposes.

Following these measures, the R&AW once again became lean and thin as it was till 1971.

CHAPTER VIII

From Negative To Positive

Within a few months of his taking over as the Director of the R&AW, Suntook managed to establish a good personal equation with Morarji Desai. He was helped in this by the fact that he (Suntook) was a Gujarati-speaking Parsi who had started his career in the Indian Police Service in the undivided Bombay State of which Morarji Desai was the Chief Minister. How successfully Suntook had managed to rehabilitate the reputation of the organization with Morarji Desai would be evident from the fact that when the Government set up a high-powered committee chaired by the late L.P.Singh, former Home Secretary, to enquire into allegations of excesses during the Emergency, its terms of reference included enquiries into the functioning of the IB and the Central Bureau of Investigation (CBI) only. The R&AW was not targeted.

There was no convergence of views among the top leaders of the new Government regarding the future shape and tasks of the organization. Morarji Desai wanted the organization to be drastically trimmed. Charan Singh was against doing anything, which could affect its professional capability. Vajpayee wanted greater attention to countries, where there were large numbers of migrants from India. As a result, the instructions from the headquarters regarding the future shape and responsibilities of the organization kept changing, depending on whose views prevailed for the moment in the Government.

Their attitude to Kao too varied. Morarji Desai was cold and disdainful. Charan Singh was initially cold, but subsequently warmed up. Kao told me long after his retirement that Vajpayee's attitude was hostile and offensive. When Kao made his farewell call on Vajpayee after handing over charge to Nair, Vajpayee accused him of spying on him when he was in the opposition and keeping Indira Gandhi informed of his personal life. When Kao strongly denied this, Vajpayee used words and expressions, which hurt Kao. He sought a meeting with Morarji Desai and complained to him about the way he was treated by Vajpayee. After listening to him, Morarji Desai replied that it was wrong on the part of Vajpayee to have spoken to him in that manner. He promised to talk to Vajpayee about it. He did. Vajpayee sent for Kao again and pulled him up for complaining about him to Morarji Desai.

In subsequent years, Vajpayee's attitude to Kao changed and he held him in great respect. After he became Prime Minister in 1998, he ran into Kao at a reception. He took the initiative in talking to Kao and enquired about his welfare. In 1999, when the report of the Kargil Review Committee (KRC) found fault with the intelligence agencies for their performance before the Kargil conflict, Kao wrote a personal letter to Vajpayee expressing his reservations over the negative remarks of the KRC on the intelligence agencies. After reading that letter, Vajpayee sent for Kao and had a discussion with him on the subject.

Morarji Desai was an interesting personality. Often, he used to bully officers, but developed a respect for officers, who stood their ground and refused to be bullied by him. He had a negative opinion of officers, who did not stand their ground. After taking over as the Prime Minister, he went on an official visit to the UK and France. During his stay in London, he asked the R&AW station chief there for a briefing on his tasks and work. The R&AW officer had prepared a written note about his tasks and operations and briefed Morarji Desai with the help of the note. Morarji Desai put the note in his pocket and said he would read it during his return flight. The R&AW officer pointed out that it would be a breach of security for Morarji Desai to carry a note giving very sensitive operational details on his person and insisted on his returning the note to him. He promised to have the note sent to him through Suntook via the diplomatic bag. Morarji Desai got irritated and told him: "Don't talk to me about security. I know more about security than you. I was Chief Minister of Bombay and Union Minister in Delhi for many years. I don't need any lessons in security from you." But the officer insisted that he should return the note and took it back from him.

He sent the note by diplomatic bag to Suntook with a covering memo explaining what happened during his encounter with Morarji Desai. He requested Suntook to hand over the note to him. Suntook later wrote to the officer that when he met Morarji Desai to hand over the note, the latter praised him for the way he had stood his ground and refused to be bullied by the Prime Minister of India.

Before Morarji Desai reached Paris from London, the R&AW officer in London rang me up and narrated what had happened to him. He said: "Raman, if he asks for a briefing on your sensitive operations, brief him only orally. Don't prepare any written note." Fortunately, Morarji Desai was in Paris only for one day. He was busy meeting the members of the local Indian community and then attended a dinner hosted by Valery Giscard d'Estaing, the then French President. He did not call me for a briefing on my work. He stayed in the Ambassador's house.

Before Morarji Desai arrived in Paris, the Elysee, as the Presidential palace is known, was in a dilemma as to what to serve him during the dinner. They had heard of his special food habits. They contacted the Embassy, which advised them to serve different types of nuts and fruits and a dessert made from cow's milk and unrefined sugar (gurh). The Elysee said they would have no problems about the nuts and fruits, but would have difficulty in preparing the dessert. The Ambassador's wife offered to prepare it herself and send it to the Elysee to have it served to him. The Elysee then asked whether Morarji Desai would have any objection to the other guests taking their normal non-vegetarian food with wine and champagne. They were told that there would be no objection at all. I was not invited to the dinner, but I was told by those who attended that they greatly admired the way Morarji Desai kept eating his nuts and fruits without any complex and without the least embarrassment on his face—as a six-course dinner with wine and champagne was being served to the other guests.

After seeing him off to Delhi the next morning, I had accompanied the Ambassador and his wife to their house. The Ambassador insisted that I take a drink before I left. As their servant served us the drink, the Ambassador's wife asked the servant: " I hope you are using new glasses?" She then turned to me and said: " I was not very sure which glass the Prime Minister was using (for drinking his urine).So, I asked them to throw away the old glasses and take out new ones."

The only other important member of the Morari Desai Cabinet to have visited Paris when I was there, was Vajpayee. The Government had transferred the Ambassador to China and the post was vacant. The mission in Paris was headed by a Charge d'Affaires (CDA), an officer of the Indian Foreign Service. The staff officer of Vajpayee told the CDA that the Minister would be keen to have an interaction with leading local journalists to explain the policies of the Government. The CDA requested the Press Counsellor to organize an interaction over drinks at the house of the Ambassador. Since I personally knew a number of important British, American and Israeli journalists posted in Paris, I was asked to help the Press Counsellor. Initially, the senior foreign journalists were reluctant to come since they did not attach much importance to India. I managed to persuade them to come. The interaction was fixed between 6 and 8 PM. All of them came in time. It was a very good gathering, but Vajpayee was nowhere to be seen. He was not in his hotel room. None of his personal staff knew where he had gone. We waited till 8 PM. He did not turn up. It was very embarrassing. We expressed our apologies to the journalists and terminated the reception. Vajpayee returned to his hotel room around 10 PM. He never apologized to the officers of the Embassy or the journalists for not keeping up his appointment. Nobody knew why he could not come and where he was. The speculation was that he had gone out of Paris to meet clandestinely an important Israeli leader, who had flown to Paris to meet him.

Vajpayee also had an interaction with the local Indian community at the Maison de l'Inde in the Cite Universitaire. In his opening remarks, he mentioned about the changes introduced by the Government in the working of the R&AW. He promised that in future R&AW officers would not harass the Indians abroad and added: "I know the R&AW officers here must have been harassing you. This would not happen in future." "No," many in the audience shouted. Vajpayee said: "I am surprised. Wherever I go, the Indian community complains about the behaviour of the R&AW officers during the Emergency. Who is the R&AW officer here? Why are you not complaining about him? Are you afraid of him?" Again, many in the audience shouted "No." Vajpayee turned to me and asked: " Is there no R&AW officer in the Indian Embassy here?" "Not that I know of, Sir," I replied. The next day, before going to the airport, Vajpayee came to the Chancery to meet the officers. I was introduced to him as an officer of the R&AW. Vajpayee said: " But you were there at the meeting yesterday. You said there was no R&AW officer posted in Paris." I kept quiet.

The R&AW's role in two events relating to Iran and the detection of Pakistan's clandestine programme for setting up an uranium enrichment plant at Kahuta with the help of Dr.A.Q.Khan helped in changing the attitude of Morarji Desai towards the organization from negative to positive. I played some role in relation to Iran.

In 1978, the agitation in Iran against the Shah and the US by a coalition of forces consisting of religious clerics, bazaris (the business class) and the students picked up momentum. Many of the students, who participated in the agitation belonged to the Iran Tudeh Party, as the Communist Party was known. Some of them were arrested and tortured by the SAVAK, the Shah's intelligence agency. Others escaped to Paris and took sanctuary there. In fact, the French gave sanctuary to all anti-Shah elements, despite their close relations with the Government of the Shah. When Saddam Hussein, the then President of Iraq, asked Ayatollah Khomeini, who was living in Iraq, to leave the country, he and his followers wanted to shift to France. The French security services were opposed to their being allowed to come to France. Giscard d'Estaing over-ruled them and allowed them to come. Khomeini and his followers reached France, took up residence at Neauphle le Chateau, near Paris, and started guiding the anti-Shah agitation from there. After his arrival, all the anti-Shah elements in Europe gathered round him and started orchestrating the Islamic Revolution from France. The students belonging to the Tudeh Party supported the Ayatollah despite their reservations about his religious views.

I met one of those students, whom I would refer to as Ali at the house of a common friend. Through him, I came to know many of the anti-Shah elements in Paris. He came from a middle class family, but was living in total penury in Paris. Frequently, he used to eat and drink with me. One night, he rang me up and said that his ulcer seemed to have ruptured and he was losing a lot of blood. He also said that he had no money to go to a hospital for treatment. I immediately rushed to his place of stay, put him in my car and got him admitted in a hospital. After he was cured and discharged, I paid all his hospital bills. He became devoted to me and, through him, I came to know many members of the Ayatollah's entourage. It used to be said in the diplomatic and journalistic circles of Paris that some Israeli diplomats and journalists and I were the only persons, who had concluded that the Shah would not be able to survive in power and that his days were numbered. The Americans and the West Europeans were still indulging in wishful-thinking that the Shah might somehow survive and crush the Islamic Revolution. I used to send my reports and assessments regularly to Suntook.

There was another person, who had come to a similar assessment, but independently. That was Morarji Desai on the basis of the reports, which he was getting from the leaders of the Shia community in India. My reports and assessments did not in any way influence Morarji Desai's assessment. What influenced it was the information and views which he was regularly getting from the Indian Shia leaders. During my service and subsequently, I have been amazed by the fact that some of the Indian Prime Ministers were very well-informed about important developments in the region and the world. I can quote many instances. Indira Gandhi was better informed about

Sri Lanka than the IB or the R&AW. In the early 1980s, she knew
before the intelligence agencies about the plan of the Sri Lankan
Government and Sinhalese extremists to secretly burn the bodies of
a large number of Tamils of Colombo killed by the extremists. When
Yuri Andropov, the General Secretary of the Soviet Communist
Party, died in February,1984, she knew of it even before an official
announcement had been made in Moscow. In August 1988, Rajiv
Gandhi knew before the R&AW that a Pakistani Air Force Plane in
which Zia-ul-Haq was traveling to Islamabad from Bahawalpur was
missing. In August,1990, V.P.Singh knew before the R&AW about
the impending dismissal of Mrs.Benazir Bhutto, the then Pakistani
Prime Minister, by Ghulam Ishaq Khan, the then President, at the
instigation of Gen.Mirza Aslam Beg, the then Chief of the Army
Staff. Chandra Shekhar was better informed about Nepal than the
R&AW. So too, Narasimha Rao about Pakistan and Iran.

Towards the end of 1978, Morarji Desai had come to his own
assessment, without any inputs from the R&AW, that it would not
be possible to stop the success of the Islamic Revolution in Iran. He
wanted to establish secret contact with Ayatollah Khomeini, in order
to convey the good wishes of the Government of India. He sent an
Indian Shia emissary to Paris to arrange a secret meeting between
the Ayatollah and Ashok Mehta, who had served as the Deputy
Chairman of the Planning Commission under Indira Gandhi. While
the Ayatollah welcomed the proposal for a meeting, he insisted
it should not be in secret. He suspected that Morarji Desai was
trying to protect himself, should the Shah succeed in crushing the
Revolution. The Shia emissary returned to India without success.

A few days later, I received a top secret message from the Prime
Minister's office stating that Ashok Mehta and an officer of the
Ministry of External Affairs (MEA) were on their way to Paris and
that I should organize a secret meeting with the Ayatollah. The
message did not even ask me whether I would be able to organize
such a meeting. It presumed that I would be able to. Such sensitive
operational instructions from the PMO normally came through the
chief of the R&AW. In this case, Suntook was not even aware that

such an instruction had been issued. I sent a reply to the PMO, with a copy to Suntook, expressing my surprise over the departure of Ashok Mehta and the MEA officer from Delhi without even asking me whether I would be able to organize such a meeting and without giving me time to prepare the ground for it. Suntook sent me a reply urging that I should take up the task. He said if I succeeded it would help the organization.

I met Ali in his house and told him about the instructions I had received from the PMO. I added: "This is a matter of my personal prestige. If I don't succeed, my reputation will be gone." Ali rushed to the place where the Ayatollah was staying and met his senior advisers. They repeated their opposition to a secret meeting. He then sought a meeting with the Ayatollah and told him how I had once saved his life. He explained to the Ayatollah that he wanted to oblige me. The Ayatollah called his senior advisers and directed them to organize a secret meeting with Ashok Mehta and the MEA officer. The meeting went off splendidly. I did not attend the meeting myself, but my No.2—a French-speaking police officer from Puducherry— attended. Ashok Mehta called me to his hotel room later and complimented me for having succeeded. He said the Ayatollah was very positive in his remarks on India and very negative in his remarks on Pakistan.

I sent a report to Suntook on how I succeeded. He sent me a long and warm letter of appreciation in which he mentioned that Morarji Desai's attitude to the R&AW had become largely positive after my success.

The other event, which changed the attitude of Morarji Desai favourably towards the R&AW, was the collection of technical intelligence (TECHINT) by its Science and Technology Division (S&T), then headed by Dr.K.Santanam. The S&T Division was started by Kao immediately after the formation of the R&AW in 1968 and he took Santanam from the Indian Atomic Energy Commission as its No.2. Over the years, he rose to be its head. It was his brilliant analysis of the tit bits of TECHINT collected by the Monitoring Division that enabled the R&AW to establish the details of Pakistan's clandestine military nuclear programme. Santanam was the first to assess that Pakistan was clandestinely constructing an uranium enrichment plant at Kahuta in addition to the plutonium reprocessing plant. The progress in the construction of the Kahuta plant and other developments relating to Pakistan's military nuclear programme-—including the full ramifications of its clandestine procurement network— were systematically monitored by the S&T Division under the leadership of Santanam. Suntook kept Morarji Desai briefed on these developments and this added to the positive change in Morarji Desai's attitude towards the R&AW.

Gen.Zia ul-Haq, who overthrew Zulfikar Ali Bhutto in a military coup in 1977 and arrested him, was anxious to avoid any fresh tensions in Pakistan's relations with India till he was able to get rid of Bhutto and consolidate his power. He kept in touch with Morarji Desai over phone in order to befriend him. Like many senior military officers of the Pakistan Army, Zia was a past master in the art of flattery. Often, he would ring up Morarji Desai under the pretext of consulting him on native medicine and urine therapy. Nothing flattered Morarji more. Zia would ask him with seeming earnestness in his voice: "Excellency, how many times one should drink the urine in a day? Should it be the first urine of the morning or can it be any time of the day?" In a disarmed and unguarded moment one day, Morarji told him that he was aware that Pakistan was clandestinely trying to develop a military nuclear capability. Indiscreet political leaders are the unavoidable occupational hazards of the intelligence profession.

Thus, by the beginning of 1979, the R&AW, under the leadership of Suntook, had considerably succeeded in diluting the negative perceptions in the minds of Morarji Desai about the R&AW. And then, there was a split in the ruling Janata Party, which led to the resignation of Morarji Desai in July,1979, and Charan Singh's taking-over as the new Prime Minister. Indira Gandhi exploited the situation in her favour, forcing new elections in January, 1980, in which her Congress (I) party returned to power and she was back as the Prime Minister of India after a gap of about three years. Charan Singh's brief tenure as the Prime Minister was uneventful for the R&AW.

CHAPTER IX

Indira Gandhi Back In Power

The return of Indira Gandhi to power in the beginning of 1980 had been anticipated by me. When I was in Paris, investigating teams of the CBI used to come there to investigate allegations that she or her party had accepted a bribe from a French oil company during the Emergency. I was not involved in the investigation, but one of the investigating officers was a close friend of mine and he used to stay as my guest in Paris. We used to discuss the result of the investigation. I remember telling him frequently: "There is hardly any evidence against her. Don't harass and humiliate her on the basis of flimsy evidence. She will win back the sympathy of the public and will be back in power." He was very confident that the case against her would end in conviction. "Her political career is finished," he used to say. Investigating officers should not have strong likes and dislikes. This would affect their objectivity and distort the investigation. Charan Singh, who was co-ordinating and supervising the various investigations against her, had carefully chosen for the investigation officers known to be critical of her. In their over-anxiety to prove something or the other against her, they spoilt the cases. She was the ultimate beneficiary. Public opinion had forgotten her perceived excesses during the Emergency and voted her back to power.

Immediately after taking over once again as the Prime Minister, Indira Gandhi removed the chiefs of the IB and the CBI, replacing officers appointed by Morarji Desai with her own nominees. Many of us in the R&AW expected that she would replace Suntook too. After all, he was the nominee of Morarji Desai and had established a very

good personal equation with him. Surprisingly, she did not replace
him. He continued as the chief of the R&AW till his superannuation
in March,1983. The credit for this should go to two factors. Firstly,
Suntook was a totally professional officer with no political leanings.
Politically, he was very non-controversial. Secondly, he enjoyed
the total trust of Kao, who had reasons to be grateful to him for
ensuring that he was not harassed or humiliated by the Morarji Desai
Government. Kao, who had retired in 1977, came back as Senior
Adviser to Indira Gandhi in the Cabinet Secretariat only in 1981. But
till, then, he was already acting as an informal adviser to her from his
house. He was already being consulted by her on all matters relating
to the R&AW and on important developments concerning national
security. It was Kao's steadfast support to him that enabled Suntook
to continue undisturbed. However, Suntook did not have the same
access to her as he used to have to Morarji Desai. He did not mind
routing things to her for orders through Kao.

Indira Gandhi's return to power was followed by a witch-hunt
of serving and retired officers of different departments, who were
associated with the various investigations against her by the CBI
and the various enquiries against her on charges of excesses during
the Emergency, conducted by the Justice Shah Commission and
the L.P.Singh Committee. The IB played an objectionable role in
helping her and her aides from her party to identify and prepare
a black list of serving officers involved in these investigations and
enquiries. Her first few months in office were spent in settling scores
with those, whom she thought had betrayed her when she was out
of power.

While Suntook himself escaped any negative consequences to
himself with the support of Kao, neither he nor Kao could protect
four senior IPS officers of the R&AW, including the late Shiv Raj
Bahadur, Suntook's No.2, from being humiliated by her. On the
basis of unsubstantiated tales carried to her and her aides that
these officers had played a very active role in the investigations and
enquiries against her, she had them thrown out of the organization
and ordered their reversion back to their respective States. Shiv Raj

Bahadur was a lovable, low profile and non-controversial officer of the Orissa cadre of the IPS, who had for some years worked as the staff officer of Kao, when he was the chief of the R&AW before 1977. Kao always held him in very great esteem. In spite of this, he could not protect him from totally unjustified ignominy. The only concession she made to Kao's entreaties about Bahadur, was to let him continue till his superannuation as the head of a central police organization without insisting on his going back to Orissa.

1980 was a bad year for the R&AW. The sins of commission and omission of some of the founding fathers of the organization since it was formed in 1968 came home to roost. When the organization came into being, Indira Gandhi gave it many special dispensations such as exempting it from the purview of the Union Public Service Commission (UPSC) in matters of recruitment and promotions, powers of sanction of foreign tours etc. The head of the R&AW wore two hats. As the head of the organization, he used to send proposals for direct recruitment, sanction of posts, foreign travel etc to the Cabinet Secretariat. As a Secretary in the Cabinet Secretariat, he had these proposals examined and sanctioned. The idea was that if the R&AW was to be effective as an external intelligence agency, it should not be subject to the usual red tape. The grant of these special dispensations demanded that the head of the R&AW exercised these powers objectively with a deep sense of responsibility. Over the years, there was a feeling among the lower and middle level officers of the organization that these special powers were being misused to promote favouritism and nepotism. Such feeling arose from the fact that among the direct recruits to the organization from the market, there were many who were related to serving and retired officers of the Government. Special posts were created in the Indian diplomatic missions abroad to accommodate relatives of senior officers such as T.N.Kaul, former Foreign Secretary. Consequently, the staff started referring to the organization sarcastically as the Relatives and Associates Wing.

The man management was also poor. There was a divide between the senior officers and those at the junior level. The R&AW had developed into an elitist organization with very little interaction between the seniors and the juniors. The juniors felt that the seniors did not bother about them and their difficulties. There were allegations that there was a lack of transparency in promotions. The organization's action in keeping many of its menial staff such as lift operators, cleaners, servers in cafeteria etc as contract daily wage staff for years, violating government rules that nobody could be kept on daily wages for more than three years, added to the unhappiness. There was also resentment among the lower and middle-level staff over the frequent security checks carried out by the Counter-Intelligence and Security (CI&S) division of the organization. The CI&S division was responsible for internal security and for the prevention of the penetration of the organization by foreign intelligence agencies. As part of its normal duties, the CI&S used to make surprise checks of the Branches and carry out periodic surprise checks at the gates to make sure no one was taking out any official document. It also made enquiries about the personal lives of the staff in order to look for evidence of living beyond one's means. There was a growing criticism of the work of the CI&S Division. It was alleged that it harassed the staff at the lower and middle levels, but did not apply the same strictness of checks against the senior officers. It was accused of acting under the presumption that only the staff at the lower and middle levels would betray the organization and the country and not senior officers.

The post-1971 years had seen the beginning of a certain permissiveness (an attitude of anything goes) inside the organization, which was overlooked by Kao and other senior officers. Incidents, which should have rung repeated alarm bells, remained under the carpet. A senior IPS officer posted in a neighbouring country got involved in a drunken brawl with a local army officer in a local club and got allegedly waylaid and beaten up by a group of local army officers while he was on his way home from the club. At the insistence of the Indian High Commissioner, this officer was withdrawn and reverted to his State. Another IPS officer of the same batch posted abroad took advantage of his position as the First Secretary (Consular) in an Indian diplomatic mission in the West to issue to himself and his family members ordinary passports without the clearance of the MEA and get long-term visas from the host government on those passports. After completing his tenure, he resigned from the organization and IPS and settled down in that country. A retired Major of the Indian Army, who went on leave to the US with his family to visit relatives, did not return. Before their departure, the CI&S Division had noticed that they were disposing off all their movable property in India and had rung an alarm bell. No action was taken to stop his going abroad. A retired military officer, posted in Europe, became an alcoholic and a compulsive gambler and developed a relationship with an American girl, much younger to him in age. She was suspected to be from the CIA. Often, he never came to office for days together and coded operational messages sent to him from the headquarters remained unattended to. When Kao visited that station, his wife met him secretly and pleaded with him to transfer her husband back to Delhi. She complained that the European posting of her husband had destroyed their marriage. He was transferred back and eased out. Two other retired military officers—one of them the son of a retired Indian Police officer— were posted abroad despite the reservations expressed by the Training Division about their suitability for foreign posting because of their known addiction to alcohol. They brought a bad name to the organization. They had to be withdrawn from their foreign postings and eased out. A member of the staff of Kao, who was posted to the US, did not return home at the end of his tenure. So too, a member of the staff of Sankaran Nair, who was posted to the UK. Another junior member of the staff settled down in West Europe after completing his tenure. The reluctance of the senior leadership of the organization to act strongly against the delinquent officers encouraged the permissive atmosphere. It also weakened the image of the senior officers in the eyes of their staff, thereby encouraging indiscipline.

A cumulative effect of all this was the appearance of trade unionism in the organization and an embarrassing strike by sections of its employees in 1980. The immediate trigger for the strike was a security check of a branch by the CI&S staff. The branch members protested and gheroed (surrounded) the CI&S staff, including the head of the Division. Ultimately, the organization had to seek the assistance of the Delhi police to have them freed. The strike continued for some days—with demonstrations outside the gates, processions and meetings, at which speeches critical of the senior officers were made. An R&AW employees' association came into being to co-ordinate such activities.

One would have thought that these developments would have created doubts in the mind of Indira Gandhi about the suitability of Suntook to continue as the chief. It did not. Such outbreaks of staff indiscipline were not confined to the R&AW alone. The IB and the CBI were also affected—though not to the same serious extent as the R&AW. On the reported advice of Kao, Indira Gandhi extended strong backing to the efforts of Suntook to put down the indiscipline and restore normalcy in the functioning of the organization. Suntook's deft handling of the situation through a policy of carrots and sticks— sacking the ring leaders and action to redress the genuine grievances of the staff—ultimately led to a collapse of the strike. The R&AW and the IB, acting jointly, managed to persuade the Government to ban trade unions in the intelligence community.

Under Morarji Desai, Suntook had remained preoccupied with rehabilitating the prestige of the organization and preserving its infrastructure. Morarji came to office thinking that the R&AW was not needed. It took many months for Suntook to convince him that it was and to persuade him to reverse some of his orders for pruning the organization. As a result, there were no new operational initiatives during this period. Once Suntook settled down under Indira Gandhi after overcoming the staff indiscipline and the strike, he was able to devote the remaining two and a half years of his service to sharpen once again the operational claws of the organization. He took advantage of the anti-Army unrest in Pakistan—particularly after the execution of Z.A.Bhutto— to network with forces in Pakistan well disposed towards India and ill-disposed towards its own Army. With the encouragement of Kao and Indira Gandhi, he started building up a covert action capability in Pakistan, similar to the capability which the IB and then the R&AW had in pre-1971 East Pakistan. He also revamped the TECHINT capability of the R&AW and considerably strengthened its Monitoring Division, as its TECHINT Division was called. The credit for creating in the R&AW a capability for closely monitoring Pakistan's military nuclear programme should go to Suntook and Santanam.

The other area where Suntook made his mark was Africa. He was the R&AW's foremost African expert. Even before 1968, one or two newly independent African countries had looked up to the IB to help them in setting up an intelligence collection capability. Kao and Sankaran Nair—one after the other—had spent some months in Accra at the request of Dr.Kwame Nkrumah, the then President of Ghana, to help that country in building up its intelligence collection capability. Indira Gandhi wanted this co-operation with the African countries to be maintained. At her instance, the R&AW organized the training of the intelligence and police officers of many African countries in India. She also encouraged the R&AW to assist the African National Congress (ANC) in its anti-apartheid struggle in South Africa and the South-West Africa People's Organization (SWAPO) in its struggle for an independent Namibia. Under Suntook, the R&AW organized the training of many of their cadres, either in India itself or in secret camps in bordering African countries. Retired officers of the R&AW were deputed to work on the faculty of the training institutes of the intelligence agencies of some African countries. It is a pity that after Suntook, no other chief of the R&AW had taken the same interest in Africa as he did and had allowed the goodwill for the R&AW in the African countries to wither away.

Bangladesh, which brought glory to the R&AW in 1971, became an embarrassing millstone round its neck. It watched helplessly as there was one surprise after another and as Bangladesh once again became the hub of anti-Indian activities directed against India's North-East. The spread of insurgency to Tripura and Assam in the 1980s from sanctuaries in Bangladesh and the seeming Indian helplessness in dealing with it strengthened India's image as a soft state. The perception that any neighbour–big or small— can defy India with impunity gained strength. It would be unfair to blame only the R&AW for this state of affairs. The political leadership and the prevailing ground realities in Bangladesh also had their contribution to make to the image of Indian weakness in dealing with Bangladesh. In India, one does not often realize the constraints imposed on Indian policy-making in Bangladesh, the like of which one does not face in Pakistan. Bangladesh still has a large number of Hindus and has substantial pockets of friendly feelings for India. Any unwise and hasty use of the big stick against Bangladesh could have negative consequences for the Hindus and the pro-India sections of its population. The resulting Indian reluctance to use the big stick is exploited by the anti-India elements in the local administration and political class to further step up their anti-India activities. We have not yet found a way of breaking up this vicious circle.

Apart from the outbreak of the insurgency in Tripura and the disturbed conditions in Assam and the support received by the anti-India elements from Bangladesh, three other developments of even greater concern to India's national security managers made their appearance during this period. The first was the entry of the Soviet troops into Afghanistan and the jihad against the Soviet troops orchestrated by the CIA with the collaboration of the ISI. The second was the outbreak of Khalistani terrorism in Punjab. The third was the unrest among the Sri Lankan Tamils and some policies of the Sri Lankan Government, which were viewed by Indira Gandhi as likely to be detrimental to Indian security. The developments in Afghanistan paved the way for the spread of pan-Islamic jihadi terrorism into India's Jammu and Kashmir (J&K) and its subsequent spread to other parts of India. The terrorism in Punjab contributed to the assassination of Indira Gandhi by two of her Sikh security guards in October 1984 and to nearly 11 years of further bloodshed caused by the Khalistani terrorists. The developments in Sri Lanka gave birth to the Liberation Tigers of Tamil Eelam (LTTE), which assassinated Rajiv Gandhi in May,1991. A common thread connecting the two developments in Afghanistan and Punjab was the role of the ISI in both and the reluctance of the US to act against Pakistan for using terrorism against India lest it weakened the support of the ISI for making the Soviet troops bleed in Afghanistan.

The Soviet intervention in Afghanistan created a dilemma for India and Indira Gandhi. Considerations of solidarity with the USSR, which had stood by India at the time of the war with Pakistan in 1971, demanded that India refrain from criticizing the intervention. Considerations of friendship with the Afghan people, who have always been well-wishers of India, demanded that India refrain from endorsing it. It was an uncomfortable situation for India, similar to what Jawaharlal Nehru had faced when the Soviet troops invaded Hungary in 1956 to overthrow an anti-Moscow Government and replace it with one, which owed its survival to the presence of the Soviet troops in Hungarian territory. Indira Gandhi was aware, through the R&AW, of the attempts of the CIA, with the help of the ISI, to destabilize Afghanistan and use Afghan territory to foment anti-Moscow unrest in the Central Asian region of the USSR. It was these attempts, which provoked the panic Soviet intervention. The intervention was not the outcome of a long-standing Soviet expansionist plan to reach the warm-water ports of Pakistan, as projected by the CIA in its PSYWAR against the USSR. It was the outcome of the nervousness caused in Moscow due to perceived threats to the stability of the Central Asian region. Indira Gandhi understood the Soviet nervousness and was unhappy with the impression given by the Charan Singh Government that it did not appreciate the Soviet intervention. One of her first acts after taking over as the Prime Minister once again was to remove any wrong impression of a lack of Indian understanding of the concerns, which forced the Soviet intervention.

At the same time, she was hoping that the Soviet intervention would be of short duration and that the Soviet troops could be withdrawn from the Afghan territory after a few months after the immediate threats to the stability of Afghanistan had been removed. Even Moscow was hoping to be able to withdraw its troops quickly. But this was not to be. In the beginning of 1981, Le Comte Alexandre de Marenches, the head of the SDECE, the French external intelligence agency, had been to Washington DC to pay a visit to William J. Casey, who had taken over as the head of the CIA in the new administration of Ronald Reagan on January 28,1981. He claimed some years later after he had resigned as the head of the SDECE that during this meeting he proposed to Casey that the Western intelligence agencies should exploit the situation to keep the Soviet troops bogged down and bleeding in Afghanistan, which could ultimately weaken the USSR itself. Among the various ideas which he suggested to Casey was to make the Soviet troops based in Afghanistan heroin addicts, in order to weaken their fighting capability. Casey was so excited by Le Comte's ideas that he took him to Reagan, who approved the entire plan for a covert operation to keep the Soviet troops bleeding except the idea to use heroin. Thus started the dirtiest of the CIA's dirty tricks, the evil consequences of which have not spared many countries of the world—not even the US as it realized on 9/11.

According to Le Comte, he wanted to give this operation the code name "Operation Mosquito". One does not know what code name was ultimately given, but the jihadis from many countries trained and armed by the CIA through the intermediary of the ISI for use against the Soviet troops started spreading like mosquitoes, if not locusts, right across the world from their breeding swamps in the Pakistan-Afghanistan region. They ultimately reached the US and West Europe. Le Comte claimed that the use of heroin in this operation was not approved by Reagan, but the fact was that it was used extensively. Within a few months of this operation being launched, Le Comte had to resign as the Director-General of the SDECE following the failure of the French President Giscard d'Estaing to win re-election in 1981. Francois Mitterrand, the French Socialist leader, who was elected the President in May 1981, and his nominee as the SDECE chief, Pierre Marion, did not share Le Comte's ill-advised enthusiasm for this operation and withdrew from it. Thereafter, it remained a covert action largely orchestrated by the Saudi intelligence and the ISI, under the supervision of the CIA.

The division of responsibilities was roughly as follows: the CIA and the Saudi intelligence provided the funds. The CIA provided the training and the arms and ammunition. Many of the arms and ammunition —barring items such as the US-made Stinger missiles

and chemical timers for the improvised explosive devices (IEDs)-
were of Chinese or Soviet origin recovered from the Vietnamese
during the war in Vietnam or subsequently procured from the arms
smugglers. The recruitment of the Afghan and Pakistani Mujahideen,
their training and motivation were handled by the ISI. The Arab
volunteers were recruited by the Saudi intelligence and got trained
in the camps of the ISI. The CIA handed over the money and the
arms and ammunition to the ISI and allowed it to decide how it
would distribute them. The ISI kept some for its own future use
against India and, in distributing the rest, it showed a favouritism
towards the Pashtun followers of Gulbuddin Heckmatyar of Hizbe
Islami and a discrimination against the Tajik followers of the late
Ahmed Shah Masood.

There were no reliable reports of the total number of Pakistani
and Afghan Mujahideen thus recruited and trained by the ISI at the
instance of the CIA. The Khad, the Afghan intelligence agency, with
which the R&AW had a cordial and productive liaison relationship
for many years, had told the R&AW that its estimate was that 80,000
Afghan and Pakistani Mujahideen and about 6,000 Arabs were
trained and armed by the ISI and the CIA during this operation.
After the withdrawal of the Soviet troops from Afghanistan in 1988-
89 and the collapse of the Soviet-backed Najibullah Government in
Kabul in April,1992, the surviving remnants of the Arab mujahideen
became the hard core of Al Qaeda and those of the Afghan and
Pakistani Mujahideen the hard core of the International Islamic
Front (IIF) for Jihad Against the Crusaders and the Jewish People
formed by Osama bin Laden in 1998.Jihadi terrorism, which has
been causing so much havoc across the world, including India, is thus
the product of two minds in the world of intelligence–William Casey
and Le Comte Alexandre de Marenches. During his secret visits to
the terrorist producing training camps and madrasas in Pakistan in
the 1980s, Casey used to address the trainees as "My sons". He died
of cancer during the second term of Reagan and, therefore, did not
live long enough to see the thousands killed by "his sons" and their
associates, including nearly 3,000 of his own countrymen on 9/11.
Some of the retired CIA officers of those days, who are now parading

themselves around the world and making money as the leading Al Qaeda watchers, were the original creators of Al Qaeda.

The long-term implications of the developments in Afghanistan to India's internal security remained inadequately analysed and appreciated in the R&AW and the IB in the beginning of the 1980s. Only after Khalistani terrorism broke out in Punjab in 1981 and thereafter spread to Delhi and training camps for the Khalistani terrorists came up in Pakistani territory was there a realization that the ISI had started diverting to the Khalistanis some of the stocks of arms and ammunition received by it from the CIA for distribution to the Afghan Mujahideen and their Arab collaborators. The Khalistanis trained and armed in clandestine training camps set up by the ISI in the Punjab and the North-West Frontier Province (NWFP) were used by the ISI in an attempt to destabilize Indian Punjab as a prelude to making another try to grab Jammu and Kashmir (J&K).

CHAPTER X

The Khalistani Terrorism

In the first few years after India's independence, the Sikh migrants from Punjab constituted the largest single group of Indian origin in the Indian diaspora in the UK, the US and Canada. Some of them had migrated even during the British rule—particularly to Canada to work in the saw mills of British Columbia. Others had gone after 1947. Most of these migrants came from poor rural families and many of them in the UK earned their living by working as drivers and conductors in the public transportation systems of the municipalities. Some of the farmers, who had migrated to the US, did extremely well in citrus farming in California. The Yuba City in California had a prosperous community of Sikh farmers. The migrants to Canada earned their living in factories and in the public transportation systems.

Despite their living in Western countries, they continued to be attached to their religion and led their lives as true Sikhs. Whenever they could save enough money, they would come to India to visit their relatives and worship in the Golden Temple in Amritsar. In the late 1950s and the early 1960s, the Sikhs, who were working abroad as salary-earners, started facing difficulties because their employers began insisting that they should shave off their beard and stop wearing turbans. This was particularly so in the public transportation companies of the UK. Moreover, the Sikh migrants in the West faced difficulties in getting permission from the municipal authorities for acquiring land and constructing gurudwaras where they could worship.

In the UK, many of the affected Sikhs took up the matter with the Indian High Commission in London and sought its intervention. The High Commission declined to intervene and advised the Sikhs to approach the local authorities for a redressal of their grievances. Jawaharlal Nehru, who was India's Prime Minister at that time, followed a hands-off policy with regard to the migrants of Indian origin living abroad. He was against the Government of India intervening on their behalf with their host governments. They were told that they should sort out matters themselves by taking up their problems with the local authorities.

The affected Sikhs compared what they thought was the indifferent attitude of the Government of India with the helpful and interventionist role played by the Government of Israel in responding to the religious sensitivities of the Jewish people, wherever they might be living and whatever might be their nationality. The Israeli Government, according to the aggrieved Sikhs, always assumed a moral responsibility for protecting the religious interests of the Jewish people. Moreover, Israeli citizenship laws permitted dual nationality, whereas the Sikh migrants, who acquired a foreign nationality, had to renounce their Indian citizenship. Another demand of the Sikhs was that the Government of India should take up with Pakistan the question of facilitating pilgrimage visits by Sikhs living in India as well as abroad to their holy shrines in Pakistan such as the Nankana Sahib gurudwara.

Dissatisfaction over the reluctance of the Government of India to vigorously take up such issues with other Governments gave rise to a feeling among some of the Sikh residents of the UK, the US and Canada that only by creating an independent State for the Sikhs would they be able to have their religious rights protected. A group of Sikh bus drivers and conductors in the UK formed an organization called the Sikh Home Rule Movement under the leadership of one Charan Singh Panchi. Some well-to-do Sikh farmers in the US floated an organization called the United Sikh Appeal, which was modeled after the United Jewish Appeal, which had actively supported the rights of the Jewish people and worked for an independent State of

Israel. However, the majority of the Sikh communities in the West kept away from these organizations. They did not support the idea of an independent Sikh State.

Before the India-Pakistan war of 1971, Dr.Jagjit Singh Chauhan, who had served for a few months between 1967 and 1969 as the Deputy Speaker of the Punjab Assembly and then as the Finance Minister of Punjab, went to London, joined the Sikh Home Rule Movement, took over its leadership and re-named it as the Khalistan movement. He wanted that the independent Sikh State to be created in Punjab should be named as Khalistan. Even before his arrival in the UK, the Pakistani High Commission and the US Embassy in London were in touch with the activists of the Sikh Home Rule Movement. They established contact with Chauhan after his arrival and started encouraging his propaganda against the Government of India in order to embarrass Indira Gandhi. Gen.Yahya Khan, Pakistan's military dictator, invited him to Pakistan. He was received warmly and lionized as the leader of the Indian Sikh community even though he had no following in the Sikh community of Punjab. During his visit to Pakistan, the Pakistani authorities presented to him some of the Sikh holy relics kept in the gurudwaras of Pakistan. He took them with him to the UK and sought to use them in order to project himself as a leader, who could protect the religious interests of the Sikhs.

Before the outbreak of the war in December,1971, the R&AW, on the instructions of Indira Gandhi, had started a PSYWAR campaign to highlight the violation of the human rights of the people of East Pakistan and the resulting refugee exodus into India. The CIA and the ISI sought to counter this by starting a PSYWAR campaign on the alleged violation of the human rights of the Sikhs in India and the indifferent attitude of the Government of India to the problems of the Sikhs living abroad. Chauhan visited New York and met the local media and others in order to brief them on the Khalistan movement. These meetings were discreetly arranged by some members of the staff of the US National Security Council Secretariat, then headed by Dr.Henry Kissinger. On October 13,1971, he had an advertisement published in the "New York Times" proclaiming the beginning of a movement for an independent Sikh State. Enquiries made by the R&AW indicated that the Pakistani Embassy in Washington DC had paid for this advertisement. This PSYWAR campaign against India and Indira Gandhi on the question of the alleged violation of the human rights of the Sikhs continued till 1977. When Indira Gandhi lost the elections in 1977 and was replaced by Morarji Desai, this campaign was abruptly discontinued by the CIA and the ISI. Dr. Chauhan returned to India and stopped campaigning for the creation of the so-called Khalistan.

In the meanwhile, a number of other Sikh organizations formed by sections of the Sikh youth in the UK, the US and Canada came into being with names such as the International Sikh Youth Federation (ISYF), the Dal Khalsa, the Babbar Khalsa etc. These advocated a violent campaign for the creation of Khalistan and repudiated the leadership of Dr.Chauhan, who was against resort to violence. By the end of the 1970s, the ISI had lost interest in Chauhan and started encouraging the new organizations. When Indira Gandhi returned to power in 1980, Chauhan went back to London and re-started his Khalistan movement. As part of his propaganda campaign, he got postage stamps and alleged currency notes of the so-called independent State of Khalistan printed in Canada and started circulating them. He went to Ottawa, met a Chinese diplomat there and allegedly sought Chinese support for his movement. The Chinese declined. He reportedly went to Hong Kong and tried to go to Beiijing in order to meet the Chinese leaders. The Chinese authorities refused him entry into China. After 1980, he was thus spurned by China and downgraded by Pakistan, but the US continued to maintain interest in him. He frequently visited Washington DC, met US officials and members of the Congress and testified before Congressional committees on matters such as India's relations with the USSR, the alleged presence of Soviet military officers in India etc. The CIA maintained a distance from the new Sikh youth organizations because they advocated violence, but it kept itself briefed on their plans and activities through journalists and other intermediaries.

After Indira Gandhi came back to power, a new Sikh leader became active in the US. His name was Ganga Singh Dhillon, who was in the Punjab Police as a junior official before he migrated to the US and settled down in Washington DC. After migrating to the US, he married a Sikh woman of Kenyan origin, who was a close personal friend of the wife of Gen.Zia-ul-Haq, and also belonged to a Kenyan family. With the help of wives, Dhillon came to know Zia and became one of his trusted friends. He formed in Washington DC an organization called the Nankana Sahib Foundation and used to visit Pakistan often. The two families became so close to each other that when Zia visited Washington DC, his physically disadvantaged daughter used to stay with the Dhillons and not in the hotel in which Zia and his wife were put up by the local authorities. Dhillon also became a strong critic of Indira Gandhi and helped the US in the propaganda campaign against her.

As a result of these activities, Suntook decided towards the end of 1980 to create a separate Division to collect intelligence about the activities of the Sikh extremist elements abroad and monitor their links with the ISI. I was put in charge of the Division. After taking over, I collected all past reports bearing on this subject, collated them and prepared a detailed background note, which I could use as a database in the Division. One day, a Joint Secretary in the Ministry of External Affairs (MEA) rang me up and asked me whether the R&AW had any background note on Sikh extremist activities abroad, particularly in the US. I sent him a few copies of the detailed note which I had prepared.

Some days later, the office of Narasimha Rao, who had taken over as the Minister for External Affairs under Indira Gandhi, rang me up and said that Rao, who was going on a visit to the US, wanted me to meet him and brief him on Khalistani activities in the US and their links with Pakistan. I met him and briefed him. He showed me the background note, which I had prepared of which he had a copy, and asked: "This is a very good background note prepared by the MEA. Why can't the R&AW prepare something like this?" I replied that I had, in fact, prepared it after going through the R&AW files on the

subject and sent some copies to a Joint Secretary in the MEA. Rao
remarked in surprise: " But the Joint Secretary said he had prepared
it!"

On September 29,1981, the then Cabinet Secretary (CS) received
a flash from the New Delhi airport control tower that an aircraft of
the Indian Airlines had been hijacked by some unidentified terrorists
and forced to fly to Lahore. The Crisis Management Committee
of the Government of India immediately met in the office of the
Cabinet Secretary. The initial assessment was that the hijacking must
have been carried out by the members of the Jammu and Kashmir
Liberation Front (JKLF), which had earlier carried out a hijacking in
1971. I was called by the Cabinet Secretary. At that time, the terrorists
had not identified themselves. The CS asked me for my assessment.
I disagreed with the view that the JKLF must be responsible for it
and added that it was most probably carried out by a Sikh extremist
organization called the Dal Khalsa headed by one Gajendra Singh.
My view was not accepted because till then the Sikh extremists—
apart from carrying out a massacre of some members of a sect known
as the Nirankaris— had not indulged in any act of terrorism.

As I reached back my office, my Personal Assistant told me that
the office of the CS was frantically trying to contact me and that
they wanted me to come back to his office. When I reached there,
an official in the CS' office told me that the terrorists had identified
themselves. It was some members of the Dal Khalsa led by Gajendra
Singh, who had carried out the hijacking. He asked me how I was
able to identify them before they had identified themselves. I replied
that a few days earlier the then "New York Times" correspondent
in New Delhi had visited the Golden Temple in Amritsar and met
some members of the Dal Khalsa. He had also interviewed Gajendra
Singh on the objectives of the Dal Khalsa and the problems of
the Sikhs. In that interview, Gajendra Singh had said: "The time
has come for the Dal Khalsa to emulate the Palestine Liberation
Organisation." The official asked me whether the "New York Times"
published the interview. I said I did not know since I did not get the
paper. He asked: "How then do you know he was interviewed by its

New Delhi correspondent?" I replied that the IB used to intercept for the Press Information Bureau all telex despatches sent by the foreign correspondents based in New Delhi to their headquarters. They used to circulate to all senior officers dealing with national security intercepts of relevant despatches. They had intercepted the telex message sent by the "New York Times" correspondent to his headquarters about his meeting with Gajendra Singh and other members of the Dal Khalsa. I also received a copy of that intercept.

The Pakistani authorities persuaded the hijackers to release the passengers and the plane and to surrender themselves. The plane with the passengers returned to India. The surrendered hijackers, including Gajendra Singh, were allowed to live in the Nankana Sahib gurudwara. The Zil-ul-Haq Government refused to hand them over to the Government of India for investigation and trial. They promised that they would try them in their court after proper investigation. They made a sham of an investigation and trial. They were convicted and sentenced to imprisonment, but instead of sending them to jail, they were allowed to continue living in Nankana Sahib. Gajendra Singh used to meet Sikh pilgrims visiting Nankana Sahib from India and abroad and carry on propaganda against the Government of India. New Delhi's protests against this used to be rejected by the Pakistani authorities.

Three more hijackings followed, with a similar course of events. The Pakistani authorities would allow the plane to land, facilitate interactions between the hijackers and the media to enable the hijackers indulge in anti-India and anti-Indira propaganda, persuade them to release the passengers and the aircraft so that they could return to India, make a pretense of arresting the hijackers and allow them to stay in a gurudwara instead of in a prison. However, in the case of the fifth and last hijacking on August 24, 1984, they did not follow this drill since their earlier fraternization with the hijackers of the previous flights had come in for criticism from some sections of the international community. When this aircraft landed in Lahore, the ISI officials found that the terrorists had hijacked it with a toy and not a real weapon. They, therefore, gave the terrorists a revolver and persuaded them to go to Dubai. When the plane landed at Dubai, the authorities of the United Arab Emirates persuaded them to terminate the hijacking, by promising that they would not be handed over to the Indian authorities. The hijackers released the plane and passengers so that they could go back to India and handed over the revolver to the security authorities of Dubai. They wanted that they should be allowed to go to the US. They seemed confident that the US would not act against them.

As soon as the Government of India came to know of the plane taking off from Lahore for Dubai, they despatched a joint team of the IB, the R&AW, the MEA and the Ministry of Civil Aviation to Dubai to interact with the Dubai authorities and persuade them to hand over the hijackers to India along with the revolver for trial as soon as the hijacking was terminated. Initially, the UAE authorities seemed hesitant to do so. Indira Gandhi deputed Romesh Bhandari, then Secretary in the MEA, who had very high level contacts in the ruling family and the bureaucracy of the UAE to go to Dubai to persuade the UAE authorities to hand over the hijackers and the revolver. He was successful in his mission. An aircraft chartered from a Western company was sent to Dubai with a joint team of officers from the IB, the R&AW, one of the central para-military forces and the MEA. It was headed by an officer of the R&AW, who was then on deputation to the MEA to be in charge of security in the Ministry and the Indian diplomatic missions abroad. After the plane landed in Dubai, all the members of the Indian team stayed inside the aircraft so that the hijackers were not able to see them.

After the aircraft had landed, the Dubai authorities told the hijackers that as desired by them they were being handed over to the US authorities and that a special plane had come from the US to take them. They were then taken to the chartered aircraft and handed over to the Indian security team inside, along with the revolver. Only then the hijackers realised that they had been misled and that they were actually being taken to India. By then, it was too late for them to do anything. The pilot and the other members of the crew of the aircraft were also taken by surprise because they did not know that the aircraft had been chartered by the Indian security establishment for flying back the hijackers. They murmured some protest, but ultimately flew back to Delhi with the hijackers.

This was a brilliant piece of operation made possible by the co-operation of the UAE authorities, the excellent contacts of Romesh Bhandari in the Gulf countries in general and in the UAE in particular and the professionalism of the Indian security team headed by the R&AW officer. However, all this would not have been possible but for the high regard in which Indira Gandhi was held in the UAE. When some terrorists belonging to the Harkat-ul-Mujahideen (HUM) of Pakistan hijacked an Indian Airlines plane from Kathmandu in December, 1999, they first took it to Lahore and then Dubai before finally going to Kandahar. The Government of the then Prime Minister Atal Bihari Vajpayee did not get the same kind of co-operation from the UAE authorities as Indira Gandhi was able to get. They allowed the plane to proceed to Kandahar after re-fuelling it. The failure of the Vajpayee Government to persuade the UAE authorities to terminate the hijacking could be attributed partly to its lack of good contacts in the UAE and partly to its image in the Gulf as anti-Muslim. Moreover, the MEA did not have in 1999 any senior officer with the kind of high-level contacts in the ruling circles of the Gulf countries as Romesh Bhandari had.

His contacts were not confined to the Gulf countries only. He had similar high-level contacts in South-East Asia. Once the R&AW received information that a Khalistani terrorist had taken shelter in the Philippines. It immediately sought the assistance of Bhandari. He was able to persuade senior officials in Manila to pick him up informally without arresting him and hand him over to the Indian security officials. In order to avoid media publicity, which might have invited judicial intervention, they picked him up and detained him in an Air Force base in the interior of the Philippines. An ARC plane flew in there and brought him to India. Such informal networking and contacts at the political and bureaucratic levels greatly help in counter-terrorism. One got an impression that the Vajpayee

Government was not able to develop such networking during the six years it was in office.

The revolver given by the ISI to the hijackers at Lahore before the aircraft was taken to Dubai was of West German make. The R&AW sent the details of the revolver to its counterpart in the then West Germany and sought its help for ascertaining to whom the West German company had sold it. After making the necessary enquiries, the West German intelligence intimated that the revolver was part of a consignment sold by the company to the Pakistan Army. The Government of India immediately shared this information with US officials and pointed out that it was a fit case for declaring Pakistan a State-sponsor of international terrorism. The US authorities did not agree. They said that there was no credible evidence to show that this revolver was given to the terrorists by a Pakistani official. The information that the revolver was handed over to the hijackers at Lahore by Pakistani officials came from one of the passengers of the hijacked aircraft, who had seen the revolver being handed over. During the interrogation, the hijackers also admitted that they got the revolver at Lahore from Pakistani officials. But, the US authorities were not prepared to accept this oral evidence as conclusive proof against Pakistan.

The action of the Dubai authorities in handing over the hijackers and the revolver to Indian officials created a scare in Khalistani circles and some nervousness in the ISI too. As a result, hijackings by Khalistani terrorists stopped completely. There were some instances of hijackings subsequently too, but these were carried out by individual elements unconnected with the Khalistan movement.

When the ISI noticed the motivation and the determination of the Khalistani elements, it decided to exploit them for its purposes to create instability in the Punjab. It set up clandestine camps for training and arming the Khalistani recruits in Pakistani Punjab and in the North-West Frontier Province (NWFP). Gajendra Singh, the hijacker of the Dal Khalsa, was put in charge of these training camps. Other Sikh terrorists such as Talwinder Singh Parmar of the Babbar Khalsa in Vancouver, who was involved in the massacre

of some Nirankaris in Punjab, Manjit Singh alias Lal Singh of the
ISYF, Canada, and Gurdip Singh Sivia of th ISYF, UK, were allowed
to visit these training camps in Pakistani territory and motivate the
Khalistani recruits. Many Khalistani elements from India were also
allowed to cross over into Pakistan and provided with safe sanctuaries.
This was the time when the ISI was in receipt of large funds from
the Saudi and US intelligence agencies and arms and ammunition
from the US for arming the Afghan Mujahideen against the Soviet
troops. These flows continued till the Soviet troops withdrew from
Afghanistan in 1988-89. The ISI diverted part of these funds and
arms and ammunition to the Khalistani terrorists.

After giving up hijackings as a weapon, the Khalistani terrorists
intensified their terrorism on the ground in Punjab and Delhi.
Initially, they committed many acts of terrorism with hand-held
weapons given by the ISI. Then, they started using improvised
explosive devices (IEDs)— timed as well as remote-controlled. The
explosives, detonators and timers were supplied by the ISI. There
were targeted killings of political leaders, officials, journalists and
innocent civilians such as farm workers from other parts of India.

During the training in Pakistan, the ISI impressed on them the
need to weaken the economy of Punjab by attacking its irrigation
canals and the farm workers from other parts of India, who go to
Punjab to work there. It also emphasized the need to extend their
operations to Delhi, Haryana, Rajasthan and other parts of India.
There was hardly any reaction from the Western Governments to
the ISI's sponsoring of terrorism against India in Punjab. The ISI
looked upon its operations in support of the Khalistan movement
as a reprisal for India's role in the liberation of Bangladesh. It also
felt that the destabilization of Punjab would weaken India's ability
to maintain internal security in Jammu & Kashmir and enable the
Pakistan Army to annex J&K. The ISI code-named its operation as
Operation K-K (Khalistan-Kashmir).

Initially, the Khalistani terrorists did not have much ground support
from the people of Punjab, but the position changed in their favour
after the Asian Games of November 19-December 4,1982, which

were held in Delhi. Around that time, the London-based Jagjit Singh
Chauhan flew to Bangkok and from there proceeded to Kathmandu
to meet some Khalistani elements from Punjab. The R&AW officer in
Bangkok detected his arrival in Bangkok from London through his
sources. The R&AW kept him under surveillance in Bangkok as well
as Kathmandu. The Government of India requested the Nepalese
authorities to pick him up and hand him over to the Indian Police.
They did not oblige. They picked him up and put him on board a
flight to Bangkok. The Thai authorities were not helpful either. They
forced him to go back to London. Before the Games, the IB and
the R&AW were in receipt of alarming reports that the Khalistani
terrorists were planning to disturb the Games through IEDs. The
Police and the central para-military forces took tight security
measures. Security barriers were set up on all roads leading to Delhi.
Cars and buses were stopped and many Sikhs were subjected to
physical search for any concealed weapons or IEDs. The feelings of
humiliation caused by these measures drove many Sikhs of Punjab
and Delhi into the arms of the Khalistani terrorists. The years 1983
and 1984 saw a serious deterioration of the situation in Punjab. The
Khalistani terrorists started using the Golden Temple in Amritsar
as a sanctuary for their operations. On April 26,1983, A.S.Atwal, a
Deputy Inspector-General of Police of Punjab, was gunned down by
the terrorists as he was coming out of the Golden Temple.

The ill-advised actions of Zail Singh, former Home Minister, who
subsequently became the President of India, in trying to use Sant
Jarnail Singh Bhindranwale to create a split among the Khalistanis
in the hope of thereby weakening them boomeranged. Instead of
weakening them, he became their leader. He acquired a religious
aura and attracted a number of Sikh peasants and other poor Sikhs
to the Khalistan cause. He and his supporters took shelter inside
the Golden Temple at Amritsar and started operating from there.
The number of incidents of terrorism started going up. Punjab
and even Delhi kept bleeding more and more. There was panic in
the Government when the trans-border sources of the IB and the
R&AW started reporting that the ISI had been infiltrating Pakistani
ex-servicemen and even some serving members of the Pakistan Army

into Punjab to help the Khalistanis. There were even some reports that some of these Pakistani mercenaries had taken up position inside the Golden Temple and were acting as advisers to Bhindranwale and other Khalistani leaders.

The alarm caused by these developments and reports made Indira Gandhi contemplate for the first time sending the Army inside the temple to arrest the terrorists and their supporters. However, before doing so, she tried frantically to find a political solution and to use the leaders of the Akali Dal for persuading Bhindranwale and other terrorists to vacate the temple. Rajiv Gandhi and two of his close associates held a number of secret meetings with Akali Dal leaders in a New Delhi guest house of the R&AW. I was given the task of making arrangements for these meetings, recording the discussions, transcribing them and putting up the transcripts to Kao for briefing Indira Gandhi. These talks failed to persuade the Akali Dal leaders to see reason and co-operate with the Government of India by persuading the Khalistani elements to vacate the Golden Temple peacefully. These transcripts, which were kept in the top secret archives of the R&AW, were very valuable records with historic value. They showed how earnestly Indira Gandhi tried to avoid having to send the Army into the Golden Temple. One hopes they are kept safely and would be available for future historians.

Simultaneously, Indira Gandhi also sent Kao abroad to contact foreign-based Khalistani elements and seek their co-operation for making Bhindranwale and other Khalistani elements vacate the Golden Temple. Two other officers of the R&AW and I accompanied him. My job was again to record the discussions secretly, transcribe them and put up the transcripts to Kao for briefing Indira Gandhi on our return to India. A Khalistani leader from the US, who met Kao in Zurich, offered to try to help if he was allowed to go into the Golden Temple and meet Bhindranwale. As proof of his goodwill, he claimed that the Khalistani elements in the US had planned to kill the R&AW officer in Washington DC, but he had prevented them from doing so. There was no way of verifying his claim. I was told that Indira Gandhi was against accepting his proposal to send him inside the temple. She felt that if this person also stayed behind inside the temple and joined Bhindranwale it could add to the problems of the Government of India.

   Things thereafter started moving inexorably towards an army raid into the Golden Temple in order to arrest Bhindranwale and all terrorists, who had taken shelter there. There was some unease in the intelligence community over the wisdom of the proposed course of action. One had an impression that Kao felt that it would be better to be patient for some weeks instead of taking any precipitate action, which might prove counter-productive or, if immediate action was considered necessary, to use the police and the central para-military forces instead of the Army. The Army is trained in a manner different from the police. Once the Army is launched into action, it has to prevail over the adversary. In the case of the police, it tunes its action to suit the circumstances. It does not have to prevail whatever be the circumstances. If it finds that the resistance of the adversary is high and that its attempts to prevail could cause high fatalities, it does not mind withdrawing and awaiting a better opportunity, when it can prevail at much less human cost. I was given to understand that at the request of Kao, two officers of the British Security Service (MI-5) visited the Golden Temple as tourists and gave a similar advice to Indira Gandhi— be patient and avoid action or use the police. There was also concern in the intelligence community over the likely repercussions of any Army raid on the discipline of the large number of Sikh soldiers of the Army, but senior Army officers were confident that there would be no negative impact on the Sikh soldiers. Ultimately, when the raid was made, their confidence was belied and the concerns of the intelligence community proved correct. There were instances of resentment openly expressed—and even violently at one place—in the Army, but these were brought under control after some initial anxiety.

   The Army's raid into the Golden Temple from June 3 to 6 ,1984, code-named Operation Blue Star, was not a totally tidy operation. It experienced more resistance than it anticipated from Bhindranwale, his followers and the terrorists inside the temple. In the prolonged exchange of fire, Bhindranwale was killed and the Akal Takht was badly damaged. There were instances of violent protests by the Sikhs in some parts of Punjab and other parts of the country. The Operation caused deep feelings of hurt in the hearts of large sections of the Sikh community in India and abroad. Its negative consequences were to be felt for another eleven years. Among these consequences was the assassination of Indira Gandhi by two of her Sikh bodyguards belonging to the Delhi Police on October 31,1984.

Lt.Gen.Sunderji, who co-ordinated the Operation, blamed the intelligence agencies for the untidy operation. He claimed that the Khalistanis were much larger in number inside the temple than he had been told by the intelligence agencies and much better armed. He blamed what he projected as the poor intelligence for the long time taken by the Army to overcome the resistance and take control of the temple. Over-confidence in his ability to score easy success before launching difficult and sensitive operations and a tendency to blame the intelligence agencies when his over-confidence was found to have been misplaced were the defining characteristics of Gen. Sunderji. One saw them during and after Operation Blue Star and one saw them again after he took over as the Chief of the Army Staff, when the Indian Peace-Keeping Force (IPKF) went to Sri Lanka.

Many ISI-trained Khalistani terrorists were arrested during the raid. Large quantities of arms and ammunition supplied to the terrorists by the ISI were recovered. But not a single Pakistani Army mercenary—serving or retired— was found inside the temple. The reports of the IB and the R&AW in this regard were found to have been wrong. Many of these reports had come from trans-border sources such as smugglers etc. In some instances, the same source was reporting to the IB, the R&AW and the Military Intelligence without these organizations being aware of it. The lack of co-ordination in trans-border operations often resulting in inaccurate, misleading and alarming reporting continues to be the bane of our intelligence community.

More than the large number of casualties, what hurt the Sikhs deeply was the damage caused to the Akal Takht by the Army action.

At the instance of Indira Gandhi, some Sikh leaders of her party organized a 'kar seva' (voluntary religious work) to have the Akal Takht repaired. But it was not that easy to repair the hurt in the hearts of large sections of the Sikh community all over the world. This lingering hurt aggravated the problem of Khalistani terrorism and led to the assassination of Indira Gandhi the same year and of Gen.A.S.Vaidya, who was the Chief of the Army Staff at the time of the operation, in 1986 in Pune, where he was living after his superannuation.

CHAPTER XI

The Assassination Of Indira Gandhi

Till 1985, the IB was the over-all in charge of the security of the Prime Minister— while he or she was in Delhi as well as during his or her travels in India and abroad. The IB's duties, inter alia, included updating from time to time the .Blue Book instructions relating to the security of the Prime Minister, issuing circular instructions on the subject, assessing threats to the security of the Prime Minister, co-ordinating physical security for the Prime Minister at Delhi through the Delhi Police, co-ordinating security arrangements for the Prime Minister during his or her travels in liaison with the concerned State agencies and foreign security agencies etc. While the IB co-ordinated and supervised the security, the actual security-related tasks, including those of bodyguards, were performed by the staff of the police concerned. India did not have a dedicated physical security agency for the Prime Minister like the US Secret Service.

Till 1975, the Division in the IB responsible for the Prime Minister's security had a very small set-up with just three officers-- a Joint Director at the head, who was of the rank of an Inspector-General of Police (IGP), a Deputy Director, who was of the rank of a Deputy Inspector-General of Police (DIG) and an Assistant Director, of the rank of a Superintendent of Police (SP). This expanded after 1975 partly due to perceived threats to Indira Gandhi during the Emergency and partly due to the Anand Marg, a Hindu spiritual group with an international following, indulging in acts of violence in order to protest against the detention of its leader by the Indian authorities. Its acts of violence, which amounted to terrorism, were

not confined to India. Its followers abroad in Australia and West
Europe indulged in violence too. The Ananda Marg had, therefore,
been included in the list of organizations capable of posing a threat
to the security of the Prime Minister.

Posting in this Division was highly coveted by officers of the Indian
Police Service— in the IB as well as in the States. It gave them a status
symbol and provided many opportunities for travel—in India as well
as abroad. The opportunities for frequent foreign travel—ahead of
the Prime Minister and along with him or her— was a very strong
attraction for the officers.

Before 1975, whenever the Prime Minister intended visiting a
foreign country, the Deputy or Assistant Director of this Division
would visit that country in advance on what used to be described
as Advance Security Liaison Visit to discuss the Prime Minister's
programme with the local authorities, inspect the place of stay
and other places to be visited by the Prime Minister, brief the local
authorities on the likely threats to the Prime Minister's security and
on the security arrangements that would be required. This officer
would then come back to Delhi and go along with the Joint Director,
who would accompany the Prime Minister, and a small number
of Delhi Police officers, who would actually perform the physical
security duties as bodyguards etc.

When the R&AW was created in 1968, Kao set up a VIP Security
Division in the R&AW too to collect intelligence on likely threats
to the Prime Minister from foreign-based elements. From 1975
onwards, at Kao's instance,one of the officers of this Division
started accompanying the IB officer going on advance Security
Liaison. Later, the MEA insisted that one of their officers should
also accompany the IB officer to discuss protocol arrangements with
the local authorities. In addition to the Advance Security Liaison
Visit, R&AW officers started going with the Prime Minister too as
part of the IB's security team in order to ensure communications
security and provide inputs regarding likely threats from elements
in the country being visited by the Prime Minister. Whenever Sonia
Gandhi and her children traveled with the Prime Minister, specially-

selected women police officers from the Delhi Police would be included in the security team accompanying the Prime Minister. The mushroom growth in the strength of the IB's VIP Security Division and in the composition of the security teams going ahead of the Prime Minister or along with him or her led to a dilution in the quality of supervision and co-ordination. There was a craze among police officers for being associated with the security teams going abroad with the Prime Minister since it gave them an opportunity for shopping and bringing back electronic and other goods without paying duty on them.

Smuggling-in of foreign goods by the staff associated with security duties almost became a racket. As soon as the Prime Minister's plane taxied to a halt, the Prime Minister and his or her entourage would leave in their cars. A vehicle of the IB and another of the Delhi Police would then go to the tarmac. The electronic and other goods bought abroad by the security personnel would be loaded into them. They would drive out of the airport without these goods being declared to the Customs. The officers would then exit in the normal manner through the Immigration and the Customs, with the bags which they had carried with them while going abroad. The Customs knew that this was happening, but did not take notice of it.

In September 1983, Indira Gandhi had been to New York to attend a session of the UN General Assembly. The Door Darshan had introduced the previous year the colour TV in connection with the Asian Games. There was a craze for foreign-made colour TV sets in all sections of our society.Many, who went abroad, came back with colour TV sets. About 15 Police officers of various ranks had accompanied her to New York. Three of them were from the R&AW and the rest belonged to the IB and the Delhi Police. During their stay in New York, all of them except one senior officer of the R&AW, bought colour TV sets and other electronic equipment. Some bought more than one colour TV set for being given to their relatives.

During the return journey from New York, there was a slight delay in the aircraft starting. Its doors were still open even after Indira Gandhi had got in and taken her seat. As she looked out through the window, she saw a large number of cardboard boxes containing TV sets and other electronic equipment being loaded into the luggage hold. She asked a member of her entourage to whom they belonged. He replied that they belonged to her security team. She did not say anything. As the plane was about to land at Delhi, she had a message sent to the Customs through the Airport Control Tower that they should check the baggage of all the security officials, who had accompanied her, and make them pay duty. After the aircraft landed, she got out and went home in her car. Two vehicles of the IB and the Delhi Police reached the tarmac and the security officers started loading the items bought by them in New York into them. In the meanwhile, a car containing Customs officers reached there and told them that everything should pass through the Customs. They said that they were acting under the instructions of the Prime Minister.

There was total panic. The officers admitted their ownership of the goods and promised to pay duty later and collect them. Those, who had brought more than one TV set, admitted their ownership of only one of them and claimed that they did not know to whom the others belonged. A senior officer of the IB, who had stayed behind in New York on a holiday, had sent the TV sets bought by him through one of his staff. This was in violation of the security regulations, which lay down that an aircraft should carry only the baggage of those traveling in it. When he later returned to Delhi, he totally denied that these TV sets belonged to him. The whole thing became an embarrassing scandal and a national daily of Delhi got the details of it from the Customs officers. It published them prominently. Normally, the hotel room and food bills of those accompanying the Prime Minister are settled by the Indian Embassy in the country visited by the Prime Minister. They were, therefore, entitled to only one-third of the normal daily allowance. This was a small amount and would not have been sufficient to indulge in a shopping spree. The Cabinet Secretary ordered that all these officers should be asked to explain how they got the money for their shopping. Most of them could not give a satisfactory explanation and got themselves tied in knots.

This was a worrisome state of affairs and was a fit case for acting against these officers and moving them out of duties connected with the security of the Prime Minister. Unfortunately, Kao, who was very kind-hearted, did not remove them. He merely expressed his displeasure to them and let them continue. This incident illustrated the kind of permissiveness, which had crept into the VIP security set-up. This permissiveness was one of the factors, which led to a dilution of the quality of supervision.

After the Army operation against Bhindranwale and the Khalistani terrorists in the Golden Temple, it was apprehended in the intelligence community that the Sikhs—even some not associated with the Khalistan movement— would attempt a reprisal attack on her for the damage suffered by the Akal Takht and for the death of Bhindranwale. In assessing the increased threats to her, one had also taken into account the danger of a reprisal attack on her by Sikh security personnel in her own entourage. Steps were initiated for revamping the intelligence collection machinery by increasing the staff in the existing R&AW stations and by setting up new stations. Requests for assistance were made to foreign intelligence agencies. The monitoring capability of the R&AW was strengthened in order to keep a better watch on the communications of the Khalistani organizations. The entire physical security arrangements for her were reviewed in order to eliminate the possibility of a threat from an insider.

While the stepped-up intelligence collection efforts resulted in a quantitative increase in reports, there was no flow of precise intelligence. There was a flow of a large number of reports of a general nature. The foreign intelligence agencies were not very helpful. Western countries such as the UK, the US and Canada had sizable Sikh population in certain constituencies. The local political leaders did not want to antagonize them by co-operating with the Government of India against the Khalistanis. An incident involving the West German authorities would illustrate the kind of non-cooperation we faced. Ever since 1981, Talwinder Singh Parmar, a sacked saw mill worker of Vancouver in Canada, who belonged to the Babbar Khalsa, had been making threatening statements against Indira Gandhi. Long before Operation Blue Star, the R&AW was worried that he might try to have Indira Gandhi killed during her foreign travels. He was wanted in India for trial in a case relating to the massacre of some Nirankaris and other cases. We had been repeatedly asking for the assistance of the Western intelligence agencies for having him arrested and brought to India for trial. They did not oblige.

At our request, the International Police Organization (INTERPOL), whose headquarters are in France, had a look-out notice issued to all member-countries, asking them to arrest him if he was found in their territory and inform the Indian Police. In 1983, he traveled by train from Zurich to West Germany. A West German Police Constable noticed that his passport particulars were the same as given in the INTERPOL look-out notice. He arrested him and the West German authorities informed the Central Bureau of Investigation (CBI) through the INTERPOL.

The CBI immediately asked the West German authorities to hand him over to the Indian Police for trial in the cases pending against him. They asked for the details of the cases in which he was wanted and the evidence against him. They were informed that a CBI team would be flying to Bonn with these details and were asked to keep him detained till the CBI team reached there. Just before the departure of the CBI team for Bonn, the MEA received a message from the Indian Consul-General in Vancouver that Talwinder Singh Parmar had addressed a religious congregation in a local gurudwara, during which he made highly threatening statements against Indira Gandhi. When we took it up with the West German authorities, they claimed that they had to send him back to Vancouver because the court had refused to give any more extention of his detention due to a delay in the arrival of the CBI team. There was no delay at all. On coming to know of his arrest and detention in West Germany, the local sikh community had exercised pressure on the Government there to release him and let him go back to Canada. The West German Government obliged them. Two years later, Parmar played an active role in the conspiracy, which resulted in the blowing-up of a plane of Air India called Kanishka off the Irish coast, which resulted in the death of over 300 passengers, many of them Canadian citizens. The West German authorities cannot escape a major share of responsibility for this colossal tragedy.

The strengthening of the monitoring efforts enabled the R&AW to intercept a large number of telephonic conversations of Khalistani elements in India and abroad. They were very critical and abusive of Indira Gandhi and the Government of India, but the IB and the R&AW did not intercept any conversation, which indicated a specific conspiracy to have her assassinated. It was believed that if the Khalistani elements had discussed any such conspiracy among themselves over the telephone or through the wireless, either the IB or the R&AW would have come to know of it . The intelligence community was worried that the ISI would exploit the widespread anger in the Sikh community for trying to have her killed in retaliation for her role in the 1971 liberation of Bangladesh. We , therefore, closely monitored the telecommunication links of the ISI too. We also stepped up our HUMINT coverage of the ISI. There were no leads suggesting a possible assassination attempt. Some members of the Congress (I) apprehended that even the CIA might exploit the Sikh anger to have her assassinated. It also came under watch —internally by the IB and externally by the R&AW.

There was thus an intense apprehension in the national security bureaucracy that some Sikh somewhere would make an attempt to kill her in revenge for the raid, but there were no answers to the questions who, when, where and how, which make a general piece of intelligence precise and actionable. Kao set up a co-ordination committee chaired by him and consisting of senior representatives of the intelligence agencies, which met daily to review the security arrangements for her. It used to discuss all intelligence inputs relating to her security and her daily programme. Rajiv Gandhi, who was then not holding any position in the Government, took close interest in the action taken for strengthening her physical security . As per his desire, two of his closest personal advisers used to attend these

meetings in order to give their suggestions and keep him informed of
the discussions and the action taken. Since they too did not hold any
position in the Government, they were not entitled to attend these
top secret meetings, in which classified information was discussed.
Despite this, in order to satisfy him that everything that was required
to be done for her physical security was being done, Kao let them
attend though they did not have the required security clearance, but
the minutes of these meetings did not show their presence.

One of the first steps taken by this committee was to ensure
that there could be no threat to her security from Sikh members
of the staff of the security set-up meant to protect her. There was
no Special Protection Group (SPG) at that time. It was set up after
her assassination. The close proximity protection group—as the
bodyguards are called—were hand-picked officers of the Delhi Police,
which was responsible for her security at her residence and during
her movements in Delhi. The work of this group was co-ordinated by
a senior IPS officer of the Delhi Police, under the overall supervision
of the head of the VIP Security Division of the IB, who was also a
senior IPS officer. There was another senior IPS officer in the IB's VIP
Security Division, who focused on the protection of Rajiv Gandhi and
his family. While the R&AW had no role in physical security for her, it
was responsible for the collection of all external intelligence, which
could have a bearing on the security of Indira Gandhi, Rajiv Gandhi
and their family. For this purpose, there were two Divisions (called
Branches) in the R&AW called the VIP Security Division and the Sikh
Extremists Division. While I headed the Sikh Extremists' Division,
another senior IPS officer headed the VIP Security Division. All these
officers reported to Kao through the DIB or the Director, R&AW or
the head of the Delhi Police as the case may be and carried out his
instructions. While the channel of command and communications
in the case of the IB and the R&AW was well laid out and clear, there
was a certain confusion in the case of the Delhi Police. This arose
from the fact that certain senior officers of the Delhi Police also
maintained a line of communication with close associates of Indira
Gandhi such as R.K.Dhawan and M.L.Fotedar. Not infrequently,
the associates of Rajiv Gandhi, who kept themselves briefed on the

security arrangements for Indira Gandhi, also interacted directly with officers of the Delhi Police. These interactions at various levels did result in a dilution in the implementation of the decisions taken and in a crossing of wires.

One of the first decisions taken after Operation Blue Star was that no Sikh officer should be deployed in close-proximity duties. All Sikh officers posted at her residence were re-deployed discreetly. There was absolutely nothing wrong about this decision. It is a rule of prudence followed by the security agencies of many countries that no officer belonging to a community, which is aggrieved against the Government, should be deployed as bodyguards of the head of the government. For many years in the US, officers from the Afro-American community were not deployed by the US Secret Service as bodyguards to the President. Similarly, Catholic officers from Northern Ireland were not deployed as bodyguards to the British Prime Minister. Unfortunately, in India, decisions taken in the interest of national security, are sought to be given an unnecessary communal colour, thereby weakening security. The withdrawal of the Sikh officers from close-proximity duties came to the notice of Indira Gandhi. Some say she noticed it herself. Others say one of her close associates noticed it, ascertained from the Delhi Police that this was done on the orders of Kao and brought this to her attention. She expressed her misgivings over the wisdom of the decision. Following this, the withdrawn Sikh Police officers were posted back to her residence. However, Kao instructed that no Sikh police officer should normally be posted alone in her close proximity and that, whenever a Sikh police officer was posted in her close proximity, he should be accompanied by a non-Sikh officer.

A number of other decisions for tightening her physical security was taken. These included strengthening the capability and arrangements for anti-explosive checks at her place of residence in Delhi and during her movements in Delhi and outside and providing her with bullet-proof cars. The R&AW, which normally had no role in physical security, came into the picture in respect of the bullet-proof cars. None of the manufacturers or garages in India had a capability for the bullet-proofing of vehicles. Till a satisfactory indigenous capability was developed, the bullet-proofing had to be got done from West Europe. It would have been simpler to have ordered bullet-proofed vehicles from famous companies such as the Mercedes of West Germany, which had a very good capability for bullet-proofing. The security agencies of many countries in the world order bullet-proof models from the Mercedes for the use of their Heads of State and Government. Indira Gandhi —like her predecessors and successors except Rajiv Gandhi— disliked moving around in a foreign-made car. They preferred the Ambassador. So, Ambassador cars bought in India used to be sent to West Europe for bullet-proofing till the R&AW developed its own capability for bullet-proofing. Kao gave the responsibility for the co-ordination of this work to the R&AW because its head, in his capacity as a Secretary in the Cabinet Secretariat, had independent powers of sanction. Financial sanctions for sending the cars, therefore, came quickly.

Two other decisions taken by Kao need to be noted. The first was that an ambulance with a competent doctor and nurses should always form part of Indira Gandhi's convoy and that this ambulance should always be stationed outside her place of stay so that it could quickly join the convoy. Indira Gandhi strongly disliked the sight of an ambulance permanently stationed outside her house or in her convoy. Despite her dislike, Kao insisted it should be there. The only concession he made to her sensitivities was to instruct that the ambulance should position itself in such a manner as not to be visible to her.

The second was to persuade her to start wearing a bullet-proof vest. Before broaching the topic with her, he decided to get a bullet-proof vest from the UK. Since nobody had the courage to ask her for measurements, he took a blouse from a lady of roughly the same body build as Indira Gandhi and asked the R&AW to get three BP vests made in the UK— one of the same size as the blouse, the second a size bigger and the third a size smaller. After they arrived, Kao rang up M.L. Fotedar and told him that he would be sending the vests through me. He asked Fotedar to request her to start wearing the size that suited her. Fotedar was hesitant to talk to her on the subject. He felt that she would refuse to wear it.Kao insisted that it was necessary. He asked Fotedar to tell the security people at her residence that I would be bringing a package and that they should not ask me to open it. I got the vests re-packed after inspecting them and took it to her residence. As the package was put through the door-frame metal detector, there was an alarm as it contained metal pieces. Since Fotedar had told the security staff in advance about me, they did not ask me to open it. One of them took me to Fotedar's room and informed him that I had come. Fotedar came out and told me that Farooq Abdullah, the leader of the National Conference of Jammu and Kashmir, was with him. He asked me to wait till Abdullah left. He asked the security guards to put a chair for me outside.

I had to keep sitting there for nearly an hour till Abdullah left. I noticed menial staff moving all over the garden without being checked or accompanied by the security personnel. A mini transport van of a well-known soft drinks company, whose owner was reportedly close to the Congress (I), entered the premises without its being subjected to anti-explosives check. No security personnel accompanied it. A couple of employees of the company went from room to room replacing used soft drink bottles with fresh ones. None of them was subjected to any security check. Nobody checked the crates of soft drinks for any concealed explosive device. The staff of the company were not escorted by any member of the security staff as they moved around the place. After about an hour, Abdullah left. Fotedar came out, took the package from me and said: " Why can't Kao do this himself? Why does he want me to do it?" We never got a feed-back from Indira Gandhi whether any of the BP vests suited her. One heard that she tried it once or twice, but felt uncomfortable as she sweated a lot. She was irregular in wearing it. I went back to Kao and reported to him what happened. I also told him about my observations regarding the very weak state of physical security inside her house. He said he would take it up with the concerned officers in the IB and the Delhi Police. I was told he did the next day, but they denied any laxity.

On October 31,1984, I went to office as usual at around 8 am. After some time, I got a phone call from G.C.Saxena, who was the head of the R&AW at that time. He said: " Raman, the Prime Minister has been shot. I am at her residence. I may be coming late to office. Take care of it." Before I could ask him for any other details, he kept the phone down. I was his staff officer. At the time she was shot, many senior officers were attending the annual parade of a central para-military organization. Kao was on a secret visit to Beijing at the instance of Indira Gandhi to meet Chinese leaders and senior officials to test the waters for a possible visit by her. I got a phone call from Dhawan. He asked: "We have been frantically trying to contact Kao. Where is he?" I told him he was in Beijing. He said that Kao should be informed that she had been shot and requested to return immediately. I told him that I would convey his message to Saxena. I did.

In the meanwhile, I started getting details from other sources. She had cancelled all her public engagements for the day and decided to spend the day with her grand-children. She had been shot by two of her Sikh security guards, who had manipulated the duty allotment in order to ensure that they would be on duty together. The two assassins were themselves shot at by other security guards immediately after the assassination. One of the assassins died. This gave rise to widespread rumours that there was a large conspiracy involving many members of the security staff and that one of the the assassins had been killed by the Police in order to prevent the truth from coming out. The instruction that no Sikh security guard should be deployed alone without their being a non-Sikh guard with him was not observed. She was not wearing her BP vest as she was spending the day in the house. There was no ambulance with qualified medical personnel and with arrangements for immediate blood transfusion available. She bled to death by the time she was taken to hospital by Sonia Gandhi. However, the announcement about her death was made by the Government of India much later, but the British Broadcasting Corporation (BBC) had announced her death much earlier.

The fact that she had been shot by her own Sikh security guards despite all the security precautions taken after Operation Blue Star to prevent such a possibility shocked everybody. The senior officers of the IB and the Delhi police responsible for her security, including the DIB, were removed. The head of the VIP Security Division in the IB was reverted back to his State. One or two officers were placed under suspension and departmental enquiries on charges of negligence were ordered against them. A full-fledged enquiry into the assassination was ordered by Rajiv Gandhi, who had taken over as the new Prime Minister.

The reputation of the Indian intelligence community and the Delhi Police sank to new depths that day. That she should have been so easily killed by her own security guards in her own house, which on paper was supposed to have been the most protected place in India, shocked Indian public opinion and the international community. Any Police or intelligence officer, who had the least qualms of conscience, would have hung his head in shame. Bravely, she had done her duty in the best way as perceived by her by ordering the Army to raid the Golden Temple and free it from the control of the terrorists. She depended on us to protect her. We failed her. It was a dark chapter in the history of the Indian intelligence and security establishment.

Rumours and conspiracy theories galore spread like wild fire in the wake of her brutal killing— that the Sikh bodyguards were acting at the behest of the Khalistanis and the ISI; that one of the conspirators had visited his village in the Gurdaspur District on leave before the assassination and from there had secretly visited Pakistan to meet ISI officers; that it was a joint conspiracy by the ISI and the CIA and so on. The fact that some months before her assassination, an American academic had undertaken a study on what could happen in India after her death added grist to the rumour mills. There was surprise and shock that the intelligence agencies were not even aware of this study. They had very little information on the background of this academic.

The judge, who conducted the enquiry, turned out to be not a good choice. Instead of a well-focused enquiry, what one had was a plethora of conjectures and speculative conclusions. There was no credible evidence to show that the Sikh officers of the Delhi Police and their instigators in a gurudwara of Delhi were acting at the behest of the Khalistani terrorists. The terrorists were hatching their own conspiracy. So too some Sikhs in the Delhi Police in association with some in a gurudwara. The Sikh police officers succeeded, where the terrorists could not. Being police officers, they knew the importance of communications security. They, therefore, avoided the use of telephones for contacting each other. As a result, it was not a surprise that no TECHINT about the conspiracy was forthcoming. The only way of collecting HUMINT would have been by keeping the Sikh police officers associated with her security under close surveillance-- at Delhi as well as during their visits to their villages on leave. This was not done. There was a shocking laxity in the supervision of the security arrangements by the senior officers. Who benefited from the assassination? Pakistan, definitely. The US,possibly. The absence of evidence of their involvement did not mean that they were not involved. If they were involved, they had covered up their tracks successfully. History is unlikely to be able to find an answer to the question of any foreign involvement.

The announcement of the death of Indira Gandhi was followed by widespread anti- Sikh riots. The R&AW had many Sikh officers at various levels in its staff. The moment Saxena heard of these riots, he asked me to contact all Sikh officers and ask them to shift to the offices of the R&AW along with their families and stay there till the riots stopped. I did so. Some, particularly at the junior levels, availed of the offer and shifted to the office. Some preferred to shift to the houses of their relatives. Others decided to brave it out in their house and requested the R&AW to arrange for physical security for them and their families in their house. We did so, with the co-operation of the Delhi Police.

Kao was informed of the tragedy immediately after the assassination. He cut short his stay in Beijing and decided to return to Delhi. There was an Air India flight from Tokyo to Delhi via Hong Kong the same evening, but there was no flight from Beijing to Hong Kong. On coming to know of his problem, the Chinese authorities graciously offered to place a special aircraft at his disposal to enable him catch the Air India flight at Hong Kong. He accepted their offer and managed to reach Delhi past midnight. Saxena received him at the airport. I went with him. He accompanied Kao to his house in the car and briefed him during the journey. I was not privy to the briefing. A day after the cremation, Kao met Rajiv Gandhi and told him of his desire to resign from his post as Senior Adviser to the Prime Minister in the Cabinet Secretariat. Rajiv Gandhi accepted his request to be relieved of the responsibility.

The assassination must have been a terrible blow to Kao for two reasons. The senior officers of the IB and the Delhi Police, whom he trusted implicitly and on whom he relied for protecting her, had let him down through their negligence and lax supervision. Indira Gandhi, whom he had known for over three decades and who had implicit trust in his judgement and advice, was brutally killed during Kao's watch of the intelligence community as its Czar. He never showed it on his face. Nor did he ever discuss with those close to him the feelings in his heart over the failure to protect her.

CHAPTER XII

Kao As Senior Adviser

The almost three-year (1981 to 84) post-retirement tenure of Kao as the Senior Adviser to Indira Gandhi in the Cabinet Secretariat did not have the brilliant dazzle of his tenure as the founder and head of the R&AW between 1968 and 1977. His main task as Senior Adviser was to advise Indira Gandhi on all matters relating to national security and to co-ordinate the functioning of the intelligence agencies. As Adviser on national security matters, he continued to be heard with respect and his advice was often followed with benefit by her and her senior officials—whether the advice related to developments in Afghanistan, the terrorism in Punjab, relations with the US, the USSR, China, Pakistan and Bangladesh and the problem of the Sri Lankan Tamils. His high-level contacts in Washington DC brought about a softening of the hostility to Indira Gandhi in the Reagan Administration. However, as intelligence co-ordinator, he was not that effective due to reservations at some senior levels in the IB regarding his suitability for this task.

Kao, who had joined the Indian Police in 1940, had initially served in Uttar Pradesh before joining the IB in 1947. He spent nearly two decades in the IB before he was asked to take over the responsibility for the creation of the R&AW. His initial years in the IB were spent in the performance of tasks relating to physical security, including the holding of the enquiry into the April 11,1955, crash of the Kashmir Princess aircraft of Air India in which a team of Chinese and East European officials and journalists was traveling to Jakarta from Hong Kong to attend the Afro-Asian summit conference at

Bandung in Indonesia. The crash was caused by an explosion on board the aircraft. The KMT intelligence was suspected. After the Sino-Indian war of 1962, he was associated with the raising of the Aviation Research Centre (ARC) as part of the Directorate-General of Security (DG&S), with the assistance of the US intelligence community. He served as the ARC's Director. This brought him into close contact with the US intelligence and helped him to build up a network of contacts, which was to stand the R&AW in good stead in subsequent years. However, his exposure to intelligence analysis and operational work in the IB was limited. He handled analysis and operational responsibilities of a real nature only for about four years in his capacity as the Joint Director in charge of external intelligence and communist activities in India before he was chosen by Indira Gandhi to be the first head of the R&AW.

A group of IB officers headed by the late M.M.L. Hooja, who was the DIB at the time of the bifurcation, strongly opposed its bifurcation and the creation of the R&AW. When their objections were overruled by Indira Gandhi, they resented her decision to make Kao its first chief. They viewed him as unsuitable for this task because of his limited exposure to analysis and operational work in the IB. After he took over as the head of the R&AW, they created difficulties for him by not making available to him all papers relating to the external intelligence divisions of the IB. It would not be an exaggeration to say that Kao had to create the organization almost from scratch without much assistance from the IB by relying on the memories of those of us, who had served in the IB's external intelligence division under him. Some of us were even arbitrarily asked by the IB to vacate our office rooms even before the R&AW could find alternate accommodation for us by hiring private buildings. Kao sent some of us on a tour of the border areas in order to get details of the trans-border posts set up by the IB for the collection of intelligence about the neighbouring countries from the IB officers posted in the field. I was sent on a long tour of the North-East. The IB officers posted there were polite, but not very communicative. Hooja and officers close to him created similar difficulties in respect of the division of the assets of the Monitoring Division of the IB, which was responsible for the collection of TECHINT.

The IB also made a determined bid to retain the liaison division, which was responsible for liaison with foreign intelligence agencies, and the Directorate-General of Security (the DGS) under the control of the DIB, but Indira Gandhi did not agree and these were transferred to the control of Kao. While the liaison division became a part of the R&AW, the DGS was maintained as a separate organization, but with Kao as its head. Thus, Kao wore two hats as the head of the R&AW and as the chief of the DGS. This practice has continued ever since.

The brilliant performance of the R&AW in 1971,the influence acquired by Kao in the policy-making circles and his emergence as a close adviser of Indira Gandhi added to the jealousies of the IB officers closely associated with Hooja. So long as these officers, who were put through their professional paces by Hooja, continued to be in service in the IB, their mental reservations regarding the advisability of Indira Gandhi's action in bifurcating the IB continued to influence their attitude towards Kao and the R&AW. They held the view that since many of India's internal security problems had trans-border linkages and arose from the state of the relations of India with its neighbours, the same organization should have remained responsible for the collection of internal and external intelligence. Long after my retirement, I once happened to travel with the then DIB by the same flight. During a chat on the internal security problems, he said that many of these problems were due to Indira Gandhi's original sin of bifurcating the IB. He strongly argued for a re-merger of these two organizations.

These reservations about Kao and the R&AW in the minds of some senior officers of the IB, who rose in the profession under Hooja, did have an impact on their co-operation with Kao after he took over as Senior Adviser in 1981. While he got excellent co-operation from the R&AW officers at all levels, one cannot say the same thing about the IB. There were officers, who had served under Kao in the IB and held him in great esteem. They extended their whole-hearted co-operation to him. There were others, who had inherited the prejudices of Hooja against him. Their co-operation left much to be desired.

During his tenure as the Senior Adviser, he continued to enjoy the total trust of Indira Gandhi as he had done between 1968 and 1977 as the head of the R&AW. She valued his advice on all national security matters. His reputation as her close adviser attracted the foreign intelligence agencies with which the R&AW had a liaison relationship and he was often in receipt of invitations from them to visit their headquarters for discussions. In certain instances, Indira Gandhi chose to operate through him rather than through the then head of the R&AW. One could cite the examples of the visits undertaken by Kao to Washington DC to remove misunderstandings in the minds of the Reagan Administration regarding her policy on Afghanistan and to Beijing, with the help of the Yugoslav intelligence, to test the waters for a possible visit by Indira Gandhi to China, which did not materialize due to her assassination. One could also cite her using him and not the head of the R&AW for resuming the dialogue with Laldenga and for discussions with one of the US-based Sikh extremist leaders in Zurich. While handling these tasks, Kao took great care to see that the authority and the importance of the head of the R&AW were not undermined.

The R&AW had two heads when Kao was the Senior Adviser to Indira Gandhi. Suntook, who had been appointed as its head by Morarji Desai in 1977, continued as its chief till his superannuation in March,1983. He was succeeded by G.C.Saxena, who functioned as the Director of the R&AW till his superannuation in March, 1986. Both of them had excellent relations with Kao, who held them in great regard. He saw to it that he did not come in the way of their independence and effectiveness.

Under Indira Gandhi, Suntook revived the R&AW's covert action capability, which had remained in a state of suspension under Morarji Desai and Charan Singh. Indira Gandhi was also keen that the organization should take active interest in meeting requests for training from the intelligence agencies and police forces of

Third World countries. Under Suntook and Saxena, the R&AW
arranged training courses for intelligence and police officers from
the Maldives, Uganda, Mozambique, Botswana, Malawi , Zambia,
Zimbabwe, Mauritius and Seychelles. It also trained the cadres of
the ANC of South Africa and the SWAPO of Namibia. Two retired
officers of the R&AW—one from the Police and the other from the
Air Force— were sent to Zambia to work as intelligence instructors.
In addition to my other work, I was also put in charge of arranging
and co-ordinating this training. In that capacity, I had visited some
of these countries. I could see the tremendous respect which Indira
Gandhi commanded among the leaders of these countries. It would
not be an exaggeration to say that they looked upon India as Indira
Gandhi's country. Despite her innumerable other preoccupations,
she found time to attend to the requests for assistance from the
leaders of these countries. Dr.Milton Obote of Uganda, who had
replaced Idi Amin, was a great admirer of Indira Gandhi. He was
very keen that India should persuade all Sindhi and other Indian-
origin businessmen, who had fled from Uganda under Idi Amin,
to come back to Uganda and re-start their business ventures. He
wanted India to run the tourism business in Uganda, including the
hotels. Unfortunately, none of the Indian businessmen was prepared
to go back.

When Suntook was the chief, the MEA for the first time raised
the issue of what they alleged was the unusually high standard of
living maintained by the R&AW officers posted abroad. The late
R.D. Sathe, the then Foreign Secretary, officially wrote to Suntook
about an R&AW officer posted to South-East Asia, who had taken
a large bank loan in order to buy a very expensive Mercedes Benz
car. " Where from is he going to find the money for paying back
the loan and the interest?" Sathe asked. The MEA also raised the
case of another officer posted to North America, who, according to
them, had ordered an expensive Mercedes Benz car and paid for
it even before he left India for his foreign posting. "How did he
raise the foreign exchange in India?" they asked. Narasimha Rao
mentioned to me that during his travels abroad, he had noticed
that R&AW and IB officers posted in the Indian Embassies had the

largest and the most expensive cars. "How do they manage to find the money?" he asked. He also pointed out that the CIA and other foreign intelligence agencies could easily identify Indian intelligence officers from the expensive cars maintained by them, since no other officer could afford to maintain such cars. Such complaints about the allegedly lavish life-style of at least some R&AW officers caused considerable embarrassment to the organization and, with great difficulty, Suntook managed to convince the Foreign Secretary that while there might be some bad eggs in the organization, the majority of the officers maintained an austere life-style.

Just before Suntook retired on March 31,1983, a traditional ally of India sought India's assistance in a very sensitive matter. After discussing this at a top secret meeting attended by a very small number of officers, Indira Gandhi accepted a suggestion of Kao to send Suntook on a visit to that country for further discussions with its Prime Minister. He returned from the visit only some days after March 31,1983. As a result, he could not formally hand over to Saxena as the chief on March 31,1983, and a farewell party arranged by the staff in his honour in a local hotel had to be postponed without giving any reason for the postponement. This gave rise to some speculation about his whereabouts. A disgruntled member of the ministerial cadre of the R&AW against whom Suntook had taken disciplinary action for his participation in the strike of 1980, told the Delhi correspondent of a leading daily published from Kolkata that there was panic in the organization because Suntook had fled to the US without properly handing over charge to Saxena and had taken with him many classified files of the organization. The newspaper published the story under an eight-column banner headline on the front page. The Editor was contacted and a strong protest was lodged over his newspaper publishing a blatantly false report fed to it by a disgruntled employee of the organization. We demanded that the newspaper should publish our denial of the story and apologise. He declined. The Government then referred the matter to the Press Council, which expressed its disapproval of the action of the newspaper in publishing a false report and, subsequently, in refusing to publish our denial and an apology.

Somehow, the US State Department in Washington DC had come to know of the sensitive request made by the Prime Minister of that country and the top secret visit of Suntook to that country at the instance of Indira Gandhi for further discussions. It got its information from the US Embassy in Delhi. A well-known American investigative journalist came to know of this from his contacts in the State Department. He contacted the Indian Embassy in Washington DC to check up whether such a request had been made by that country to New Delhi and, if so, what would be the response of India. The Embassy sent a message to the MEA in Delhi. Everybody in Delhi was surprised as to how the US Embassy had come to know of the discussions at a top secret meeting convened by Indira Gandhi, which was attended by a very small number of senior officers. One was told that enquiries by the IB on her orders gave strong grounds for suspicion that the leakage had probably occurred from a senior officer of the Army, who had attended this meeting. This came in the way of his promotion and affected his chances of rising to the top despite his reputation as an excellent professional.

Girish Chandra Saxena, popularly known as Gary, took over as the head of the R&AW in the first week of April,1983, after Suntook returned from his top secret foreign trip. He was the last of the "Gentlemen Professionals" of the R&AW— the others being Kao himself, Sankaran Nair and Suntook. They were not only brilliant professionals, but also lovable individuals with endearing personal qualities. There was nothing small or mean about them. They did wonders and were very close to the Prime Minister of the day. Their role in influencing government policy on national security matters was phenomenal. They had a wide network of contacts in the international intelligence community at the highest levels. They imparted a sense of pride to the R&AW officers. They never bragged about themselves and their role and contacts.

Saxena, an IPS officer of the Uttar Pradesh cadre, came to the R&AW at its very inception from the UP and was appointed as the head of the analysis division dealing with Pakistan and the rest of the Islamic world. In the initial years of his career in the R&AW, he turned out to be an excellent analyst. In the months leading up to the 1971 war, his assessment of the political developments in West and East Pakistan and his predictions for the future turned out to be uncannily correct. He was one of the legendary Kaoboys. After the liberation of Bangladesh, he was posted out as the head of the R&AW station in Rangoon. After completing his tenure, he came back to headquarters and took over the responsibility for analysis as well as operations relating to Pakistan. Suntook posted him to London , where he was responsible for liaison with the British intelligence. During his posting there, co-operation in counter-terrorism had not assumed the kind of importance in the liaison relationship as it did after 1985. The focus was more on exchange of intelligence on China, Pakistan and other countries of common interest and concern to India and the UK.

Suntook recalled him from London in 1980 before he completed his three-year tenure so that he could take over as No.2 in the place of Shiv Raj Bahadur, who was removed from the organization by Indira Gandhi. Saxena supervised and co-ordinated on behalf of Suntook the working of all administrative, analysis and operational divisions. He devoted special attention to the analysis and operational divisions covering Pakistan and once again laid the foundation for an effective covert action capability.

Kao's tenure as the Senior Adviser saw the beginning of an activist policy by India in Sri Lanka. Indira Gandhi's close interest in Sri Lanka and concerns about it went back to 1971, when, to her annoyance, the then Sri Lankan Government allowed planes of the Pakistan Air Force to re-fuel at the Katunayake airport while on their way to and from East Pakistan after she had banned their flights through the Indian air space. Her strong expression of unhappiness over the Sri Lankan action led to a discontinuance of the re-fuelling. Despite her cordial relations with Sirimavo Bandaranaike, Indira Gandhi did not close her eyes to the threats that could be posed to India's security by Sri Lanka's close relations with China. However, her unhappiness over Sirimavo Bandaranaike's flirting with the Chinese did not inhibit Indira Gandhi from promptly responding in April, 1971, to an SOS from the Sri Lankan leader for Indian assistance when the then ultra-Marxist Janata Vimukthi Peramuna (JVP) launched simultaneous attacks in many places and came very near to capturing power. On the instructions of Indira Gandhi, Kao, who was then heading the R&AW, rushed to Colombo an IPS officer of the Maharashtra cadre serving in the R&AW, who had acquired an expertise in counter-insurgency. He had also been trained by the British security services, which had successfully put down the communist insurgency in Malaysia. This officer stayed in Colombo for some time and closely advised her and her officers on how to deal with the JVP insurgency. He returned to Delhi after the initial JVP threat had been overcome by the Sri Lankan security forces. Collection of intelligence about the JVP, its contacts with China and North Korea and its likely contacts with Marxist elements in India became an important task for the R&AW.

More than the Pakistani, the Chinese and the Marxist threats to India through Sri Lanka, what caused a major concern to Indira Gandhi was the possibility of American threats. After she returned to power in 1980, reports started coming in of increasing American activities in Sri Lanka and the hobnobbing of the United National Party (UNP) Government with the US. Indira Gandhi as well as Kao were concerned over the implications of an American interest in the hiring of a large number of petrol storage tanks in Trincomallee, which had been constructed by the allied forces during the Second World War. After the war, these tanks had remained unutilized. After the Indo-Pakistan war of 1971, the US Navy started showing interest in expanding its presence and activities in the Indian Ocean region——mainly to monitor and counter the activities of the Soviet Navy and also to keep an eye on the movements of a large number of Soviet fishing trawlers in the Indian Ocean. The CIA suspected that they were being used by the TECHINT division of the KGB, the Soviet intelligence agency, for intercepting the communications of the US naval ships in the Indian Ocean region. Apart from developing Diego Garcia as a US naval base, the US started showing an interest in acquiring a presence in Trincomallee. After the war of 1971, Kao ordered an exercise to examine the various possibilities of strengthening the R&AW's capability for the collection of maritime intelligence about the US Naval activities in the Indian Ocean region. One of the decisions taken was to enter into a triangular co-operation agreement with the French and Iranian intelligence agencies, to which a reference has already been made in a previous chapter. Another was to acquire a fishing trawler to be manned by officers of the R&AW and the Indian Navy and use it for the collection of TECHINT with equipment and technical advice to be obtained from the TECHINT Division of the KGB. The first project did not produce satisfactory results. The second for a fishing trawler was a non-starter due to mental reservations in the Navy and the Finance Ministry. After Morarji Desai came to power in 1977, the project report was given a quite burial. It was not revived again since there was not much enthusiasm for it in the R&AW itself. The IPS officers, who constituted the majority in the organization, tended to be over-cautious and to avoid ideas beyond their comprehension.

Some months after Indira Gandhi returned to power in 1980, reports started coming in that a Singapore-based company was negotiating with the Sri Lankan authorities for taking the petrol storage tanks on hire. Enquiries made by the R&AW indicated that the Singapore company was acting as a front for the US intelligence community— for either the CIA or the NSA (the National Security Agency). The R&AW, which had a long-established liaison relationship with the intelligence division of the Sri Lankan Police and the Sri Lankan Ministry of Defence, immediately took up the matter with them. They denied the report. The MEA took it up with its counterpart in Colombo with negative results. The negotiations with the Singapore-based company slowed down, but were not called off. In the meanwhile, another report was received that the Voice of America (VOA), which is funded by the US State Department, was negotiating with the Sri Lankan authorities for permission to considerably expand its presence and broadcasting capabilities in Sri Lanka. The ostensible reason given by the VOA was that it wanted to expand its broadcasts to Asia. The R&AW's TECHINT officers suspected that the real purpose was to enable the CIA use the VOA set-up to monitor the communications of the Indian naval establishments in South India and of the Indian and Soviet naval ships in the Indian Ocean region. This matter too was taken up with the Sri Lankan authorities, but with similar negative results.

   Though the Sri Lankan authorities ultimately abandoned the petrol storage tanks proposal and considerably scaled down the expansion of the VOA, Indira Gandhi was upset over the frequent instances of their insensitivity to India's security concerns. In the meanwhile, the relations between the majority Sinhalese and the minority Sri Lankan Tamil communities kept deteriorating. This resulted in widespread anti-Tamil riots in Colombo in 1983 and the start of the movement for an independent Tamil state to be called Tamil Eelam under the leadership of the Liberation Tigers of Tamil Eelam (LTTE). The riots and the Tamil Eelam movement had their echo in Tamil Nadu. Indira Gandhi always had a soft corner for South India in general and for Tamil Nadu in particular. They had stood by her in the best of times and in the worst of times. Reports of the sufferings of the Sri Lankan Tamils at the hands of the Sinhalese moved her to go to their help. The R&AW was asked to start an activist policy in Sri Lanka to assist the Sri Lankan Tamils. Indira Gandhi's unhappiness over the insensitivity of the Sri Lankan authorities to India's security concerns and her desire to help the suffering Sri Lankan Tamils both influenced her decision to embark on an activist policy. This activist project of the R&AW, which started during the tenure of Kao as Senior Adviser, under the over-all supervision of Saxena, continued after his exit, despite some embarrassment caused by a media leakage of some aspects of the project.

   There was considerable nervousness in the Pakistani Armed Forces over the return of Indira Gandhi to power and her action in recalling Kao from retirement and appointing him as Senior Adviser. Zia-ul-Haq, the military dictator who had overthrown Zulfikar Ali Bhutto and seized power in 1977, and other Armed Forces officers had not forgotten what happened to Pakistan and its Army in December 1971, when Indira Gandhi was the Prime Minister and Kao headed the R&AW. Zia was very happy with the Morarji Desai Government, which refrained from any fraternization with the opponents and critics of the military regime in Pakistan. Moreover, Morarji Desai, A.B.Vajpayee and Charan Singh hardly knew any Pakistani political leader. The Pakistani political leaders did not think much of them. Those, who had escaped from Pakistan and gone into exile in Afghanistan, the UK and other countries of West Europe, were greatly excited by her return to power and by the appointment of Kao as her Senior Adviser. The Pakistani political class in Sindh, Balochistan and the North-West Frontier Province (NWFP) admired her and began hoping that she would help them in their movement against the military regime for the restoration of democracy in Pakistan. They started visiting India—many secretly, some like the late Khan Adul Wali Khan, the son of Khan Abdul Ghaffar Khan, the Frontier Gandhi, openly. They came either to meet her or Kao or Saxena. The R&AW made discreet arrangements for these visits and for their meetings with Indira Gandhi and others. Many of the Pakistani leaders had a wide circle of friends in the Congress (I) party, originating from the days of the party's freedom struggle against the British before 1947. They renewed their contacts and old friendships during their visits.

Since its inception in 1968, the R&AW had a close liaison relationship with the Khad, the Afghan intelligence agency, which was an important source of information for the Indian intelligence on Pakistan. This relationship was further strengthened after Indira Gandhi and Kao returned to office and Saxena took over as the head of the R&AW. The foundation was laid for a trilateral co-operation involving the R&AW, the Khad and the KGB. Many of the training camps for the Khalistani terrorists run by the ISI were located in the tribal areas of the NWFP. The arms and ammunition for them came from the Pakistan Army stocks kept in the NWFP. The R&AW, therefore, greatly valued the co-operation of the Khad for monitoring the Khalistani activities in that area.

The R&AW was also greatly interested in details regarding the covert operations of the CIA in Afghanistan—how the CIA and the ISI were training the Afghan Mujahideen, what kind of arms and ammunition and explosives were being given to them etc. Under the leadership of William Casey, the CIA started following in Afghanistan a policy of using the methods practised by the Hezbollah, the terrorist organization of the Lebanon, for making the Soviet and Afghan troops bleed. To avoid Congressional allegations of their resorting to terrorism in their proxy war against the Soviet troops, the CIA avoided directly training the Afghan Mujahideen and the Arab terrorists, including Osama bin Laden, who had flocked to Afghanistan via Peshawar. Instead, they helped the ISI in creating a covert action division headed by Brigadier Mohammed Yousef to train the Afghan Mujahideen and the Arab volunteers in the techniques of the Hezbollah and other terrorist organizations. Brig. Yousef and his officers were secretly taken to the US and imparted the necessary training. Experts of the U.S. Special Forces trained the ISI officers in the fabrication of high-tech explosive devices such as the ammonium nitrate-fuel oil (ANFO) vehicular bombs and in sabotage techniques. The CIA supplied to the ISI large quantities of explosive material of different kinds, detonators and timers. The ISI officers trained by the CIA and the US Special Forces, in turn, trained the Afghan Mujahideen and the Arab volunteers. The ISI, while carrying out the instructions of the CIA, secretly transferred some of these techniques and materials to the Khalistani terrorists in the camps run by it for them. The Khalistanis started using these techniques and materials against the Indian security forces and civilians, when they stepped up their acts of terrorism after Operation Blue Star. Thus, while the CIA-ISI collaboration was supposedly directed against the Soviet and Afghan troops in Afghanistan, India too started feeling their effect on its internal security. The R&AW's co-operation with the Khad and the KGB had two purposes— to get information regarding the ISI-imparted techniques and the ISI-supplied materials being used by the Afghan Mujahideen and the Arab volunteers and to get details of the equipment captured by the Soviet and Afghan troops from them.

While keeping a wary eye on the activities of the CIA and the ISI in Afghanistan, Kao, Suntook and Saxena did not allow concerns over this come in the way of the R&AW's liaison relationship with the

CIA. In fact, the R&AW sought the assistance of the CIA for training some of its officers as well as some from the IB in counter-terrorism techniques such as dealing with hijackings, hostage negotiations etc. The CIA happily obliged. Thus, one had one more bizarre example of how international intelligence co-operation works. The CIA trained the officers of the ISI in the use of terrorism against an adversary. At the same time, it trained the officers of the R&AW and the IB in some of the techniques of countering that terrorism.

Even while actively co-operating with the CIA against the Soviet presence in Afghanistan, the military dictatorship in Pakistan pressed on with its efforts to acquire a military nuclear capability, without facing any serious opposition from the US. Its dependence on Pakistan for its operations in Afghanistan made the Reagan Administration close its eyes to Pakistan's feverish quest for acquiring a military nuclear capability. Pakistan not only continued with its clandestine procurement activities in the West, but it also entered into a secret collaboration project with China on this subject. The Science and Technology (S&T) Division of the R&AW, headed by Dr.K.Santanam, did outstanding work in closely monitoring Pakistan's clandestine activities in this regard.

Shortly after the formation of the R&AW in September 1968, Kao, with the approval of Indira Gandhi, had set up a secret liaison relationship with Mossad, Israel's external intelligence agency. This relationship used to be handled through R&AW officers posted in West Europe.Senior officers of the two services, including the chiefs, periodically used to exchange visits. The main purpose of this liaison relationship was to benefit from Israel's knowledge of West Asia and North Africa and to learn from its counter-terrorism techniques. The secrecy of India's contacts with Israel and of the liaison relationship between the R&AW and the Mossad was successfully maintained till 1977. Some aspects of it leaked out during the Prime Ministership of Morarji Desai. The media had come to know of a clandestine visit by Gen.Moshe Dayan, the legendary military hero of Israel, to Kathmandu. It did not take them long to establish that the main purpose of the visit was for a clandestine meeting with representatives of the Government of India.

When an operationally more activist policy towards Pakistan was resumed after the return of Indira Gandhi to power, the Pakistani military dictatorship was not worried over its impact on the political situation in Pakistan. It was confident that the US, which was totally dependent on Pakistan for its Afghan operations, would not allow India to destabilize Pakistan, which could weaken its Afghan operations. What the military dictatorship was worried about was regarding the dangers of a joint Indo-Israeli operation to destroy Pakistan's uranium enrichment plant that was coming up at Kahuta. The successful Israeli air raid in 1981 to destroy the French-aided Osirak nuclear reactor in Iraq before it could be commissioned added to the Pakistani fears of a similar raid on Kahuta by India and Israel.

The CIA and the ISI stepped up their monitoring of the activities of the R&AW, each for its own reason. The CIA wanted to find out more about the R&AW's contacts with the Khad and the KGB. The military dictatorship in Pakistan wanted to find out more about India's contacts with Pakistani political exiles and its clandestine co-operation with the Mossad. Consequently, there was a steady increase in the number of CIA and ISI officers posted in the diplomatic missions of the two countries in India. The CIA stepped up its efforts to penetrate the R&AW and the IB through CIA operatives posted in the US Embassy in New Delhi and in the US Consulates in Mumbai, Kolkata and Chennai.

The 1980s also saw an increase in the presence and activities of intelligence officers of West European countries in India. They all co-operated with each other. The French intelligence penetrated the Prime Minister's office and shared with its West European and American counterparts the intelligence and documents collected by it. The West German intelligence co-operated with the CIA by establishing secret contacts with Afghan Government leaders and officials visiting Delhi for talks with their Indian counterparts or for medical treatment and collecting intelligence from them. The CIA felt that because of Indira Gandhi's well-known distrust of the US and paranoia about it, its officers would be under close surveillance by the IB. It, therefore, often operated through the intelligence agencies of the West European countries, which were not under similar surveillance till the detection of the penetration of the PMO by the French intelligence. Much later, in 1987, the IB detected a CIA penetration of the R&AW's office in Chennai to collect intelligence and documents about the R&AW's activities in Sri Lanka. The greatest damage was caused by the French intelligence agency's penetration of the office of the Prime Minister. It had access to a large number of top secret reports sent by the R&AW and the IB to the Prime Minister on their sensitive operations.

Continuing weaknesses in the counter-intelligence capability of the R&AW were a matter of concern during this period. It came to notice that an Australian woman, who used to work in a UN-aided project in South-East Asia, was living with a promoted (not a direct recruit to the IPS) police officer (a widower) on deputation with the R&AW at his house in Delhi without the Counter-intelligence and Security Division (CIS) of the organization being aware of it for some time. The wife of another promoted police officer on deputation was found having lunch with the wife of an identified Australian intelligence officer posted in their High Commission in New Delhi for liaison with the R&AW. Enquiries indicated that her husband had been associated by the organization for a liaison meeting with the Australian officer. Thereafter, the police officer and his wife had maintained a social relationship with the Australian couple without the knowledge of the organization. There were reasons to suspect that the couple was exploring the possibility of migrating to Australia with the assistance of the Australian intelligence officer. Both the promoted police officers were reverted back to their respective States. A diplomat from a Gulf country posted in Delhi was killed at his residence by a suspected terrorist. The media described the slain diplomat as a tenant of an R&AW officer. Enquiries indicated that a retired and re-employed Army officer of the organization had given out his house on a high rent to the diplomat without the knowledge of the organization and in violation of the security regulations. A distinguished IPS officer from the Kerala cadre, known for his personal integrity and who also had a reputation as a strict disciplinarian, was posted as the head of the CIS Division. He tightened up the CIS procedures and played an important role in the 1987 detection of the penetration of the Chennai office by the CIA.

Weaknesses in the linguistic capability of the staff of the organization also came in the way of analytical and operational work. At a time when Khalistani terrorism had become a highly worrisome problem, the organization found itself without the services of an adequate number of staff at various levels knowing the Punjabi language in the Gurumukhi script. The organization had many officers, who were very proficient in the Chinese and Arabic languages, but had very few officers with a good proficiency in the languages spoken in Pakistan and Afghanistan. It had some officers, who could speak and understand Urdu, but very few who could read and write that language. It had one officer with a good knowledge of Pushtoo and none, who could read, write or speak in Sindhi and Baloch. As a result, it had to depend on the staff of the external services of the All India Radio and other outsiders for monitoring the Pakistani language press. Their work was often unsatisfactory since they did not have a good idea of the requirements of an intelligence organization. They were also not prompt in meeting the requirements.

Before the R&AW was formed in 1968, the undivided IB had built up a very good cadre of linguists with adequate proficiency in the languages spoken in India's immediate neighbourhood. The credit for this should go to Mallik. The credit for building up an excellent cadre of Chinese and Arabic knowing linguists should also go to him. Till I retired in August 1994, the best linguists with proficiency in Chinese, Arabic and the languages spoken in the neighbourhood were mostly of IB vintage. In the R&AW, there was a needless fascination for West European languages, with the result that it had more officers knowing them than the languages spoken in the neighbourhood. For the direct recruits, proficiency in a foreign language was compulsory before they were confirmed in service and promoted, but linguistic proficiency was not obligatory for the officers of the IPS, other All-India and Central services and military officers, who came to the organization on deputation. I do not know whether this state of affairs has been rectified since my retirement.

Another issue, which came to the fore during this period, was regarding the induction of Muslim officers into the intelligence community—either as direct recruits or as deputationists. While all other religious minorities were well represented and well regarded in the intelligence community, there was a glass partition to keep out Muslim officers without seeming to do so. The decision to keep out Muslim officers was taken by Sardar Vallabhbai Patel, when he was the Home Minister of India after independence. It was endorsed by Jawaharlal Nehru and all the Prime Ministers, who succeeded him, including Indira Gandhi when she was the Prime Minister between 1966 and 1977. Unhappiness reportedly expressed by a senior Muslim officer belonging to an All-India Service over what he viewed as attempts by the IB and the R&AW to keep out his son, who belonged to the IPS, under some pretext or the other was among the factors, which contributed to a review of this practice during the second tenure of Indira Gandhi. It was decided that Muslim officers should no longer be kept out of the intelligence community. If we have to deal effectively with jihadi terrorism, it is important to increase the intake of Muslim officers into the intelligence and security agencies and give them important analytical and operational positions.

Kao's tenure as the Senior Adviser saw three other important developments in the intelligence community. The first was the resumption of direct recruitment to the R&AW from the open market, which had remained suspended under Morarji Desai and Charan Singh, and the initiation of action to constitute the Research & Analysis Service (RAS). When Indira Gandhi decided to bifurcate the IB and form the R&AW in September 1968, she wanted that the new organization should shed the police image, which the external intelligence division of the IB had acquired. It was her view— and correctly too— that while IPS officers might do well in an internal intelligence organization, they might not have the aptitude for the collection, analysis and assessment of external intelligence, which needed a different kind of expertise and aptitude. She, therefore, suggested that the proportion of IPS officers in the organization should be diluted and that more officers should be taken from other government services and the Armed Forces as well as directly from the open market. While there was no problem in increasing the intake of officers on deputation from other services, the direct recruitment from the open market initially posed difficulties since all Government departments were required to make all recruitment through the Union Public Service Commission (UPSC). Kao succeeded in persuading Indira Gandhi to exempt the organization from the purview of the UPSC. She also accepted a suggestion of Kao to constitute a separate central service for the organization to be called the RAS. The RAS was to consist of all direct recruits as well those among the deputationists from different services, who were considered worthy of inclusion in the RAS, provided they were willing to resign from their parent services and to be permanently absorbed in the organization.

Action to constitute the RAS could not be completed till Kao retired in 1977 due to many reasons. There were allegations that the exemption from the purview of the UPSC granted to the organization was being misused to directly recruit sons and daughters of senior serving and retired Government servants, who had either failed in the UPSC examinations for All India and Central Services or who would have never passed if they had appeared for the examinations. It so happened that some of the initial recruits were the sons of senior officers of the Armed Forces. This led to allegations that the organization was trying to soften criticism of its performance by the Armed Forces by recruiting the sons and daughters of their senior officers. There were also difficulties in fixing the inter-se seniority of officers, who had been taken in from different services as well as from the open market. After Morarji Desai took over as the Prime Minister in 1977, the organization thought it wise not to proceed further with the constitution of the RAS cadre since he would have been hostile to it—particularly since he was questioning the very need for such a large organization and wanted it trimmed.

When Kao took over as Senior Adviser in 1981 after Indira Gandhi's return to power, he was very keen to take up once again the discontinued work relating to the cadre. One had an impression that Suntook was not very enthusiastic about it since he felt troubled by the kind of allegations that were being made by the staff at the junior and middle levels about nepotism and favouritism in the matter of direct recruitment. In his own gentle manner, Kao kept pressing for the resumption of direct recruitment and for early completion of the constitution of the cadre. Ultimately, Suntook agreed to it. Kao had a one-man committee consisting of Sankaran Nair, who had retired in 1979, set up to recommend how to fix the inter-se seniority of officers from different services and the direct recruits in the RAS cadre. The recommendations of Sankaran Nair were accepted and the RAS cadre was constituted. There was some unhappiness among the civilian officers—particularly among those from the IPS— over the recommendations of Nair regarding the inter-se seniority. They felt that undue advantage had been given to officers from the Army in the matter of seniority. The manner in which officers from different services were taken into the organization, the direct recruitment from the open market was made and the inter-se seniority was determined left a bitter taste, which has continued till today.This has come in the way of the R&AW officers developing an esprit de corps even 39 years after the formation of the organization. Persisting frictions — -RAS vs non-RAS, IPS vs the rest, military officers vs civilian officers- – and the failure of different chiefs, including Kao, to address these frictions and pockets of unhappiness in a manner satisfactory to all should explain the unfortunate practice of different officers or groups having grievances relating to their career planting negative stories about the organization in the media. In the IB too, as in any other government department, grievances exist at various levels, but instances of dog eating dog are less. There is greater inter-service and inter-rank harmony among the officers of the IB than among those of the R&AW.

The second important development related to the bifurcation of the Joint Intelligence Committee (JIC) of the Government of India. After the war over the Falkland Islands between the UK and Argentina in 1982, there were allegations of intelligence failure against the British Secret Intelligence Service (SIS). An enquiry by Lord Franks, a member of the House of Lords, ordered by Margaret Thatcher, the then Prime Minister, absolved the SIS of any responsibility for the intelligence failure. It held that since the SIS did not have a presence in Argentina it could not be blamed for failing to anticipate the Argentine invasion of the Falkland Islands. Instead, it blamed the British JIC for its failure to adequately analyse the open information available on the likelihood of an Argentine invasion. It recommended the strengthening of the JIC by appointing an independent person not connected with either the intelligence collecting or consuming agencies as its Chairman. After reading its report, Kao suggested to Indira Gandhi that the Indian JIC should also be strengthened. He also told her that since internal security was assuming increasing importance in view of the continuing insurgency in the North-East and the worsening terrorism in Punjab, it would be advisable to create a separate JIC for assessing internal intelligence to be headed by an officer of the Indian Administrative Service.

She accepted his recommendation. Two JICs were created—one to assess external intelligence headed by an IPS officer from the R&AW and the other to assess internal intelligence headed by an IAS officer from the Ministry of Home Affairs. Many in the intelligence community and in the other departments of the Government were not convinced of the wisdom of creating a separate JIC for internal intelligence. They felt that internal and external security could not be artificially separated and that there was a continuing need for a holistic assessment of both. There were also reservations regarding Kao's recommendation to appoint an officer of the R&AW to head the JIC in charge of assessing external intelligence. Since the JIC assesses the intelligence supplied by the agencies and monitors their performance, it was felt that appointing an intelligence officer as its Chairman could affect its independence and objectivity. But, their reservations could not come in the way of Indira Gandhi implementing Kao's recommendation. Rajiv Gandhi, who succeeded her, reversed the bifurcation and restored the original position of a single JIC to assess internal and external intelligence. However, he did not reverse the practice of appointing an IPS officer—either from the R&AW or the IB— as the Chairman of the JIC. This practice was reversed only after the Kargil conflict in 1999.

The third important development was the creation of a Policy and Research Staff in the Cabinet Secretariat under him. It had one officer of the Indian Foreign Service and three from the R&AW. It had little expertise in internal security. This became the precursor of the National Security Council Secretariat, which came up in 1999. None of the three policy initiatives of Kao as Senior Adviser was well thought of and they did not add to the strength of national security management.

Analysis and assessment are important components of the intelligence process, but too many analysis and assessment points led to an overload of assessments leading to confusion in policy-making. There were five assessment points—the IB, the R&AW, the JIC (Internal), the JIC (External) and the Policy and Research Staff, when Kao was the Senior Adviser. His practice of often not keeping other senior officials responsible for national security management such as the Principal Secretary to the PM, the Cabinet Secretary, the Home Secretary, the Foreign Secretary and the Defence Secretary in the picture regarding the advice given by him to the PM created pockets of unhappiness in the national security bureaucracy, but thanks to his endearing personal qualities, this did not give rise to any resentment or jealousy against him. But, after his exit as the Senior Adviser, this question came up again and again, that is: While the PM has every right to consult his or her intelligence chiefs directly and while the intelligence chiefs should have the right of direct access to the PM, is it not important to keep the other senior officials in the national security establishment informed of the advice given so that they could take up with the PM any reservations they might have regarding the advice given by the intelligence chiefs?

This issue has remained unresolved. It was raised by some of the senior officials before the Special Task Force for the Revamping of the Intelligence Apparatus headed by G.C.Saxena set up by A.B.Vajpayee in 2000, of which I was a member. After discussing this, the Task Force decided that this was an important prerogative of the PM, which should not be disturbed. While the de jure position thus continued undisturbed, Brajesh Mishra, as the Principal Secretary to Vajpayee and as, concurrently, his National Security Adviser established the practice of all advice to the PM—either from the intelligence chiefs or other senior officials— going through him. That is why he strongly opposed the repeated demands that the same person should not wear two hats as the Principal Secretary to the PM and as the National Security Adviser.

He diluted the role of the intelligence chiefs as advisers to the PM on national security matters and kept their roles restricted to the collection, analysis and assessment of intelligence and its dissemination. In national security policy-making, the intelligence chiefs—particularly the chief of the R&AW—were reduced to the role of being his direct subordinates and advisers and not the direct subordinates and advisers of the PM. However, the DIB managed to acquire a little more space and significant role for himself by using his political contacts such as L.K.Advani, the Home Minister and the Deputy Prime Minister, who jealously guarded his turf from any encroachment by Brajesh Mishra, and Ranjan Bhattacharya, the son-in-law of Vajpayee.

Without any such political contacts, the R&AW chiefs found their status and role diluted. One is given to understand that under Dr. Manmohan Singh too, the role of the intelligence chiefs remains reduced to that of the subordinates and advisers of the NSA, with little direct access to the PM. During a lunch with senior R&AW officers in the R&AW headquarters in September,2005, Dr.Manmohan Singh reportedly expressed his admiration for Kao, whom he knew personally, and said that the intelligence chiefs were welcome to approach him directly whenever they felt the need to do so. But his offer remained largely unutilized due to a fear of rubbing M.K. Narayanan, the present NSA, on the wrong side by doing so.

After resigning as the Senior Adviser in the wake of Indira Gandhi's assassination, Kao devoted the rest of his life to sculpture, in which he was deeply interested and other pursuits. He had a large circle of friends and admirers in the intelligence community and other government departments as well as in the political class, particularly in the Congress (I). They kept in touch with him. He kept himself well-informed on matters concerning national security, but had very limited access to Rajiv Gandhi and his successors as the Prime Minister. However, when he felt strongly on any issue, he did not hesitate to convey his views to the Prime Minster of the day through a letter. He was a greatly and universally admired icon of the Indian intelligence community when he was the chief of the R&AW. His tenure as the Senior Adviser was less distinguished than his tenure as the head of the R&AW, but he still maintained a certain aura round his head. He would have left office with this aura intact but for the assassination of Indira Gandhi.

CHAPTER XIII

Terrorism Continues In Punjab

The widespread resentment in the Sikh community in India and abroad over Operation Blue Star led to an aggravation of Khalistani terrorism. More people started supporting the Khalistanis. The situation became worse in the wake of the atrocities committed on the Sikh community after the assassination of Indira Gandhi and the failure of the Government to prevent it. There were serious allegations that some leaders of the Congress (I) had instigated the atrocities. The ISI took full advantage of the resentment to further fuel the anger in the Sikh community to serve Pakistan's own purpose. It set up more training camps for the Khalistanis in its territory and started imparting to them training in the fabrication and use of improvised explosive devices (IEDs), through timers and remote control. Before Operation Blue Star, the ISI's training was mainly confined to the use of hand-held weapons. It started supplying high-grade explosives, detonators and chemical timers. Many of these came from the stocks given by the CIA for use by the Afghan Mujahideen against the Soviet troops. The ISI advised them to float non-governmental organizations in West Europe to agitate on the alleged violation of the human rights of the Sikhs during and after Operation Blue Star and after Indira Gandhi's assassination. It funded them. It stressed upon them the importance of attacking economic targets. It wanted them to damage the agricultural economy of Punjab. It brought them into contact with fundamentalist organizations such as the Jamaat-e-Islami (JEI) of Pakistan and asked them to co-operate with the extremist elements in Jammu & Kashmir. It provided sanctuaries to terrorists and others, who had escaped from the Golden Temple and crossed over into Pakistan. The Zia-ul-Haq regime rejected repeated complaints of the Government of India regarding the ISI's assistance to Khalistani terrorism.

Protection of Rajiv Gandhi and the members of his family from the wrath of the terrorists received the urgent attention of the Government of India. Till Indira Gandhi's assassination, India did not have a dedicated service or force for the protection of the Prime Minister—similar to the US Secret Service, which is responsible for the protection of the US President. The IB performed the role of the co-ordinator of security arrangements for the Prime Minister. Unsatisfactory co-ordination   and ineffective supervision had contributed to her assassination. It was, therefore, decided to set up a dedicated force called the Special Protection Group (SPG) for the protection of the Prime Minister. It was taken out of the control of the IB, which became one of the input feeder agencies for the protection of the PM instead of the principal agency as it was before Indira Gandhi's assassination. Dr. S.Subramanian, a highly distinguished officer of the IPS from Andhra Pradesh, who had served for some years as Assistant Director in charge of the PM's security in the IB in the late 1960s and early 1970s, was appointed the first Director of the SPG. He organized the SPG with great competence and won the trust of Rajiv Gandhi and his family. He was a no-nonsense type of officer, who was thorough in his supervision. He commanded the respect and the implicit obedience of his officers. He was professional to his finger tips and did not allow any interference by the political class or by the IB or the other senior officers in the work of the SPG. He ensured that in matters concerning the physical security of the Prime Minister his word was the law.

The R&AW continued to be responsible for co-ordinating the work relating to the bullet-proofing of the PM's cars and for the maintenance of the cars used by the PM. For reasons which were not clear, Rajiv Gandhi wanted the initial crop of officers of the SPG to be trained by Italian experts—though the Italian security services were not particularly known for their expertise in this field. They used to impart the training in a guest house owned by the R&AW

away from Delhi. There were complaints of rude behaviour by the Italian experts towards the trainees. It was even alleged that one of the Italian experts slapped a trainee. The R&AW brought these things to the notice of Rajiv Gandhi and told him that the rude behaviour of the Italians towards the trainees could create feelings of resentment in the minds of the trainees. This was not desirable. Thereafter, Rajiv Gandhi terminated the training arrangements with the Italians.

The situation in Punjab and Delhi kept going from bad to worse. The ISI expanded a provocative programme over the external services of Radio Pakistan, whose only purpose was to strengthen the feelings of alienation in the minds of the Sikh community in India and abroad. It kept pressing the Khalistanis to blow up the Bhakra Nangal dam and to damage the irrigation canal system in Punjab. Between 1981 and 1984, the Khalistanis mainly resorted to aircraft hijackings and targeted killings with hand-held weapons for drawing attention to their cause and for intimidating the Government and the people. After the assassination of Indira Gandhi, they started using IEDs frequently. Initially, they were detonating the IEDs through mechanical timers such as a clock. And then, they started using chemical timers of US-make given by the ISI. Thereafter, they showed considerable skills in remote-controlled activation of IEDs. Their ability to innovate was of great concern to the Indian security agencies. Coinciding with the first anniversary of Operation Blue Star in June,1985, they carried out a number of explosions in different parts of Delhi with what came to be known as transistor radio bombs. They concealed IEDs inside transistor radio sets and left them in public places. When passers-by picked them up and switched them on, there were explosions causing casualties. There was considerable panic. The security agencies appealed to the public not to touch transistor radios if found anywhere, but to report their presence to the Police.

Rajiv Gandhi refrained from traveling abroad for about eight months after taking over as the Prime Minister. In June,1985, he undertook his first official visit abroad. He paid a State visit to

France, the US and Algeria. On his way back to Delhi from Algeria, he stopped over in Geneva to address the annual session of the International Labour Organization (ILO). On coming to know of this, Khalistani elements in the UK, the US and Canada conspired to kill him during his travel. The Indian as well as foreign security agencies took extraordinary precautions to foil their conspiracies. Some of these precautions, which were necessary, added to the resentment in the Sikh community. One of these precautions was to ensure that no Sikh would be deployed on any duty near Rajiv Gandhi and his family.

I was at that time posted as Counsellor in the Indian Permanent Mission to the UN organizations based in Geneva. I held concurrent charge as the Indian Consul-General in Geneva accredited to the Cantonal Government of Geneva. Since I had previously served in Paris in the 1970s and had a good knowledge of the French language, I was asked to act as the interface with the security agencies of France and Geneva, co-ordinate the arrangements and assist the SPG in whatever way I could. I felt many embarrassing situations in this role. A clean-shaven Sikh of foreign origin was occupying a senior position in one of the Air India Offices. I was asked by Delhi to persuade the Air India to send him out on tour so that he would not be present during Rajiv Gandhi's visit.

In Geneva, I had prepared the entire security plan. There was a charming, young Sikh officer belonging to the Indian Foreign Service who was posted in the Indian Permanent Mission. I had made him in charge of co-ordinating the arrangements at the airport during the arrival and departure of Rajiv Gandhi, in association with the Geneva authorities. On coming to know of this, Delhi asked me not to associate him with any security- related duties. I pointed out that this would amount to a humiliation of the officer who had already been told by me that he would be in charge of the airport arrangements. Moreover, when every other officer in the Indian mission was being associated with the security arrangements, not to associate one officer just because he was a Sikh would be incorrect and exploited by the Khalistanis in their propaganda against the

Government of India. Delhi then ordered that he should be put in charge of the 24-hour Control Room, which had been set up in the Permanent Mission so that he would not be anywhere near Rajiv Gandhi and his family during their stay in Geneva.

It was obvious this young officer felt very hurt when his duties were changed. However, he did not show it outwardly and performed his duties in the Control Room with great diligence. He never spoke to me even once about it. Three years later, on the eve of my transfer back to Delhi, there was a farewell party for me in the Mission. After Dr.J.S.Teja, the then Permanent Representative, had spoken praising me, this young officer asked for Dr.Teja's permission to say a few words. After praising me very warmly, he made a reference in very polite language to his hurt over his removal from airport duty to Control Room duty during the visit of Rajiv Gandhi. I felt a very small man. How I wished I had resisted the pressure from Delhi and insisted on his performing the airport duty as originally scheduled.

One of the engagements for Rajiv Gandhi at Geneva was a reception hosted by the Indian association in a local hotel. The President of the association was a distinguished Sikh officer of one of the UN organizations. I had deliberately not kept Delhi informed of this fact after the embarrassment over this young IFS officer. I could sense a feeling of nervousness among some of the officers, who had accompanied Rajiv Gandhi when they saw a Sikh welcoming him as he arrived at the hotel for the reception. Another India-based Sikh used to come to Geneva often to attend multilateral meetings. Fortunately, Delhi did not ask me to keep him also away from Rajiv Gandhi. His name was Dr.Manmohan Singh.

One of the unfortunate, but understandable consequences of the assassination of Indira Gandhi by two of her Sikh security guards was the over-cautiousness of the intelligence and security agencies and the paranoia about the Sikh community, which came to grip many of us, including me. We started playing safe by looking with suspicion at many Sikhs— often even our closest friends. We started taking seriously all reports on alleged activities of Sikh extremists without proper verification. The sources and even some unscrupulous intelligence officers took advantage of this paranoia by feeding all sorts of reports of likely threats from Khalistani terrorists. Any Sikh— however reputed and distinguished— who criticized the Government or the Prime Minister, was looked upon with suspicion as a hidden Khalistani. When not only sources, but also junior officers found that credence was being given to any report which spoke of a threat from the terrorists, there were attempts at fabrication. A directly-recruited telecommunications expert of the R&AW working in its Monitoring Division claimed to have intercepted a conversation between two Sikhs, which indicated a conspiracy to kill Rajiv Gandhi. Fortunately, a retired Army Colonel, who was his supervisory officer, managed to establish that this expert had fabricated the intercept. He was sacked.

The IB and the R&AW used to prepare a collation of terrorist and other extremist suspects from whom threats could arise to the security of the Prime Minister. Many names were included in this list on the basis of single-source reports. It became bulky with hundreds of names. Often, these names did not have any identifying particulars such as the full name or the address or the passport particulars etc. Before the Prime Minister's travels abroad, IB and R&AW officers accompanying the Advance Security Liaison Teams used to carry this list, hand it over to the local authorities and request them not to let any of the suspects figuring in the list enter their country before and during the visit of the Prime Minister. This bulky list and the lack of identifying particulars in many cases became an object of ridicule in many countries.

Before one of the visits of Rajiv Gandhi to Islamabad, when Benazir Bhutto was the Prime Minister , an Advance Security Liaison Team had visited Islamabad. At a joint meeting of intelligence and security officials from the two countries chaired by the Pakistani Interior Secretary, the R&AW representative, before handing over the bulky list to the Interior Secretary, read out the names of suspects, who were resident in Pakistan—particularly in Islamabad and Rawalpindi. After he had finished reading, the Pakistani Interior Secretary mockingly said: "Alok (not the real name), I was very nervous as you were reading out the names. I was worried my name might also figure in your list. In that case, I might have been obliged to tell Benazir that our Indian friends look upon me as a security suspect and request her to remove me from all duties connected with Rajiv Gandhi's visit. I am relieved my name is not in your list." Everybody laughed—the Pakistanis heartily and the Indian officials with great embarrassment.

A similar drill was followed before a planned visit of V.P. Singh, when he was the Prime Minister, to Kuala Lumpur. When the suspects' list was handed over to a senior security official of the Malaysian Government, he remarked: " This is the suspects' list? I thought it was the dictionary!" He then glanced through the list and found there were many names like "A.Singh", "S.Singh", "I.Ahmed" etc. Many names had no identifying particulars. The Malaysian official asked for the expansion of the names or the identifying particulars. Neither the IB nor the R&AW had them. They had just included these names because they figured in some source report or the other. The Malaysians were surprised. They asked: " Do you mean to say you have included these names without even verifying whether such persons existed or not?" At that time, the Indian High Commission in Kuala Lumpur had a senior Sikh official from the IFS. One Malaysian officer remarked jocularly: " We hope you have not put his name also in your list. We will face a mighty embarrassing situation." After the return of the team from Kuala Lumpur, the IB and the R&AW undertook a drastic revision of the list and pruned it considerably.

Every year, before the Independence Day and the Republic Day, the headquarters of the IB and the R&AW receive a large number of reports on likely threats from their sources and their junior officers. All these reports used to be conveyed to the Commissioner of Delhi Police, the Home Secretary, the Director of the SPG and other officers involved in making the security arrangements. A co-ordination group consisting of representatives of the various security agencies met almost daily and discussed these reports in order to decide whether any additional security arrangements were called for. Once the IB reported about the possibility of a terrorist strike on the route of the Republic Day parade. After discussing this, the co-ordination group decided to take additional security measures along the parade route. A few days later, the IB reported that in view of the strengthening of security measures along the parade route, the Khalistani terrorists were likely to strike away from the parade route in old Delhi. When this report came up for discussion before the co-ordination group, the Commissioner of Police of Delhi literally blew up at the IB officer and said: " If we take additional security measures in Old Delhi too, you will report after a couple of days that in view of the tight security in Old Delhi, the terrorists are likely to strike in Karolbagh. We can't function like this."

Some years later, when P.V.Narasimha Rao was the Prime Minister, even A.N.Verma, his Principal Secretary, used to accuse the IB and the R&AW of play-it-safe reporting. He used to even allege that the intelligence agencies were preparing their assessments of threat perceptions before domestic and foreign travels of the Prime Minister without applying their mind to the reports. He complained that the two organizations had ready-made omnibus assessments of threat perceptions, which would suit any country and any occasion. He accused them of sending these omnibus assessments even without making them country-specific. He once pointed out that an assessment of likely threats sent by the R&AW before the Prime Minister's visit to the US contained many paragraphs, which seemed to have been lifted from an earlier assessment on likely threats in Thailand.

Such instances of over-cautiousness and "play-it-safe" reporting could seem ridiculous in retrospect today when viewed against the wisdom of hindsight. But, it was not so in the 1980s when there was a sudden increase in the number and lethality of the Khalistani terrorist strikes and after the brutal assassination of Indira Gandhi by two of her own security guards and the assassination at Pune of Gen. A.S.Vaidya, who was living there after his retirement as the Chief of the Army Staff. The intelligence agencies had to disseminate to the physical security agencies reports indicating a likely threat of terrorism even before verifying them. It was not play-it-safe reporting, but prudent reporting. In fact a rule of prudence followed by the intelligence agencies all over the world is to alert the physical security agencies immediately after the receipt of a report indicating the likelihood of a terrorist strike without waiting till the verification process is completed. Report-and-simultaneously-verify is the rule of the thumb invariably followed by all intelligence agencies in respect of reports indicating a likely threat to a VVIP instead of verify-and-then-report.

In 1987, a source of the R&AW had reported that a Khalistani terrorist would be attempting to kill Rajiv Gandhi with a pistol when he visited the Rajghat and that he would take up position on the branch of a tree the previous night. There was no way of getting the report verified through a second source. A retired officer of the Air Force, who was then in charge of the VIP Security Division, immediately conveyed the information to a Joint Secretary in the MHA. Since there was no way of getting the information independently verified before communicating it, he sent it only to a Joint Secretary and not to a senior officer of the rank of a Secretary. The Joint Secretary and the Commissioner of Police, who also received a copy, treated it as one of the play-it-safe instances. They did not act on the report with all the seriousness it deserved. The security for Rajiv Gandhi at Rajghat was not tightened up by the Delhi Police and there was no proper search of the trees and other places where the terrorist could have concealed himself. Exactly as mentioned in the report, the terrorist had managed to sneak into Rajghat the previous night before the Police took up position and to conceal himself in the thick branch of a tree. He managed to remain unnoticed even after the Police took up position and opened fire with a pistol after Rajiv Gandhi reached Rajghat. He had a lucky escape because of the limited range of the pistol and its malfunctioning. Instead of complimenting the R&AW officer for collecting the intelligence and promptly disseminating it, the explanation of that officer was called for by T.N.Seshan, who had enquired into the incident, for disseminating the report only at the level of a Joint Secretary and not at the level of a Secretary to the Government of India. Later when Seshan became the Cabinet

Secretary, he saw to it that this officer was not promoted to the rank of Joint Secretary despite his excellent record. In sheer disgust, the officer went on premature retirement.

This incident illustrates the dilemma faced by intelligence officers while dealing with reports indicating a likely threat to the security of a VVIP. If the information proves to be incorrect, they are accused of frivolous reporting without proper verification. If the information proves to be correct, but had not been reported in time since the verification process was incomplete, they are accused of tardy reporting. It is true that the practice of reporting unverified information has two inherent risks. The first is that if instances of threats not materializing occur frequently, there would be a tendency on the part of physical security agencies not to take intelligence reports seriously. The second is that the practice of reporting unverified information could lead to instances of over-assessment of threats and consequent over-reaction by the physical security agencies. Repeated instances of over-reaction could aggravate terrorism due to the anger in the community from which the terrorists have arisen. This is a dilemma to which no satisfactory answer has ever been found. One has to live with it.

When Rajiv Gandhi undertook his first visit abroad in June,1985, coinciding with the first anniversary of Operation Blue Star, the R&AW was in receipt of reliable reports from sources in the UK that the Khalistani terrorists were planning to kill him in Geneva and that Gurdip Singh Sivia, a Khalistani extremist leader from the UK, had been visiting Geneva in this connection. There were apprehensions that the terrorists could emulate the Provisional Irish Republican Army (IRA), which on October 12, 1984, had unsuccessfully tried to kill Margaret Thatcher, the then Prime Minister, by blowing up a hotel at Brighton in the UK where she and other senior leaders of the Conservative Party were to stay while attending the annual conference of the Conservative Party. The day before the arrival of Rajiv Gandhi , the Geneva Police, therefore, decided that he and his family should stay in the house of Ambassador Muchkund Dubey, the then Indian Permanent Representative to the UN at Geneva, and not in Hotel Inter-continental, where arrangements for their stay had been made.

After Rajiv Gandhi and his family reached Geneva, the local Police took them straight to the Ambassador's house. The members of his entourage such as his Principal Secretary, the Foreign Secretary, Arun Singh and others were taken to the hotel where arrangements for them had been made. The arrangements, which had been made for the stay of Rajiv Gandhi and his family in the hotel, were not cancelled. Only the Principal Secretary, the Foreign Secretary, the Press Adviser and Arun Singh were told that Rajiv Gandhi and his family were staying in the house of Dubey. They were allowed to visit him for consultations there. The others were kept in the dark about his actual place of stay. Even the senior officials, who were allowed to visit Rajiv Gandhi in Dubey's house, were not permitted to go up to the house in their cars. They were asked by the Geneva Police to get down from their cars at a short distance away from the house and then walk.

Some of these officials protested to Dr.S.Subramanian, the then Director of the SPG, and insisted that he should ask the Geneva Police to allow them to come in their cars up to the house of the Ambassador. He declined to do so. He told them that the local Police on the basis of the inputs provided by the Indian intelligence had decided upon a certain security drill for Rajiv Gandhi and his family. He would not like to interfere with that drill. As the officials were discussing the restrictions imposed by the Geneva Police with Subramanian, Rajiv Gandhi came there and asked them what it was about. On coming to know of the objections raised by the officials, he supported Subramanian's stand that the arrangements made by the Geneva Police should not be interfered with. This incident illustrates a difficulty faced by physical security agencies in making effective arrangements for the protection of VVIPs because of the practice of officials with no security background interfering with the arrangements for their own reasons. This happens again and again despite the various tragedies suffered by us at the hands of terrorists. Subramanian was a no-nonsense type of officer, who stood his ground and was supported by Rajiv Gandhi. There are other officers, who are not that strong and tend to succumb to pressures to change the security drill to suit the convenience or ego of somebody or the other close to the VVIP.

Before Rajiv Gandhi's arrival in the US, the Federal Bureau of Investigation (FBI) discovered a plan by Lal Singh alias Manjit Singh of the International Sikh Youth Federation (ISYF), Canada, to kill him during his stay in the US. The local Khalistanis had also planned to kill Bhajan Lal, the then Chief Minister of Haryana, who had preceded Rajiv Gandhi on a visit to the US. Lal Singh managed to evade arrest by the FBI and fled to Pakistan, where he was given shelter by the ISI. All of us, who were associated with making security arrangements for Rajiv Gandhi during his first visit abroad as the Prime Minister, heaved a sigh of relief after he returned to Delhi without any mishap. The President of the Indian Association in Geneva had hosted a party in his house on June 23,1985, for the office-bearers of his association and for the officials of the Indian Mission, who were associated with the visit. Muchkund Dubey and I were there. As all of us were congratulating each other for a successful and incident-free visit, there was a breaking news on the British Broadcasting Corporation that Kanishka, an India-bound aircraft of Air India from Toronto via Montreal, had been blown up in mid-air off the Irish coast.All the 329 passengers and crew were killed.

We were shocked. We knew that the Khalistanis would try to stage a spectacular terrorist strike coinciding with the first anniversary of Operation Blue Star. Physical security for all VIPs in India had been tightened up. So too for Rajiv Gandhi and his family during their travel abroad. We had innumerable reports from our sources about likely threats to Rajiv Gandhi and his family. We also had reports about the possibility of terrorist strikes at planes of Air India. In the beginning of June,1985, the Air India had, on the basis of inputs from the intelligence agencies, sent the following telex to the Royal Canadian Mounted Police (RCMP), which was responsible for making physical security arrangements : "Assessment of threat received from intelligence agencies reveal the likelihood of sabotage attempts being undertaken by Sikh extremists by placing time-delay devices in the aircraft or registered baggage.It is also learnt that Sikh extremists are planning to set up suicide squads who may attempt to blow up an aircraft by smuggling in of explosives in the registered or [carry on] baggage or any other means."

While seeking the assessment of the Canadian Security Intelligence Service (CSIS) on the likelihood of threats to Air India planes from Khalistani terrorists based in Canada, the RCMP did not tell the CSIS that the Indian assessment warned of such a threat. In its reply to the RCMP, the CSIS ruled out any threat. Even at that stage, the RCMP did not consider it necessary to tell the CSIS that the Indian intelligence had assessed that there was a threat and request it to re-consider its assessment. No attempt was made to reconcile the two assessments. The RCMP disregarded the Indian assessment and acted on the CSIS assessment that there was no threat. The RCMP officer in charge of airport security said in a June 5 telex to his headquarters: "I do not feel there is a need for extra security by this force."

The shocking inaction of the RCMP on the Indian warning cost the lives of 329 innocent civilians. This incident illustrated the kind of non-cooperative attitude from some Western intelligence agencies that India faced while dealing with Khalistani terrorism. While the physical security agencies of many other countries, including the UK, the US and Switzerland took Indian warnings of possible terrorist strikes coinciding with the first anniversary of Operation Blue Star seriously, the CSIS and the RCMP chose to ignore the Indian warnings. The Sikhs have a considerable political clout in some constituencies of Canada and the CSIS was not prepared to concede that the Khalistanis were indulging in terrorism. Their attitude changed only after the tragedy because many of those killed were Canadian citizens of Indian origin. Till today, no proper enquiry has been made by the Canadian authorities and no responsibility has been fixed for this criminal negligence. Compare it with the alacrity and thoroughness with which enquiries were made into the crash of a Pan Am aircraft in Lockerbie in Scotland on December 21, 1988, and the responsibility was fixed.

In fact, the Babbar Khalsa of Canada had planned to blow up two Air India planes on the same day—one starting from Toronto and the other from Tokyo. While they had successfully smuggled the Improvised Explosive Device (IED) into the luggage hold of the plane which started from Toronto without being detected by the airport security authorities, their attempt at Tokyo failed due to a premature explosion of the IED before the piece of baggage containing it could be loaded into the aircraft. As a result, only two ground personnel were killed. The passengers had a lucky escape.

The investigations indicated that Talwinder Singh Parmar of the Babbar Khalsa, Canada, had played an active role in orchestrating both these strikes. He too fled to Pakistan and was given sanctuary there by the ISI. Thus, Lal Singh alias Manjit Singh, who was involved in the plot to kill Rajiv Gandhi in the US, and Talwinder Singh Parmar, who was involved in the blowing-up of the Kanishka and the unsuccessful attempt to blow up another Air India aircraft in Tokyo, lived clandestinely as the guests of the ISI in Lahore from 1985 to 1992. From there, they were guiding the Khalistani terrorists operating in India and orchestrated terrorist strikes in India and abroad. They used to visit the training camps set up by the ISI in Pakistani territory for the Khalistani terrorists and give them motivational talks. Everytime the Govt. of India asked Islamabad to arrest and hand them over for prosecution and trial, we got the same reply: "We have searched for them. They are not in Pakistani territory." Look-out notices by the INTERPOL were ignored by the ISI.

The assassination of Indira Gandhi and the blowing-up of the Kanishka brought about a change in the attitude of the UK and Canada to Khalistani terrorism. Till then, they were not prepared to treat the Khalistanis as terrorists despite their involvement in many incidents of hijacking of Indian aircraft. It was partly due to the political clout wielded by the Sikh diaspora in some of their electoral constituencies and partly due to their lack of sympathy for the problems faced by India—particularly by Indira Gandhi.

On the day Indira Gandhi was assassinated, some of the Khalistanis in the UK headed by Jagjit Singh Chauhan gathered outside the Indian High Commission in London, sang and danced and drank and distributed champagne to the passers-by. This was shown on the British TV. Large sections of the British, who viewed this, were disgusted. So too Margaret Thatcher, the then British Prime Minister. It was reported that she asked the head of the MI-5, the British Security Service, to extend all co-operation to the Indian intelligence agencies in dealing with the Khalistanis. She also rang up Rajiv Gandhi and told him how disgusted she was by the behaviour of the Khalistanis in the UK. She also told him that she had asked the MI-5 to extend all co-operation to the Indian intelligence. Thus started the co-operation of the MI-5 with the R&AW and the IB in dealing with Khalistani terrorism. The British determination to deal with these terrorists was further strengthened by the blowing-up of the Kanishka by the Babbar Khalsa.

Following this, the co-operation of the MI-5 and the MI-6 with the IB and the R&AW in dealing with Khalistani terrorism improved considerably. This co-operation was in the form of exchange of hard intelligence and assessments through written reports and meetings twice a year in New Delhi and London of the experts of the four services to pick each other's brains on the subject. A hot line between the MI-5 and the R&AW was also set up for quick exchange of intelligence, which called for immediate action. The MI-5 and the MI-6 readily shared not only intelligence regarding the activities and plans of the Khalistani terrorists, but also regarding the role of the ISI in assisting the terrorists. I cannot think of a single instance in which the British agencies excised references to Pakistan or the ISI in the source reports shared by them with us.

During my meetings with them, I could see that the MI-5 had a larger budget, a larger staff in the headquarters and more Punjabi-Gurumukhi-knowing experts than the Branches of the IB and the R&AW put together, which were dealing with this subject. Moreover, the British agencies persuaded their Home Office to amend their Prevention of Terrorism (Special Provisions) Act in order to make it applicable to terrorist organizations other than the Irish Republican Army (IRA) too. Till the required amendments were adopted by their Parliament, this Act was applicable only to terrorism emanating from Northern Ireland.

After this amendment, they were able to use the provisions of this Act against the Khalistani terrorists too. The MI-5 also advised the Charities Commission of the UK to make periodic checks of the accounts of gurudwaras in the UK, which were suspected of funding the Khalistani organizations. However, despite this, co-operation to stop the flow of funds from the UK to the Khalistani terrorists was not satisfactory due to the British insistence that they could legally proceed against those in the UK funding terrorism in India only if the Indian intelligence provided a continuous chain of evidence linking the remittance of an amount from the UK with the commission of a specific act of terrorism in India. This was an impractical request. After 9/11, they have themselves frozen many bank accounts of jihadi extremist organizations purely on the basis of strong suspicion, even in the absence of a continuous chain of evidence.

The Canadian services, which were unco-operative till 1985, started co-operating as vigorously as the British after the Kanishka disaster, in which many of those killed were Canadian citizens. Like the British, they too readily shared with the R&AW and the IB all the important intelligence coming to their notice regarding the activities of the Khalistani terrorists as well as the role of Pakistan and the ISI.

In sharp contrast to the co-operative attitude of the British and the Canadians, the intelligence agencies of the US and the continental European countries were unhelpful. The lack of co-operation from the US agencies was particularly deplorable. While they positively responded to requests for training assistance and for strengthening physical security during the visits of Indian VVIPs to the US, they rarely shared any worthwhile intelligence on the activities and plans of the Khalistani terrorists. Even when they did share any report, they took care to excise from it all references to Pakistan and the ISI. Our repeated requests to the US administration to declare Pakistan a State-sponsor of international terrorism met with a negative response.

The IB and the R&AW collected a lot of intelligence regarding the ISI training camps in Pakistani Territory for the terrorists, the arms and ammunition supplied by the ISI to the terrorists etc. Whenever we produced this intelligence before the US authorities and requested them to act against Pakistan, they would reject it on the ground that the intelligence was gathered during interrogation of suspects, who must have been tortured by the Indian police. When we produced technical intercepts, they would reject them on the ground that it was difficult to prove their authenticity. We requested the British and the Canadian agencies to share with the CIA the intelligence collected by them regarding the Pakistani sponsorship of terrorism. I told my counterparts: "Look, I have not been able to convince the CIA about the Pakistani sponsorship. Every time I produce any intelligence, the CIA rejects it on some ground or the other. You have collected your own independent intelligence. If you share it with the CIA, it would find it difficult to reject it."

My interlocutors in the two agencies gave me identical replies: "We know the CIA has more intelligence regarding the Pakistani sponsorship of terrorism against India than all of us together have. The CIA was convinced a long time ago about the ISI's sponsorship of terrorism. The problem is not with the CIA. It is with the State Department, which does not want to act against Pakistan."

In the early 1990s, Lal Singh alias Manjit Singh came to India from Pakistan. The Gujarat police arrested him. He was wanted in a number of cases in India, the US and Canada. I informed my counterparts in the Canadian and US intelligence that they could send their officers to interrogate him. I assured them that no Indian officer would be present during the interrogation. The Canadians availed of the offer and sent a police officer to interrogate him. The US agencies decided not to avail of the offer. I came to know later that the State Department had advised them not to send anybody to interrogate him. It was apparently afraid that if Lal Singh gave the US interrogator details of the ISI's role, it would find it difficult to reject his evidence as possibly obtained through torture.

The co-operation of the US and the continental European countries improved after two incidents in 1991. The first incident related to the failed attempt of some Sikh terrorists based in West

Europe to kill Julio Ribeiro, the Indian Ambassador in Bucharest, who had earlier served as the chief of the Punjab Police after the outbreak of the Khalistani terrorism. The investigation brought out that the conspiracy to kill him was hatched by the terrorists at a clandestine meeting held at Zurich in Switzerland from where the entire operation was co-ordinated by the Khalistan Liberation Force (KLF).

In the second incident, terrorists of the Khalistan Liberation Force (KLF) kidnapped Liviu Radu, a Romanian diplomat posted in Delhi, kept him as a hostage in a hide-out and demanded the release of some Khalistani terrorists from detention. The Government of India rejected their demands. Independently of each other, the intelligence agencies of India, the US and Germany intercepted telephone conversations of terrorists based in Lahore with their associates in Frankfurt and New York. The IB also managed to detain a member of the KLF, who had some knowledge of the kidnapping. From the intercepts and the interrogation of the detained person, it emerged that the KLF had initially planned to kidnap a French diplomat, but it found he had some physical security. It, therefore, picked up the Romanian, who had no physical security. The terrorists were greatly disappointed that the international media did not show much interest in the kidnapping. They, therefore, decided to release him and to target in future an American or someone from an important country in order to get more publicity.

These intercepted conversations and the interrogation report set the alarm bell ringing and the intelligence agencies of the US, France and Germany started paying more attention to monitoring the activities of the Khalistani terrorists. While the co-operation of the agencies of these countries improved, it was still not comparable to the co-operation extended by the agencies of the UK and Canada. Moreover, the US continued to avoid sharing any intelligence on the links of the terrorists with the ISI.

Encouraged by the reluctance of the US to act against Pakistan, the ISI stepped up its training and arms assistance to the Khalistani terrorists. There were reports that it had even given them shoulder-fired missiles capable of bringing down aircraft. Security for Rajiv Gandhi's aircraft was tightened up. The Mossad, the Israeli external intelligence agency, responded positively to a request from the R&AW for the supply of jammers to neutralize remote-control devices. This request was made to the Mossad following a British refusal to supply similar jammers. During a visit by Rajiv Gandhi to Canada where the threat to him from remotely-controlled improvised explosive devices (IEDs) was very high, the British sent a team with the jammers, but they refused to train the SPG staff in the use of the jammers and to supply one for use in India. India's repeated requests for arresting and handing over the hijackers of Indian aircraft, Lal Singh alias Manjit Singh and Talwinder Singh Parmar were rejected by Islamabad, which continued to insist that they were not in Pakistani territory. The British and Canadian intelligence confirmed their presence in Pakistan and yet the US refused to act against Pakistan.

The internal security situation in Pakistan started deteriorating. The Sindhudesh Movement for an independent Sindh picked up momentum. The late G.M.Syed, the father of the Sindhudesh movement, openly visited India and met Rajiv Gandhi and other Indian leaders. In Pakistan, he made a famous statement that he had committed a historic blunder by co-sponsoring at the annual conference of the Muslim League at Lahore on March 23, 1940, a resolution for the partition of India and the creation of Pakistan. He and his associates started traveling all over Sindh to propagate the cause of Sindhudesh. Sindhi human rights organizations sprung up in the UK, the US and Switzerland and started highlighting the violation of the human rights of the Sindhis.

Altaf Hussain, who was working in the US, returned to Karachi and was instigated by Zia ul-Haq and the ISI to form a Mohajir Students' Organisation to counter the movement for an independent Sindhudesh. The ISI created tensions and instigated acts of violence between the Sindhis and the Mohajirs. There were clashes between the Mohajirs and the large number of Pashtun truck-drivers in Karachi. The suppression of the Mohajirs by the Army to protect the Pashtuns turned the Mohajirs too against the Army. The Mohajir

Students' Organisation became the Mohajir Qaumi Movement (MQM). The MQM started demanding that Karachi should be given a status similar to that of Hong Kong. The attempt of the Army and the ISI to divide and rule by playing the Mohajirs against the Sindhis misfired.

There was a steady increase in the number of Bangladeshi illegal migrants infiltrating into Karachi and settling down there. Many of them took up jobs as manual workers in the Karachi port. Frequent strikes by them badly disrupted the work at the port. International shipping companies started avoiding Karachi. Cargo insurance rates for Karachi went up. The Baloch nationalist leaders, who had been given shelter by the Najibullah Government in Afghan territory, started visiting Delhi and meeting Indian leaders. Khan Abdul Wali Khan, son of Khan Abdul Ghaffar Khan, the Frontier Gandhi, continued to openly visit India and meet Rajiv Gandhi and other Indian leaders. The chiefs of the R&AW and the Khad, the Afghan intelligence agency, started visiting each other and sharing intelligence and assessments on Pakistan. Though these visits were supposed to be secret, the ISI came to know of them through its sources in Kabul.

The situation in Sindh in general and in Karachi in particular started deteriorating and the deterioration continued till 1996. The ISI and the Army started accusing the R&AW of trying to destabilise Pakistan. This was not true. Pakistan had started stewing in its own Islamic and sectarian juice. This was bound to happen. R&AW did not have to cause it. The only thing it did, with the approval of Rajiv Gandhi, was to help the All India Radio expand its external services in the Sindhi and Baloch languages and encourage the Khad to expand the Afghan radio's external services in the Pashtun language. A proposal was initiated to set up TV Stations in Rajasthan to telecast programmes in the Sindhi and Baloch languages. It could not take off.

On April 10,1988,there was a huge explosion in a military storage depot at Ojhri in Rawalpindi, killing 5,000 persons—civilians and military personnel. The arms and ammunition and explosives supplied by the CIA for distributing to the Afghan Mujahideen used to be kept there. The ISI used to divert part of this stock to the Khalistani terrorists. Zia ul-Haq was forced to order an enquiry following widespread allegations by the Pakistani political exiles that the ISI itself had caused the explosion before a visit by a CIA team from Washington DC to enquire into charges that ISI and other Army officers had earned millions of dollars by selling some of the stocks, including Stinger missiles, to the Iranians and the Libyans for use against the Americans. Muhammad Khan Junejo, a respected Sindhi, who was Zia's Prime Minister, turned against him and demanded that the Ojhri enquiry report be released to the public and action taken against the Army and ISI officers responsible for this disaster. Zia sacked Junejo on May 29,1988, dissolved the National Assembly and ordered fresh elections. The Shias of Gilgit rose in revolt against the Pakistan Army. The Zia regime had them violently suppressed in August 1988, with the help of pro-Osama bin Laden Sunni tribals from the Waziristan area of the Federally-Administered Tribal Areas (FATA), who were brought into Gilgit.

On August 17,1988, Zia-ul-Haq, accompanied by Gen.Mirza Aslam Beg, a Mohajir, who was the Vice Chief of Army Staff, Arnold Raphel, the US Ambassador, and other senior officers flew to Bhawalpur to watch the demonstration of a new US-made tank, which had been offered to the Pakistan Army. After the demonstration and lunch, Zia and party took off for Islamabad. Gen.Beg decided not to fly with them. He took off in another plane. As he was flying, his pilot heard frantic conversations by the staff of the airport control tower, which indicated that they had lost contact with Zia's plane.These conversations were also picked up by a monitoring station of the Indian Air force, which immediately informed Rajiv Gandhi about it. Gen.Beg asked his pilot to fly back to Bhawalpur. As it was flying back, he noticed fire and smoke coming from the ground. He asked his pilot to come down and circle over the spot. He noticed that Zia's plane had crashed. He informed the Bhawalpur airport control tower to send a rescue party to the spot. He asked his pilot to continue flying to Islamabad. The rescue party reached the spot and reported that there were no survivors. Beg assumed charge of the Army and advised Ghulam Ishaq Khan, the Chairman of the Senate, the upper house of the Parliament, to take over as the acting President and go ahead with the elections. A few hours later, the death of Zia was announced. Large sections of the people of Sindh came out into the streets, sang, danced, hugged each other and distributed sweets to the passers-by.

Ghulam Ishaq Khan ordered an enquiry into the crash of Zia's plane. There were speculations and rumours all over Pakistan as to what caused the crash. Some said it was an improvised explosive device (IED) concealed inside a basket of mangoes. Some others said that it was disorientation of the crew due to a Shia airman from Gilgit suddenly releasing tear-smoke or some other gas into the cockpit. A few alleged that the R&AW had brought down the aircraft in retaliation for the blowing up of the Kanishka by the Khalistani terrorists assisted by the ISI. The enquiry report was not released to the public by the army. Only the Pakistan Army and the US' Federal Bureau of Investigation knew the contents of the enquiry report. Even the political leaders of Pakistan were not shown the report. It was widely believed that the plane crash was caused by a Shia airman from Gilgit.

There were some intriguing questions, which have remained unanswered till today. Why did Gen.Beg choose not to travel in Zia's plane when everybody else traveled in it? Did he have advance information that the plane was going to crash? When he noticed the fire and smoke, why did he not land immediately and organize the rescue effort instead of leaving it to the Airport Control Tower staff, who took nearly an hour to do so?

The Pakistan People's Party (PPP) of Benazir Bhutto won the elections held on November 16, 1988. The Army and the ISI were initially reluctant to allow her to take over as the Prime Minister. They suspected her and her associates of being R&AW agents. Under US pressure, they relented and agreed to let her form the Government, but imposed severe restrictions on her.

A reliable source of the R&AW reported that at one of her meetings with her senior officials, she was bold enough to tell Lt.Gen.Hamid

Gul, whom she was forced to keep as the head of the ISI : " You are playing the Sikh card against India. They have started playing the Sindh card against us. Stop using the Sikh card and hand over to India all the Sikh leaders living in Pakistan, who are wanted by the Indian Police for investigation and trial." According to the source, Lt.Gen.Gul replied: " Madam, keeping Indian Punjab destabilized is equivalent to the Pakistan Army having two extra Divisions at no cost. If you want me to drop the Sikh card, you have to sanction the creation of two new Divisions." She found his argument compelling and kept quiet. Gul assured her that Sindh would soon be under control. She would not have to worry about it.

There was one interesting development under Zia, which continued under Benazir after she took over as the Prime Minister. The then Crown Prince Hassan bin Talal of Jordan was a good personal friend of Rajiv Gandhi and Zia. Hassan's wife was of Pakistani origin, and he had known Zia from the days when Zia, as a middle level officer, was posted in Amman as the commanding officer of a Pakistani army unit based there. He contacted Zia and Rajiv Gandhi separately and suggested that the chiefs of the ISI and the R&AW should meet secretly and discuss the issues relating to the Indian allegations of Pakistani support to Khalistani terrorists away from the glare of publicity. He offered to arrange the first meeting at Amman. His offer was accepted and he arranged a meeting at Amman between Lt Gen Hamid Gul and A K Verma, who was the head of the R&AW. He introduced the two to each other and then disappeared from the scene. The two had two meetings – the first at Amman and the second at Geneva. The atmosphere in the two meetings was positive. The agenda included not only the question of stopping the ISI's support to the Khalistani terrorists and handing over the terrorists given shelter in Pakistan, but also ways of solving the Siachen issue.

While there was progress in the discussions on the Siachen issue because the Pakistan Army was keen to have the Indian Army withdrawn from there, on the terrorism issue Lt.Gen Gul took up the standard position that the Sikh terrorists wanted by India were not in Pakistani territory. However, through a carefully worked-out operation, he enabled the Indian authorities to get the custody of four Sikh soldiers of the Indian army who had deserted while they were posted in Jammu and Kashmir and sought sanctuary in Pakistan. He wanted the operation organised in such a manner that it would not appear that the ISI had handed over these deserters to the R&AW. The R&AW agreed to this and kept its word of honour to Lt.Gen Gul that it would not tell the media about it.

After Zia's death and the elections, Benazir was allowed by the Army and the ISI to take over as the Prime Minister only after she had accepted three conditions imposed by them: First, Gen Mirza Aslam Beg would continue as the Chief of the Army Staff; second, Lt.Gen Gul, who was functioning as the chief of the ISI since March, 1987, would continue in that post; and third, Pakistan's nuclear establishment headed by Dr.A.Q. Khan would work directly under Gen. Beg. It would not report to Benazir. Crown Prince Hassan as well as Lt Gen Gul kept her informed of the exercise for a dialogue with the R&AW. She agreed that it should continue.

In March 1989, Lt Gen Gul, without consulting her, organised a raid on Najibullah's Afghan Army post at Jalalabad with the help of Afghan Mujahideen, Osama bin Laden's Arab followers and Pakistani ex-servicemen. The raiding party managed to surround the Jalalabad post for some days. Everybody thought that they would ultimately capture Jalalabad and that would be the beginning of the end of the rule of Najibullah. It did not happen that way. Najibullah's Army post managed to repulse the raiders, inflicting heavy casualties.

Benazir took advantage of this fiasco, which was the creation of Lt Gen Gul, to have him replaced as the Chief of the ISI in June 1989 by Maj Gen Shamshur Rahman Kallue, a retired officer, who was close to her father and had been very loyal to the Bhutto family. Surprisingly, Beg did not oppose the removal of Gul. Some years later after he had retired from the Army, Beg claimed that Gul had not consulted him either before undertaking the disastrous raid on the Jalalabad post. Beg opposed her selection of a retired officer to succeed Gul, but she managed to have her way.

After taking over, Kallue abolished the political division of the ISI, then headed by Brig Imtiaz. It was responsible for keeping a watch on Pakistani political leaders and civilian bureaucrats and also for assisting the Khalistan movement. On the advice of Lt Gen Gul, Nawaz Sharif, who was then the Chief Minister of Punjab, took Imtiaz into the Special Branch of the Punjab police to continue the ISI's operation for assisting the Khalistani movement. Lt Gen. Gul sent a message to all Khalistani leaders that in future they should contact Imtiaz in the Punjab Special Branch for any assistance and not Kallue.

Lt Gen Gul also leaked to Nawaz Sharif and some members of the media the information about the handing over of four Sikh deserters to India. He did not admit that he did it. He alleged that Benazir, who was in close touch with Rajiv Gandhi, did it despite his strong opposition. There was a big campaign mounted by the Pakistan Muslim League, then headed by Nawaz Sharif, against her on this issue. Lt Gen Gul also told her detractors that Kallue, on her orders, had handed over to the R&AW some files of the ISI on the Khalistani leaders. Benazir was accused of being an R&AW agent and of betraying the Khalistan movement. Embarrassed by these allegations, Benazir asked Kallue for the files relating to Lt Gen Gul's meetings with Verma. After checking, he reported to her that there were no papers on the subject in the ISI headquarters.

Benazir's close friendship with Rajiv Gandhi, her alleged links with the R&AW and her alleged betrayal of the Khalistan movement were some of the secret charges used by Ghulam Ishaq Khan, the then President, to dismiss her on August 6, 1990, at the instance of Gen Beg and Lt Gen Gul.

While Benazir tried to cut down, if not totally stop, the assistance to the Khalistanis, she wanted to go down in Pakistan's history as the Prime Minister who succeeded in annexing J&K. She asked Kallue to step up financial, training and arms assistance to the jihadi terrorists from J&K. Kallue set up a number of training camps for them in the Pakistani territory near the Afghan border. Some of the jihadis from J&K were also taken into Afghanistan by the ISI to have them motivated by the Mujahideen. Najibullah kept sending messages about the visits of the Kashmiris to the training camps of the Mujahideen in Afghan territory. His wake-up calls were not given serious attention because of Rajiv Gandhi's almost total trust in Benazir. Because she tried to be helpful on Punjab, it was presumed she would not create any trouble for us in J&K. She did create and with what vengeance. Our troubles in Kashmir started when she was the Prime Minister before August, 1990. Just as A.B.Vajpayee totally trusted Nawaz after his meeting with him in Lahore in February, 1999, and we paid a heavy price for it in Kargil, Rajiv Gandhi totally trusted Benazir. He did not have to pay a price for it, because the Congress (I) lost the elections at the end of 1989 and V.P.Singh replaced him as the Prime Minister. V.P.Singh and his successors paid a heavy price in J&K for Rajiv Gandhi's folly in trusting Benazir. However, Benazir's action in instigating terrorism in J&K could not save her from dismissal.

After dismissing her, Ghulam Ishaq Khan, on the advice of Gen. Beg, appointed Ghulam Mustafa Jatoi, a Sindhi who used to belong to the PPP, as the caretaker Prime Minister. In the elections held in October, 1990, Nawaz Sharif's PML, in coalition with the anti-India, Jamaat-e-Islami (JEI), came to power and Nawaz was appointed the Prime Minister. He transferred the work relating to the assistance to the Khalistanis back to the ISI from the Punjab Special Branch and appointed Imtiaz as the Director of the Intelligence Bureau. Reliable sources of the R&AW reported that the Habib Bank of Pakistan, the Saudi Intelligence and Osama bin Laden contributed generously to the election funds of the PML and the JEI.

As all these things were happening, the ground situation in Punjab continued to be bad. It even started deteriorating. In May, 1988, a group of Khalistanis once again occupied the Golden Temple. Rajiv Gandhi reacted differently from Indira Gandhi, who had faced a similar situation in 1984. She had consulted her close advisers in the PMO and the Cabinet Secretariat and they had advised her to send the Army in. Rajiv Gandhi sent for K.P.S.Gill, who had taken over as the Director-General of the Punjab Police only three weeks earlier, and consulted him. Gill advised him against entering the

Golden Temple. He suggested that, instead, the temple should be surrounded by the Police and the para-military forces and they should tire out the occupiers of the temple. Rajiv Gandhi liked his idea very much and asked him to implement it. It came to be known as Operation Black Thunder. It was actually the Gill Plan as outlined to Rajiv Gandhi. Gill's idea was very simple. Surround the Temple with forces from the Punjab Police, the National Security Guards (NSG), the Central Reserve Police Force (CRPF) and other para-military units; don't allow anyone to enter or go out; don't allow food to go in; issue only small arms and ammunition to the deployed forces; no heavy weapons; have some sharp-shooters with quick reflexes outside, who can kill any terrorist inside the temple from outside, whenever he exposed himself in order to fire at the police; play a game of patience and tire out the terrorists; and allow the media to be present to watch and report the entire thing.

His plan worked admirably and after seven days (May 11 to 18), the terrorists vacated their occupation of the Temple, came out and surrendered. As the media personnel entered the Temple with the police, they saw with their own eyes how the terrorists had been misusing the Temple. They had defecated at many places and the whole place was stinking. The media reported this in detail—on the basis of their own personal observation and not on the basis of spins put out by the Police. The Sikhs in Punjab were disgusted with the Khalistanis after reading this. Those sections of public opinion in Punjab, which had started sympathizing with, if not supporting, the Khalistanis after Operation Blue Star in 1984, started turning away from them after Operation Black Thunder. This was a brilliant Operation by K.P.S.Gill and Ved Marwah, who then headed the NSG, and marked the beginning of the process of withering away of the Khalistani terrorism. There was a slight set-back under V.P.Singh, who removed Gill from Punjab in order to placate the Khalistanis and started adopting a soft policy towards the terrorists in order to win some cheap popularity.

The process of withering away again picked up momentum under Narasimha Rao. After taking over as the Prime Minister on June

21,1991, he sent Gill back to Punjab as the DG of Police and ordered elections to the State Assembly, which were held in February,1992. The State had been under the President's rule without elections since May,1987. Gill and the Punjab Police ensured that the terrorists were not able to disrupt the elections. An elected Government under Beant Singh as the Chief Minister took over.

The year 1992 was the election year in the US. The Jewish community in the US started pressurising the administration of President George Bush, the father of the present President, to act against Pakistan.The Bush Administration was still reluctant to declare Pakistan a State-sponsor of international terrorism. Nor was it prepared to exercise pressure on Islamabad to stop meddling in J&K, which it regarded as a disputed territory. But it started exercising pressure on the issue of the ISI support to the Khalistanis. Nawaz Sharif, who had succeeded Benazir as the Prime Minister in 1990, asked the ISI to scale down the support to the Khalistanis. The ISI asked Lal Singh, Talwinder Singh Parmar and Sohan Singh, the head of the Second Panthic Committee, to leave Pakistani territory. Lal Singh flew from Karachi to Mumbai in 1992 and was arrested as he was traveling to Gujarat. Talwinder Singh Parmar, who reached Punjab via Singapore and Chennai in October 1992, was shot dead by the Punjab Police in an encounter. Sohan Singh, who returned quietly to Punjab via Kathmandu, was arrested.

Sukhdev Singh Babbar, the head of the Indian Babbar Khalsa, was killed in an encounter in Punjab on August 19,1992. His encounter with the Punjab Police took place in public view with many members of the public watching. After the encounter, the watching public was disgusted to find that Sukhdev Singh, who used to enforce rigid codes of conduct on the public, had a woman companion in his car, which had a mini bar. This also contributed to turning public opinion away from the Khalistanis. The followers of Sukhdev Singh retaliated brutally against the Punjab Police for the death of their leader. They killed many relatives of junior police officers. They also shot dead many members of the public, who were assisting the police as volunteers in the capacity of what was known as Special

Police Officers. But, their killing spree for a couple of days could not demoralize the Punjab Police and weaken their determination to put an end to the Khalistani terrorism.

Before losing steam under the relentless pressure maintained by Gill and the Punjab Police, they managed to commit one last spectacular act of terrorism on August 31, 1995, when they killed Beant Singh, the brave Chief Minister of Punjab, as he was leaving office at the end of the day at Chandigarh. Since then, the Khalistanis have not been able to recover, but one cannot say that their terrorism has been eliminated once and for all so long as some surviving remnants continue to live in Pakistan under the protection of the ISI. Pakistan continues to deny their presence in its territory. Since the beginning of 2006, there have been attempts to revive the Khalistani movement in the UK.

What were the factors, which contributed to the success of our counter-terrorism operations against the Khalistanis? Firstly, the valiant fight of the Punjab Police and other para-military forces, which assisted it. Secondly, the brilliant leadership of Gill. He led from the front and built up a team of officers, many of them Sikhs, who braved the brutalities of the terrorists and fought against them. Thirdly, the political leadership of Beant Singh in Punjab and Rajiv Gandhi, Narasimha Rao and Rajesh Pilot in New Delhi, who gave full backing to Gill and his Police and a free hand in dealing with the situation. Fourthly, the inputs provided by the IB and the R&AW from their human sources and the excellent work of their technical intelligence divisions. Fifthly, the co-operation from the intelligence agencies of the UK and Canada. And sixthly, the patriotism and broad-mindedness of the Sikh community, which overcame its anger over the results of Operation Blue Star and the atrocities committed on many Sikhs after the assassination of Indira Gandhi, and turned its back on the Khalistanis.

It was a brilliant piece of counter-terrorism operation. One hopes when the dramatis personae are still around, the National Police Academy at Hyderabad would undertake an exercise to document their experience and insights so that these are available for future generations of police officers.

The control of terrorism in Punjab was followed by a number of non-governmental organizations of dubious background descending on the State and harassing many of the police officers, who had bravely fought against the terrorists, by leveling allegations of human rights violations against them and chasing them from court to court. It is a matter of shame that neither the political leaders nor the public have stood by these officers but for whom normalcy might not have been restored in Punjab. One of the officers even committed suicide.

CHAPTER XIV

Geneva And Bofors

I was posted in Geneva as Counsellor in the Permanent Mission of India (PMI) to the UN organizations based in Geneva from April 1985 to May,1988. I handled work relating to the International Telecommunications Union, the Inter-Parliamentary Union (IPU), the Commission for Environment and Development, the World Meteorological Organization and the International Committee of the Red Cross (ICRC). Concurrently, I also held charge as the Indian Consul-General (CG) in Geneva.

As the Counsellor in the PMI, I worked under the Indian Permanent Representative (PR) to the UN Organizations in Geneva and as the CG, I took orders from the Indian Ambassador to Switzerland, who was based in Berne, the capital. Ego and jurisdictional clashes between the two often created difficult situations for me. Rajiv Gandhi's visit to Geneva in June,1985, was mainly to address the annual session of the International Labour Organization and to visit the headquarters of the ICRC. It was not a bilateral visit to Switzerland. The PR was totally in charge. Hence, I had no problem.

R.Venkatraman, the then President of India, visited Geneva in 1987, to inaugurate a Festival of India. After doing so, he visited Berne before returning to India. It was a purely bilateral visit and he had no engagements connected with the UN. The then Ambassador in Berne said he would handle the entire visit to Geneva and Berne, but the PR refused to let him handle the visit to Geneva. He insisted that since he was the representative of the President of India in Geneva, he would handle the Geneva part of the visit. Caught between the two, I went through many tense moments. The PR would forbid me from going to Berne to attend the co-ordination meetings held by the Ambassador, who insisted that I would take orders only from him in respect of the President's engagements in Geneva too. Somehow, I managed and the visit went off smoothly.

The President's visit came at the height of the controversy over the Bofors deal of the Government of India with the Bofors company in Sweden. A Swedish non-governmental organization had alleged that the company had paid commissions to certain persons, allegedly close to Rajiv Gandhi and his family. It had also been alleged that the Hinduja brothers, a Sindhi business family, were one of the beneficiaries of the commission payments. The headquarters of their business ventures were located in London and looked after by Srichand Hinduja, the eldest brother. They had a big office in Geneva, which was being looked after by Prakash Hinduja, his brother. Srichand used to visit Geneva often.

I knew Prakash quite well. Frankly, despite the allegations against the family, I found Prakash and Srichand to be likable and patriotic persons. The entire family had very wide contacts at very high levels in Iran, where they had originally started their overseas business career, Europe and the US. They never hesitated to be of any legitimate help to the Government of India, whenever they were approached. Even though they had been living abroad for many years, they were Indians by heart and by mind. Even if they had accepted commissions from the Bofors company as it was alleged they had, it did not make them any the less Indian or any the less patriotic. I do not hesitate to put this on record even at the risk of being misunderstood and vilified.

The Hinduja brothers —particularly Prakash— were in the permanent list of invitees of the PR in Geneva and the Ambassador in Berne and were invariably invited to any reception or dinner hosted by them in honour of visiting dignitaries from India. A few weeks before the visit of the President, H.K.L.Bhagat, who was then Minister for Parliamentary Affairs in the Rajiv Gandhi Cabinet, had visited Geneva to attend a meeting of the IPU. I had co-ordinated

the arrangements for the visit under the guidance of the late Alfred
Gonsalves, the then PR. The PR requested Prakash to host a dinner
for Bhagat and invite all the senior members of the Swiss Federal
Cabinet in Berne and of the Cantonal Government in Geneva.
Prakash happily agreed and issued the invitations. Everbody invited
by him accepted.

Before the PR asked Prakash to host the dinner, I had drawn his
attention to the controversy relating to the Bofors and pointed out
that it might not be advisable to ask Prakash to host a dinner for
Bhagat. I suggested to the PR that he should ask Bhagat whether he
would have any objections to attending a dinner hosted by Prakash.
The PR summarily rejected my suggestion saying: " Raman, I know
more about our politicians than you do. I have handled more
foreign visits by our politicians than you have. They are all corrupt
without exception. They all like to wallow in the comforts and riches
provided by businessmen. I know Bhagat. He will happily go to
Prakash's house." I kept quiet.

Gonsalves and I received Bhagat at the airport and took him to
Hotel Inter-Continental where he was put up. Gonsalves hosted a
lunch for him at a hotel restaurant, which was attended by senior
officials of the IPU. After the lunch, the PR took him on a sight-
seeing visit to Lausanne. The PR and Bhagat traveled in one car. I
followed them in another. When we were half way to Lausanne, the
PR's car stopped. My car also stopped. The PR came literally running
towards me. I came out. He said: " Raman, you were right. The old
man was furious when I told him he would be attending a dinner
hosted by Prakash. He said I should not have accepted the invitation
and has refused to attend. You go back to Geneva and tell Prakash
that the Minister is indisposed and hence would not be coming. Tell
him, I also won't come because I have to look after the Minister."

At that time, two important conferences of the ILO and the World
Health Organisation (WHO) were going on in Geneva. Half a dozen
senior officials of the Government of India had come to Geneva
to attend them. Prakash had invited all of them and also all the
diplomatic officers of the Permanent Mission. Gonsalves asked me

to ring up all of them and tell them that the Minister would not be attending the dinner due to indisposition and that it was up to them to decide whether they would attend or not.I did so. All the senior officials from Delhi and all the officers of the Permanent Mission guessed that Bhagat's decision not to attend must have been due to the Bofors controversy. They all rang up Prakash's office and said they would not attend due to indisposition.

On coming to know of this, I contacted the PR in Lausanne and told him that this amounted to humiliating Prakash. I told the PR: "Prakash did not offer to host this dinner. You asked him to do so because you thought that if he hosted the dinner senior leaders of the Federal Government would attend. All of them have agreed to attend because they were told it was a dinner in honour of a senior Indian Minister.If they find that neither the Minister nor the PR nor any Indian official was attending the dinner, they would start wondering what had happened. There will be unnecessary gossip." Gonsalves agreed with me and said: "You contact all visiting officials from Delhi and all officers of the Permanent Mission and tell them that this is an important dinner and that I desire that they should attend." I did so. Some officials from Delhi and some diplomatic officers attended. Many did not. What a messy situation it was !

Another VIP who visited Geneva before the President was Dr.Farooq Abdullah, the then Chief Minister of J&K. I got a message from the Indian High Commission in London that Dr.Abdullah and his staff officer would be visiting Geneva for 24 hours. The message did not say why they were coming, whether it was an official or a private visit and whether any hotel arrangements for them were required to be made. I contacted the Indian Mission in London. They replied: " We have told you what we were asked to communicate.The Chief Minister's staff officer did not tell us anything about hotel bookings."

As the Consul-General, I went to the airport to receive him and waited for him at the place through which normally VIPs exit. He and his staff officer did not come. I made enquiries with the airport Police. After checking, they told me that a member of the staff of the

Hindujas had taken a car to the tarmac and taken them directly to the hotel. I then went to the hotel and called on him.

A diamond merchant of Indian origin, with some links to South Africa, hosted a lunch in honour of Farooq Abdullah attended by a small number of dignitaries from the local Indian community. I was also there. It was a sit-down lunch. During the conversation, there was a reference to the situation in India and the role of the intelligence agencies. Farooq Abdullah started criticizing the R&AW in very strong language, "Kuch nahin karthe hain. Secret service paisa kathe hain (They don't do any work. They just eat the secret service money)," he remarked. He did not know I was from the R&AW. I just kept listening to him without reacting.

The host was embarrassed. He wrote something on a piece of paper and passed it across to Abdullah. He had obviously written that I was from the R&AW. Abdullah was not the least embarrassed. "Raman Saheb, you are from the R&AW? Kao is a great man. Your organization taught the Pakistanis a lesson in 1971. The time has come to do it again. Otherwise, they will keep interfering in Punjab." I replied that I would convey his views to my headquarters.

That evening, he had been invited by the Hindujas for a dinner in their house. As he was discussing his programme with his staff officer, the latter pointed out that there could be a controversy if it came to be known in India that the Hindujas had hosted a dinner for him. Abdullah replied: " So what? I would myself inform the Government of India that I had attended a dinner by the Hindujas. He has been my friend for long. I can't suddenly boycott him socially just because there has been a controversy over his role in the Bofors deal."

Dr. J. S. Teja, the then PR in Geneva who had succeeded Gonsalves, hosted a reception for the President when he came to Geneva. He intended inviting, among others, the Hindujas too. I mentioned to him what had happened when H.K.L. Bhagat had come and suggested that he should consult the President's office before inviting the Hindujas. He sent a message. Prompt came the reply that they should not be invited.

The next day, Prakash rang me up and said that the President's office had asked him to arrange a check-up for the President by a local ear specialist since he wanted to change his hearing aid. Prakash requested me to keep an empty slot in the President's programme for this. I immediately sent a message to the President's office asking them to confirm that they had asked Prakash to arrange a check-up for the President. His office replied denying that they had made any such request to Prakash and told me that there was no need to include this in the President's programme. I informed Prakash suitably. After inaugurating the Festival of India in Geneva, the President went to Berne and from there returned to India. Later on, I came to know that the ear specialist had gone to Berne and examined the President there. The President's office was apparently embarrassed when Prakash told me that he had been asked to organize the check-up. They, therefore, decided to have it in Berne instead of in Geneva, without the knowledge of the Indian Embassy in Berne.

While visiting dignitaries thus started exercising caution about interactions with the Hindujas after their names cropped up in connection with the Bofors scandal, I did not notice any inhibitions coming in the way of the interactions of senior officers of the Central Bureau of Investigation (CBI) with the Hindujas during their visits to Geneva. Even after the scandal broke out, I had occasionally seen senior CBI officers having lunch with Prakash or Srichand or both in Geneva restaurants. After the scandal broke out, Narasimha Rao had once come on a visit to some West European countries. During his stay in West Europe, the Hindujas had hosted their annual Diwali dinner, which was always attended by many dignitaries of the UK and other countries. The Hindujas were very keen that Narasimha Rao should attend. He was reluctant to do so. He sent a message to the PMO asking whether he should attend. Prompt came the reply that he should.

Before the Bofors scandal broke out, there were no such inhibitions. In fact, Prakash was even better informed about the happenings in New Delhi than the Indian diplomatic mission was. He came to know in advance— even before the Indian mission — the details of the programmes of all visiting dignitaries—whether political leaders or senior bureaucrats. Almost everybody—political leaders, senior bureaucrats, judges and others— socially interacted with him during their stay in Geneva.

There were only two leaders who kept away from them even before the Bofors scandal broke out. One was Narasimha Rao. The other was V.P.Singh. He was the Minister for Commerce in the Cabinet of Rajiv Gandhi at that time. He used to attend meetings of the GATT (General Agreement on Trade and Tariffs). He had given strict instructions to the Indian mission that the Hindujas should not be informed of his programme and that no invitation from them should be accepted.

Once Prakash came to know of his presence in Geneva. He found out in which hotel he was staying and rang him up there in order to invite him for a dinner. V.P.Singh declined the invitation. He then strongly protested to the Indian mission for telling Prakash about his programme. The Indian mission told V.P.Singh that Prakash always came to know of the programmes of visiting dignitaries from his contacts in Delhi and not from the Indian mission in Geneva.

An Indian journalist based in Geneva played a very prominent role in exposing the Bofors scandal initially through the columns of "The Hindu", a daily of Chennai, and then of the "Indian Express". She had very good sources in the Federal Police Department of Switzerland and in governmental and non-governmental circles of Sweden. According to some people in the Indian community of Geneva, a Swedish student, who was living Au Pair in her house and helping her in her domestic chores, also helped her in her coverage.

The personal relations of this journalist with the Indian diplomats posted in Geneva and with large sections of the local Indian community were somewhat strained. They tended to keep away from her. Though I cannot claim to have been her friend, I had better contacts with her, thanks to the fact that her mother, a well-known musician, was a close friend of my family in Chennai. I had been to her house on a couple of occasions for taking a meal with her and her husband, an Italian-speaking Swiss national. Often—but not always—she used to share with me the salient points of her despatches to her paper on the Bofors scandal. I had some well-informed friends in the local community of Afghan political exiles and I used to share with her—not as a quid pro quo— interesting information gathered by me about developments relating to Afghanistan. Whatever information about the Bofors scandal she shared with me, I used to pass on to the R&AW headquarters, who used to pass it on to Rajiv Gandhi. On such occasions, Rajiv Gandhi used to know in advance what "The Hindu" was going to carry the next day.

Once this journalist contacted me and alleged that she had heard that at the instance of the Government of India, the Hindujas were planning to have her killed in order to silence her. I told her she was imagining things. I assured her that the Government of India was not in the habit of indulging in such things. On two more occasions, she came back to me with the same allegation. I told her that I did not believe it was true and added that if she believed it was true, she was free to seek the protection of the Geneva Police. Thereafter, she did not raise the topic again. I did not think she sought the assistance of the Geneva Police either.

I continued in Geneva for about a year after the Bofors scandal broke out. Many of my friends had asked me while I was still in Geneva and subsequently too whether I thought Rajiv Gandhi was corrupt and whether he or any member of his family had accepted a commission from the Bofors company. My reply has always been as follows: "I had never come into contact with Rajiv Gandhi in Delhi, but I was associated with his visit to Paris, Lyon and Geneva in June,1985, and to The Hague in October,1985. He had some expensive tastes like his love for fast cars and fancy electronic gadgets. He had reportedly accepted an expensive Mercedes Benz car as a gift from the King of Jordan, who felt concerned about his personal security when he found him moving around in Delhi in a slow-moving Ambassador car. He used to drive around in this

Mercedes sometimes, but when he lost the elections towards the end of 1989, he promptly transferred it to the President's garage for being used when foreign Heads of State and Government visited India. Similarly, he transferred to the Government all the other gifts which he had received from foreign leaders when he lost the elections. His personal habits were very simple and austere and he made it a point to settle all his bills while traveling. I formed a strong impression that he was not corrupt. However, he lost his cool when allegations were made in Stockholm that commission had been paid by the Bofors company to some people, one of them an Italian businessman, who was well known to be close to his family. He frantically mounted a cover-up operation and personally got involved in the cover-up exercise, thereby creating unnecessary and incorrect doubts in the minds of some people about his own integrity. Indira Gandhi would have handled a similar situation differently. She would have maintained a regal distance from any cover-up exercise and let her senior officials handle it, without personally getting involved. Rajiv Gandhi not only personally got involved in the cover-up, but he also encouraged officials and others close to him to create pin-pricks for V.P.Singh, who was in the forefront of those against a cover-up. As examples of such pin-pricks, one could cite the allegations of the involvement of the son of V.P.Singh in a scandal, the childish attempts with the alleged help of the IB to delay from the New Delhi airport the take-off of a hired aircraft in which V.P.Singh wanted to fly to his constituency to file his nomination papers in the 1989 elections etc. As a result of all this, Rajiv Gandhi unnecessarily got himself tied in knots. Instead of giving him the correct advice to let the truth about the Bofors come out even at the risk of some personal and political embarrassment to him, the IB, the R&AW and the CBI vied with one another in giving ideas to Rajiv Gandhi as to how to do the cover-up." I still hold this view.

At the instance of Rajiv Gandhi, a Joint Parliamentary Committee (JPC) chaired by B. Shankaranand, a Congress (I) member of Parliament, had been set up to enquire into the allegations of the commission payments. The JPC had deputed to Geneva and London a team of investigators consisting of officers of the CBI, the

Directorate of Revenue Intelligence and other concerned agencies to make enquiries and record the statements of a number of persons in Geneva and London. The R&AW headquarters had advised me that I would have no role in their investigation. I was told that my role would be restricted to providing them with back-up support such as acting as their interpreter (French-English) when required, placing the services of my Personal Assistant at their disposal for typing work etc. But they insisted that I should meet before them all the persons figuring in their list of possible witnesses, have a preliminary chat on what he or she knew and then tell them before they met the person formally and recorded his or her statement. I got the impression that they met only those who had little or no knowledge of the Bofors payments and avoided meeting those, who claimed to have knowledge of the payments.

One of the persons, whose name they gave me for a preliminary chat, did not live at the address mentioned by them. Through my sources, I found out his correct address and gave it to them, but they did not meet him. They recorded in their report that no person by that name was living in that address. They did not meet either Prakash Hinduja or the journalist, who had done the investigative reporting. They told me that they would be recording the statement of Srichand Hinduja at London. They had a sanction from the Finance Ministry for a stay of five days in Geneva, but their work was over in three days. The head of the team rang up the then Director of the CBI, who was co-ordinating the investigation on behalf of the JPC, and asked him what they should do. After consulting Shankaranand, he advised them that they should not cut short their stay since this could lead to allegations that they were not serious about the enquiry. Despite this, they cut short their stay by a day and left for London.

The Bofors scandal brought out some of the worst traits in our intelligence and investigative agencies. The very same officers, who placed their services at the disposal of Rajiv Gandhi for assisting him in his cover-up exercise and advised him as to how to do the cover-up, volunteered their services to V.P.Singh, when he succeeded Rajiv Gandhi as the Prime Minister after the elections of 1989, for bringing out the truth and having Rajiv Gandhi fixed. While he was the Finance Minister, V.P.Singh and Vinod Pandey, who had served under him, had shown a penchant for relying more on private detective agencies such as Fairfax than the intelligence agencies of the Government of India for making confidential enquiries. They exhibited this penchant even after V.P Singh became the Prime Minister and appointed Vinod Pandey as his Cabinet Secretary.

By making payments from the secret service fund of an intelligence agency, Pandey had the services of an European private detective hired for making enquiries about the Bofors payments. The reports sent by this detective—not independently verified or often unverifiable— were given by Pandey to journalists for publishing in their newspapers as coming from "privileged sources". If a US President had recruited a foreign detective to make enquiries about his predecessor or a Congressman and if this had leaked, he might have faced impeachment proceedings. I was amazed how highly reputed newspapers—including one of Chennai—unquestioningly accepted what Pandey fed them on the basis of the uncorroborated reports of this European private detective and carried them as coming from "privileged sources" in order to discredit Rajiv Gandhi.

I was transferred back to Delhi in May,1988, after I had completed three years. I was succeeded at Geneva by the late S.A.Subbiah, an outstanding IPS officer from the Karnataka cadre. Unfortunately, his relations with the Geneva-based journalist, who was playing an active role in exposing Rajiv Gandhi's alleged cover-up of the Bofors scandal, were not good due to no fault of his. After V.P.Singh took over as the Prime Minister, she developed direct and easy access to him and Vinod Pandey. She became their blue-eyed investigative journalist and anything she said or reported to them was believed without proper verification. She reportedly felt that Subbiah was not giving her the importance she deserved under the new dispensation headed by V.P.Singh. She allegedly carried baseless tales about Subbiah's behaviour towards her to Vinod Pandey and Satish Chandra, who was Subbiah's boss at Geneva as the Indian Permanent Representative.

While Satish Chandra reportedly did not believe her allegations and took no notice of them, Vinod Pandey did and ordered Subbiah's premature transfer back to Delhi, allegedly for trying to create difficulties in the way of the Bofors investigation. It must be said to the credit of A.K.Verma, the then chief of the R&AW, that he resisted the orders of Vinod Pandey. He called back Subbiah to headquarters for consultations for a month and, during this period, managed to convince Vinod Pandey that he was an outstanding professional with unimpeachable integrity and that the journalist's allegations against him were baseless. Vinod Pandey agreed to his going back to Geneva and resuming his work.

My tenure in Geneva (1985 to 1988) as an intelligence officer was professionally not as satisfying as my earlier tenure (1975 to 1979) in Paris. In Paris, I was in what was known as an open liaison post. I was responsible for liaison with the French external intelligence agency, which knew that I was from the R&AW. There was a gentleman's agreement that I would not take advantage of my position to recruit sources in the French Government. I observed it strictly, but I was free to recruit and run sources, who were not French nationals or public servants. There were no restrictions on my running operations to collect intelligence about other countries such as Pakistan, China, Iran etc so long as I did not use French nationals or public servants. This gave me opportunities for professional satisfaction. Moreover, the liaison work itself was quite interesting.

In Geneva, I worked in a secret, non-liaison post. The Federal authorities of Switzerland and the Cantonal authorities of Geneva were not told that I belonged to the R&AW. Instead, they were given the impression that I was an offcer of the Ministry of External Affairs of the Government of India belonging to the Indian Foreign Service posted in the Indian Permanent Mission to do multilateral work relating to the UN and other international organizations and, concurrently, to function as the Consul-General of India. The Standing Instructions of the R&AW lay down that in order to protect what is called the diplomatic cover—that is, their story that they are officers of the Indian Foreign Service— of the R&AW officers when they are posted in the Indian diplomatic missions abroad, they should not be given security or criminal investigation related duties.

These instructions were not strictly followed in Geneva due to the enhanced threats to the security of visiting Indian dignitaries because of the Khalistani terrorism and due to the investigation into the Bofors scandal. I was closely involved in the co-ordination of the security arrangements for Rajiv Gandhi when he visited France and Switzerland in June,1985, and Holland in October,1985. I was also directly involved in the co-ordination of security arrangements for President R.Venkatraman, when he visited Switzerland in 1987. I had to liaise closely with the intelligence and security agencies of France, Switzerland and Holland in this connection.

I was also involved with the visit of the team of investigating officers sent to Geneva by the JPC on the Bofors Affair. As a result, my cover was blown and it became an almost open secret in Geneva that I was a police officer belonging to the R&AW and not an IFS officer from the MEA. In fact, some mischievous members of the Indian community in Geneva used to refer to the house near the Geneva airport where I lived as the "R&AW House". Fortunately, the Swiss authorities were not bothered about my being from the R&AW so long as I did not work against their interests and I was not worried so long as the Swiss authorities were not.

The R&AW post in Geneva was one of the first to be created by Kao immediately after the R&AW was formed in September,1968. His idea was to use the post for secret liaison with the MOSSAD, Israel's external intelligence agency, and as a secret rendez-vous point for sensitive meetings with sources and political, military and diplomatic contacts from India's neighbourhood. There was resistance from the MEA to the creation of the post on the ground that Switzerland was of no interest from the point of view of India's national security. Kao explained to Indira Gandhi why the R&AW needed this post. These reasons could not be spelt out in the proposal sent to the MEA for its creation. After listening to Kao, Indira Gandhi asked the Foreign Secretary to sanction this post.

The post served as the contact point with the MOSSAD for about
10 years after its creation. Thereafter, the need for this diminished
since the MOSSAD posted one of its officers in New Delhi under the
cover of a businessman from one of the South American countries.
For nearly 12 years, successive MOSSAD officers posted under
the cover of businessmen in New Delhi acted as the contact point
between the R&AW and the MOSSAD. After the establishment of
diplomatic relations between India and Israel in 1992, the need for
a non-diplomatic cover diminished.

Many sensitive meetings were held in Geneva such as those with
Bengali-speaking diplomats of Pakistan before 1971 in order to
motivate them to support the independence struggle by staying in
their posts till Bangladesh was liberated and keeping the R&AW and
the leaders of the liberation movement informed of the goings on
in the Pakistan Foreign Office and in its diplomatic missions abroad.
The initial negotiations with Laldenga, the leader of the MNF, were
held in Geneva in 1975 by a joint team of senior officers from the
R&AW and the IB.

By the time I took over at Geneva in 1985, such needs had
considerably diminished. The R&AW had started using other cities
outside Switzerland too as contact points. Despite this, Geneva
acquired a new importance as a listening post on Tibet, the Xinjiang
region of China, South Africa and Sri Lanka. In the 1980s, it used to
have the largest community of Tibetan refugees after India. Some of
them were very well informed on developments in Tibet. Germany,
bordering Switzerland, had a small, but politically active community
of Uighurs from Xinjiang, who had initially fled to Turkey and from
there migrated to the then West Germany. Some of these Uighurs
used to work as translators and broadcasters for the CIA in the radio
station run by it from Munich under the name Radio Liberty. These
Uighurs often used to come to Geneva to attend meetings of the UN
Human Rights Commission.

While many of the overseas-based leaders of the African National
Congress (ANC) were mostly operating from the Scandinavian

countries, they often used to come to Geneva for attending meetings of the UN Human Rights Commission and the World Council of Churches, both of which have their headquarters in Geneva. After the Liberation Tigers of Tamil Eelam (LTTE) started its independence struggle in Sri Lanka in 1983, there was an exodus of Sri Lankan Tamils to foreign countries. Switzerland was their favoured destination in West Europe. Many of their leaders too used to come to Geneva for attending meetings of the UN Human Rights Commission and the World Council of Churches and for interactions with the officials of the International Committee of the Red Cross (ICRC), which had an active programme of humanitarian assistance in Sri Lanka.

Indira Gandhi and Rajiv Gandhi took an active interest in assisting not only the newly-independent countries of Africa, but also the liberation movements such as the ANC of South Africa and the SWAPO of Namibia. The assistance extended by India to the newly independent African countries was not only for their economic development, but also in security-related matters such as the training of their police and intelligence officers. The project to help the African countries had been started even before the formation of the R&AW. The IB played a role in helping newly-independent Ghana in strengthening its capability in the fields of intelligence and security. It had deputed Kao and Sankaran Nair—one after the other—to Accra for this purpose.

Such work was intensified after the R&AW came into being. The R&AW played an active role in organizing training assistance in Uganda after the overthrow of Idi Amin Dada, Mozambique, Zimbabwe, Zambia, Botswana and Malawi. Very often, Indira Gandhi preferred senior R&AW officers for sensitive missions of a political nature to African countries. When President Milton Obote of Uganda sought India's guidance for putting his country back on its feet after the exit of Idi Amin Dada, she asked the R&AW to take the initial steps. In such matters, she and Rajiv Gandhi had greater confidence in the R&AW than in the MEA.

The R&AW played a very active role in helping the ANC in its anti-apartheid struggle and the SWAPO in its struggle for the independence of Namibia. Many of their cadres were trained either in India or Zambia. Geneva and Lusaka played an active role as contact points with the leaders and cadres of the ANC and the SWAPO. It is a great tragedy that the R&AW has not built up a record of its role in Africa. It does not even have a list of all its officers, who distinguished themselves in Africa.

The African leaders looked at Indira Gandhi and Rajiv Gandhi with respect and admiration. They never hesitated to ask her for any assistance. They were confident of a positive response. Those were the days when India and Indian officials stood 20 feet tall in Africa—thanks to Indira Gandhi and Rajiv Gandhi. The decline in Indian interest and influence in Africa started under V.P.Singh and has continued non-stop since then. Today, the Indian influence has been replaced in most countries by that of China. You will need a powerful magnifying glass to locate India in Africa.

The meetings of the UN Human Rights Commission in Geneva attract the intelligence officers of many countries, who are included in the delegations of their countries. Dissident, separatist and insurgent groups from all over the world, which have the money for travel, send their representatives to Geneva to canvass support for their cause. Interactions with them used to provide useful intelligence.

When the Khalistan movement was started in 1981, the Khalistani leaders did not realise the importance of human rights work to project their cause. It was the LTTE more than any other organization in Asia, which started paying attention to human rights work—with rich dividends. Others, including the Khalistanis, started emulating it. The LTTE had organized its human rights network in a professional manner—with separate organizations for human rights work. It took care to see that office-bearers of the front organizations floated by it were not involved in its acts of violence.

The Khalistanis did not take a similar precaution. Very often, the same people, who were involved in acts of violence, also exercised responsibilities as office-bearers of the front organizations for human rights work. As a result, whereas the front organizations of the LTTE had easy access to the meetings of the Human Rights Commission, the Khalistanis faced difficulty in getting permission to attend the meetings. They, therefore, adopted the tactics of getting themselves included as members of delegations of organizations of Red Indians from the US and Canada, which were accredited to the Human Rights Commission through the UN Economic and Social Council. While the Red Indian members of the delegations would criticize the Governments of the US and Canada for violating the human rights of the Red Indians, the Khalistanis would attack the Government of India for allegedly suppressing the Sikhs.

By constantly interacting with the leaders of these Red Indian organizations, I managed to persuade them not to include the Khalistanis in their delegations. This prevented them from gaining access to the meetings of the Commission, but they were still able to interact with delegations from the other countries in the lobbies and cafeterias. I did not mind it since I felt it was advisable that they had an opportunity of letting out steam against the Government of India through such interactions. There is less chance of people taking to violence if they are able to let out steam. Generally, only people who keep boiling inside take to violence. The terrorist movement in Jammu & Kashmir had not yet started when I was in Geneva and, hence, no Kashmiris used to come.

Even before I joined at Geneva, Switzerland had started becoming an important centre for the activities of Pakistan. The Pakistani Army had started procuring artillery pieces and sophisticated communication equipment from Zurich. Pakistan's clandestine nuclear procurement work was being co-ordinated from Geneva. The BCCI had a large branch in Geneva mainly staffed by Pakistanis. The Habib Bank had an active branch in Zurich, again staffed by Pakistanis. The payments for the nuclear material procured in the UK, West Gemany and other countries used to be remitted from these branches. A Pakistani shipping company, which was being used by Pakistan's nuclear establishment for the clandestine transport of the military and nuclear equipment procured in West Europe, had its head office in Geneva. There was an increasing flow of political refugees from Pakistan into Zurich—mainly Ahmadiyas and supporters of the Bhutto family, who were being harassed by the Zia-ul-Haq military regime in Pakistan.

After I joined in Geneva, a number of Afghan political exiles close to ex-King Zahir Shah, who himself was living in Rome, settled down in Geneva and Zurich and started interacting with the Human Rights organizations. Geneva was chosen as the venue for the UN-sponsored proximity talks between the Afghan-Soviet authorities and the Pakistanis and the Mujahideen. These talks paved the way for the exit of the Soviet troops from Afghanistan. Many important delegations from Pakistan, Afghanistan and the USSR used to visit Geneva for the proximity talks.

I developed a reputation as a fairly well-informed Indian in Geneva on the proximity talks. I had some good contacts amongst the Pashtun as well as the Tajik exiles. During this period, K.Natwar Singh, who was the Minister of State for External Affairs, visited Geneva. As the Indian Consul-General, I was taking care of the arrangements for his visit.

He had a reputation in his own service for being abrasive and somewhat uppish, but I had a lot of personal admiration for him. He was one of the few intellectuals with wide interests produced by the Foreign Service. No other Foreign Service officer was better known and respected in the Third World countries—particularly in the African countries—than Natwar Singh. After Indira Gandhi and Rajiv Gandhi, he was the most respected Indian public servant in Africa. He had served as the Indian High Commissioner in Zambia at a time when the interactions of the R&AW with the ANC were increasing. He encouraged them. He was totally loyal to Indira Gandhi and her family. How do you judge loyalty to a leader— not when the leader is shining, but when he or she seems down and out. When Indira Gandhi appeared down and out once and for all between 1977 and 1980 and was being harassed and humiliated by the Morarji Desai Government, there was only a small number of public servants , who resisted the temptation to throw stones at her in order to ingratiate themselves with the Morarji Desai Government— Natwar Singh was one of them.

When Natwar Singh came to Geneva, the Afghan political exiles with whom I was in touch came to know of his visit. All of them knew him and respected him. One of them told me that he would like to make a discreet courtesy call on him without the Pakistanis and other exiles coming to know of it. He said: " We are unhappy with the Government of India for not supporting the Afghan people and for supporting the Soviet troops. But that has not lessened our admiration and affection for Indians, who were close to us and who had helped us before the Soviet invasion and occupation. Natwar Singh is one of them." I told Natwar Singh about it. He asked me to bring him for breakfast in his hotel suite.

I took him to Natwar Singh's suite, left him to have a one-to-one breakfast with him and went back to my office. As the Afghan exile left Natwar Singh's suite after the breakfast, the Minister came out to see him off. Just then, Ambassador J.S.Teja, who was the Indian Permanent Representative in Geneva, reached there. He saw the warm and cordial manner in which Natwar Singh and the Afghan were taking leave of each other. Later, he enquired from Natwar Singh's staff who was that visitor. They gave him his identity and said I had brought him.

After meeting Natwar Singh, Teja came to his office and rang me up: " You never told me you know this man. Please bring him to my office for a cup of tea. In future, I will remain in touch with him. You need not." I avoided taking him to Teja. He reminded me on two or three occasions. I gave him some excuse or the other. He understood that I was reluctant to introduce him and stopped reminding me. Teja was a very fine gentleman. He took my reluctance in the right spirit and did not hold it against me. He was very cordial to me throughout my stay and did not allow this to affect the high opinion in which he held me. At a farewell party hosted by the staff on the eve of my transfer, Teja said in his speech in the presence of many Foreign Service officers: " I wish we had officers like you in our Foreign Service." I was greatly touched.

This incident illustrates the difficulties often faced by the R&AW officers in their relations with their heads of missions, when they are posted abroad. There are clear instructions laid down since the days of Kao, with the approval of Indira Gandhi, regarding these relations. These instructions lay down that immediately after joining a diplomatic mission, the R&AW officer working under diplomatic cover in a mission would meet the Ambassador and show to him a written note on his story regarding his previous career, which he would be telling the local people, and request him that he and his officers should corroborate his story and protect his cover.

Many IFS officers rarely do. The worst threat to an R&AW officer posted abroad comes from the wives of the IFS officers. Many of them take a sadistic delight in going around telling people. "This officer is not from the IFS. He is actually from the R&AW." If an officer of the CIA or the ISI or any other intelligence agency wants to find out whether there is any R&AW officer posted in an Indian mission, all he has to do is to ask the wife of one of the IFS officers. Without any hestitation, she will reveal the identity. Once, when I was in Paris, at a party the wife of an IFS officer got totally drunk, came and stood by my side and announced to the gathering: "Ladies and gentlemen, meet the most charming officer from India's external intelligence." Fortunately, all the guests were from the local Indian community. There were no foreigners.Indiscreet IFS officers and the even more indiscreet wives of some of them are constant occupational hazards for R&AW officers posted abroad.

R&AW officers posted abroad do not collect TECHINT. They collect only HUMINT and send them to their headquarters. They also prepare analytical reports based on open information. The instructions to them are that all these reports should be shown to the head of mission without revealing the identity of the source where it is a HUMINT report and that any comments made by him— positive or negative— should be conveyed to headquarters. Generally, most heads of missions do not make enquiries about the source. However, some, when they find a particular HUMINT report good, try to find out the identity of the source and insist that they should handle him or her. Friction creeps into personal relations if the R&AW officer declines to reveal the identity of the source. I was, therefore, impressed when Teja took my hesitation to introduce my source to him in his stride and did not allow this to affect his positive opinion of me. Such instances are rare.

Professionally, for an intelligence officer under cover, Geneva was a challenging station—with considerable scope for job satisfaction. Despite this, I enjoyed my stay in Paris better than my tenure in Geneva. In Paris, my Embassy-related work was light. I had all the time I needed to devote to my intelligence tasks. In Geneva, my Permanent Mission related work was quite heavy. Moreover, my additional charge as the Consul-General kept me busy with protocol related work such as receiving and seeing off dignitaries and fulfilling social responsibilities. As a result, the time available for intelligence work was limited. Moreover, the fact that I had to work under two senior Ambassadors based in Geneva and Berne created some tension. Unfortunately, intelligence officers cannot be choosers.

My three-year term was to end in May,1988. In October, 1987, I received a message from A.K.Verma, the then chief of the R&AW, that he had decided to extend my stay by one more year till May,1989. Three weeks later, I got another message from him saying that my presence in headquarters was needed to deal with a very important and sensitive project. Therefore, the extension was being cancelled and I should return in May,1988.

I handed over to Subbiah in May,1988. I was 52 years old, with six more years of service left. I knew I would not get any more field postings. On the flight back home, I was thinking of all the interesting things I had done during my 20 years in the R&AW— a little over seven of them abroad. Little did I realise that in the remaining six years, I would be doing even more interesting things than I had done till then— administering to the ISI some of its own medicine. Nothing gave me greater satisfaction. I felt 10 years younger.

CHAPTER XV

Rajiv Gandhi & R&AW

During the little over five years he was the Prime Minister, Rajiv Gandhi had three chiefs of the R&AW. G.C.Saxena, an IPS officer of the UP cadre,who had taken over as the chief in April, 1983 when Indira Gandhi was the Prime Minister, continued till his superannuation in March 1986. S.E.Joshi, an IPS officer of the Maharashtra cadre, who succeeded him, retired in June 1987, after having served as the chief for 15 months. Rajiv Gandhi was keen that he should continue so that he had a tenure of three years like his predecessor, but Joshi felt it would be unfair to his successor. An officer of the Tamil Nadu cadre was to succeed him, but Rajiv Gandhi reportedly got annoyed with him because he was unaware of the Bofors scandal when it broke out in the Swedish electronic media. He had him shifted as the Chairman of the Joint Intelligence Committee and designated A.K.Verma, an IPS officer of the Madhya Pradesh cadre, as the chief. He had a full tenure of three years—partly under Rajiv Gandhi and partly under V.P.Singh.

Saxena, like Kao and Suntook, was suave in his behaviour and gentle in his words, but hard-hitting in action. Joshi and Verma were more like Sankaran Nair—anything but suave, blunt in words and hard-hitting in action. Like Sankaran Nair, Saxena, Joshi and Verma were experts on Pakistan and political and militant Islam. Saxena, Joshi and Verma knew more about Pakistan than any other expert in India or abroad. Saxena had never served in the Islamic world, but he had been dealing with Pakistan right from the day he joined the R&AW shortly after its formation. He did not have much to do with

Pakistan only during his posting in Rangoon in the 1970s. Joshi was the only chief of the R&AW to have served in Pakistan. Verma had served in Kabul and Ankara and had been dealing with Pakistan and the Islamic world during most of his postings in the headquarters.

Sankaran Nair and Verma were held in awe and respect in Pakistan's intelligence and policy-making communities. They knew of the active role played by Nair under Kao in the liberation of Bangladesh and of Verma's reputation as a mirror image of Nair—as an officer who would like nothing better than to break Pakistan again if he was given the go-ahead by India's political leadership. During my posting in Geneva and subsequently in headquarters, I had much to do with Pakistan and with various sections of the Pakistani civil society and Government. I could see for myself that those, who had an opportunity of interacting with Verma, looked upon him as one of the very few Indians who had a really good understanding of the Pakistani psyche and of the Pakistani military mind-set. I have no doubt in my mind that if Rajiv Gandhi had not lost the elections in 1989 and if Verma had continued as the chief of the R&AW under Rajiv Gandhi for two or three years more, Pakistan would not be existing in its present form today and innocent civilians in our country would not be dying like rats at the hands of jihadi terrorists.

There was a strong convergence of views between Rajiv Gandhi and Verma that unless Pakistan was made to pay a heavy price for its use of terrorism against India, India would never be free of this problem. The process of re-activating the R&AW's covert action capability, which had remained in a state of neglect under Morarji Desai, started after Indira Gandhi returned to power in 1980. Suntook, Saxena and Joshi played an active role in carrying forward this process, but it was Verma, who gave the R&AW once again the strong teeth, which it was missing since 1977, and made it bite again.

Well-deserved tributes have been paid to the Punjab Police under K.P.S.Gill, the IB under M.K.Narayanan, the National Security Guards under Ved Marwah, the other central para-military forces and the Army for their role in restoring normalcy in Punjab. But, the Indian public and the political leadership as a whole barring the Prime

Minister of the day hardly knew of the stealth role played by Saxena, Joshi and Verma in making our counter-terrorism success in Punjab possible. While Saxena and Joshi laid the foundation for an active and strong liaison network and for improving the R&AW's capability for the collection of terrorism-related HUMINT, Verma gave the R&AW the teeth which made Pakistan realize that its sponsorship of terrorism would not be cost-free.

All the three of them were fortunate in having Rajiv Gandhi as their Prime Minister. Rajiv Gandhi came to office as the Prime Minister with very little knowledge of the intelligence profession and of the Indian intelligence community. When Indira Gandhi was the Prime Minister, Rajiv Gandhi used to take an active interest in the physical security arrangements for her after Operation Blue Star. She used him often in her attempts to find a political solution to the problem in Punjab. Many of his clandestine meetings in this connection were organized by the R&AW when Saxena was the chief. Beyond that, he had very little interaction with the R&AW and very little knowledge of it before he became the Prime Minster.

It used to be said that after he took over as the Prime Minister, he was amazed—even somewhat disturbed— when Saxena briefed him at a one-to-one meeting on the sensitive on-going operations and covert actions of the R&AW. It was also said that while he did not have the least hesitation in approving the continuance of all the R&AW operations relating to Pakistan, China and Bangladesh, he was somewhat confused in his mind regarding the wisdom of the operational policies followed under his mother in relation to Sri Lanka . He took some time to make up his mind on Sri Lanka. Ultimately, he decided to continue on the lines laid down by his mother in relation to Sri Lanka too.

It would be incorrect to characterize his operational policy towards Pakistan as a carbon copy of the policy followed by Indira Gandhi. There were nuances, which differed from those of his mother. Indira Gandhi came to office with a strong dislike and distrust of Gen.Zia-ul-Haq, which continued till her death. She was convinced in her mind that Zia was not a genuine person and that his expression of warmth and bonhomie towards Indians was contrived. And the fact that Zia and Morarji Desai got along comfortably with each other prejudiced her mind against him.

Rajiv Gandhi did not inherit his mother's anti-Zia prejudices. He was fully aware of the role played by the ISI in supporting terrorism in Punjab. The suspicion that the ISI under Zia might have been behind the assassination of Indira Gandhi by her security guards was never proved, but it kept haunting the minds of some persons (including me) during the 1980s. Despite this, Rajiv was prepared to consider meaningful ideas for a co-operative relationship with Pakistan. His ready acceptance of the offer of the then Crown Prince Hassan of Jordan to arrange a dialogue between the chiefs of the ISI and the R&AW to which a reference had been made in an earlier chapter was a typical example of his open mind to such initiatives.

At the same time, Rajiv Gandhi was convinced—as strongly as his mother was— that India's preoccupation had to be not with individual Pakistani leaders, who are a passing phenomena, but with the Pakistani mindset, which was an enduring phenomenon right rom the day Pakistan was born in 1947. In India, there is no such thing as an enduring Indian mindset towards Pakistan. The mindsets keep changing with leaders and circumstances. It is not so in Pakistan. The compulsive urge to keep India weak, bleeding and destabilized influences policy-making in Pakistan— whoever be the leader, civilian or military. It has nothing to do with its humiliation in Bangladesh in 1971. It was there before 1971 and it has been there since 1971. Some leaders such as those of the fundamentalist parties openly exhibit it, but others manage to conceal it behind seeming warmth in their behaviour. Till that mindset changes, India has to adopt a mix of incentives and disincentives in its operational policies towards Pakistan—incentives towards a co-operative relationship and disincentives to discourage hostile actions.

On the need for a mix of incentives and disincentives, Rajiv Gandhi, Saxena, Joshi and Verma were on the same wavelength. Rajiv Gandhi's ready acceptance of Crown Prince Hassan's offer was an example of such an incentive. It was fully backed by the R&AW without any mental reservations, though it did not ultimately produce the desired results. As examples of disincentives, one could mention the timely and effective pre-emption of Pakistani designs to use the Siachen glacier to weaken the Indian position in the Kargil and Ladakh areas and the use of the R&AW's covert action capability to make Pakistan realize that it would have to pay a heavy price for its use of terrorism against India in Punjab.

Another component of the operational policy followed under Rajiv Gandhi was to frustrate Pakistan's goal of a strategic depth in Afghanistan. The policy of frustrating Pakistan's goal in Afghanistan was actually initiated under Indira Gandhi by Kao immediately after the formation of the R&AW in 1968. Strong relationships at various levels—open as well as clandestine— were established not only with the people and the rulers of Afghanistan, but also with the Pashtuns of Pakistan. India's desire for close relations were readily reciprocated by the Afghan people and rulers and by large sections of the Pashtun leadership. The networks established in the 1970s continued to function even after the occupation of Afghanistan by the Soviet troops and the installation in power of a succession of pro-Soviet regimes in Kabul.

The Soviet Union blessed and welcomed this networking and helped it grow in strength in whatever way it could. This networking created misunderstanding in India's relations with the Afghan Mujahideen leaders. They were hurt and disappointed by India's reluctance to support their struggle against the Soviet occupation, but these feelings of hurt and disappointment did not turn them hostile to India. Many Afghan Mujahideen leaders—Pashtun as well as Tajik— maintained secret contacts with the R&AW even while co-operating with the ISI and the CIA against the Soviet troops in Afghanistan. Rajiv Gandhi fully supported this policy. Thus, Saxena, Joshi and Verma under Rajiv Gandhi's leadership followed a triangular strategy towards Pakistan—co-operative relations where possible, hard-hitting covert actions where necessary and close networking with Afghanistan.

This policy started paying dividens in Punjab even when Rajiv Gandhi was the Prime Minister in the form of reduced ISI support for the Khalistanis, but this did not prevent the ISI from interfering in a big way in J&K from 1989. The successors of Rajiv Gandhi as the Prime Minister had the good sense to realize that this was an argument not for discontinuing Rajiv Gandhi's policy, but for further strengthening it. This triangular strategy was continued with varying intensity under the successors to Rajiv Gandhi, but, unfortunately, Inder Gujral, who was the Prime Minister in 1997, discontinued it under his Gujral Doctrine. He ordered the R&AW to wind up its covert action division as an act of unilateral gesture towards Pakistan. His hopes that this gesture would be reciprocated by Pakistan were belied. His policy towards Pakistan became one of unilateral incentives with no disincentives. However, he had the good sense not to change the operational policy in respect of Afghanistan as laid down by Indira Gandhi and Rajiv Gandhi. It continued to pay dividends. So far as dealing with Pakistan is concerned, we have had no coherent strategy since 1997. The innocent civilians of India are paying a heavy price for this at the hands of the jihadi terrorists trained, armed and used by the ISI to keep India bleeding.

The PSYWAR division of the R&AW, which had been wound up under the budgetary cut imposed by Morarji Desai, was revived after the return of Indira Gandhi to power and further strengthened under Rajiv Gandhi. An officer of the Indian Information Service, who had worked in the R&AW before 1977, was re-inducted to revive the PSYWAR Division. The work of this Division was largely focused on countering the ISI's disinformation campaign against India and providing the dissident elements in Pakistan with the means of having their views disseminated inside and outside Pakistan. This revived PSYWAR Division was to do very good work when jihadi terrorism broke out in a big way in J&K in 1989, when V.P.Singh was the Prime Minister. This would be discussed later.

Rajiv Gandhi took great interest in the modernization and computerization of the R&AW. Under the modernization programme, its TECHINT capability was considerably increased. This was made possible through adequate investments for strengthening its capability for satellite communications monitoring, for aerial surveillance through the ARC and for the use of technical means in the collection of HUMINT. Prior to 1980, the R&AW's capability for the collection of communications intelligence (COMINT) was largely confined to tapping landline telephones, which needed a human intervention to get access to the line. Before and during the 1971 war, its Monitoring Division was also able to intercept telephone conversations between the two wings of Pakistan. However, its capability for the interception of Pakistan's overseas telephone communications was limited. The investments in satellite monitoring in the 1980s overcame these limitations to a considerable extent.

While the investments in the ARC improved the R&AW's capability for the collection of electronic intelligence (ELINT), those in its technical laboratories added to its capability for the collection and dissemination of HUMINT. These investments were in fields such as secret writing, clandestine photography, wireless communications under hostile conditions, clandestine recording of communications and scrambling of telephone communications. Its Science and Technology Division continued to do good work in the collection of intelligence regarding Pakistan's nuclear and missile programmes.

The R&AW's Pakistan Division was the main beneficiary of the improvements brought about by the fresh investments under Indira Gandhi and Rajiv Gandhi. Morarji Desai's budget freeze had resulted in a stagnation of the organization's TECHINT capability. This process was reversed and then the capabilities further improved. However, the Armed Forces continued to voice dissatisfaction over the gaps in the collection of military intelligence relating to Pakistan. Their constant complaint was that while the R&AW was able to collect Pakistani military intelligence relating to overseas procurement, new raisings, deployments etc, its ability to collect intelligence regarding the future plans of the Pakistani Armed Forces, their military exercises, the deficiencies noticed during those exercises, their war games, their future intentions etc remained inadequate. Our Armed Forces—particularly the Army—therefore started demanding that

they should also be permitted to collect external intelligence outside
the Indian territory through human sources and to make similar
investments for strengthening their TECHINT capability.

When Indira Gandhi set up the R&AW in 1968, she had laid
down that it would be exclusively responsible for the collection of
external intelligence. Kao and those, who followed him as the chief,
interpreted this to mean HUMINT as well as TECHINT. In respect of
HUMINT, they took up the stand that while the Army could collect
tactical military intelligence upto a limited depth across India's
international borders through intelligence collection posts set up
along the borders, it could not run clandestine source operations
outside Indian territory through military officers posted under cover
outside the country. They insisted that any military officer posted
outside the country for clandestine intelligence collection had to be
from the R&AW.

A practice also grew up under which all proposals from the
Armed Forces for substantial investments for improving their
TECHINT capability were referred to the head of the R&AW for his
concurrence. The R&AW particularly was adamant in its refusal to
let the Army develop its own capability for satellite monitoring to
supplement that of the R&AW. These issues, which were a source
of dissatisfaction to the Armed Forces, were agitated upon by them
much more vigorously under Rajiv Gandhi than they were able to
do under his mother. When Indira Gandhi was the Prime Minister,
Kao was able to see that any differences between the R&AW and the
Armed Forces regarding their respective roles in the collection of
military intelligence were always sorted out in favour of the R&AW.

After her assassination and the final exit of Kao from the intelligence
community, the R&AW did not have the same kind of clout with Rajiv
Gandhi as it had with Indira Gandhi. As a result, while Rajiv Gandhi
ruled in favour of the R&AW in respect of HUMINT, he was more
open to the arguments of the Armed Forces in respect of TECHINT.
Proposals from the Armed Forces for substantial investments for
improving their TECHINT capability—particularly in the field of
satellite monitoring— received a sympathetic consideration from

Rajiv Gandhi. While the R&AW continued to maintain its monopoly —approved by Indira Gandhi— in respect of HUMINT, the process of weakening its monopoly in respect of TECHINT started under Rajiv Gandhi. But its progress was slow and reached its culmination only after the Kargil conflict of 1999 when a decision was taken to set up a separate agency for future investments in TECHINT and to allow not only the Armed Forces, but also the IB to improve their TECHINT capabilities without making their proposals subject to a veto by the R&AW.

After the exit of Kao, not only the Army, but also the IB started questioning the exclusive authority for the collection of external intelligence—HUMINT as well as TECHINT— entrusted by Indira Gandhi to the R&AW in 1968. The IB expressed dissatisfaction over the R&AW's coverage of external intelligence having a bearing on India's internal security. It was particularly critical of what it projected as the inadequate intelligence flow from the R&AW on the activities and plans of the Khalistani terrorists. Some officers of the IB, who were unhappy over the bifurcation of the IB by Indira Gandhi in 1968, now started insisting that the Government should have a second look at the orders passed by her in 1968. They even questioned the wisdom of her orders that the R&AW would be responsible for liaison with foreign intelligence agencies and that all contacts of other agencies such as the IB with foreign intelligence agencies would be only through the R&AW. Their argument was that since many of India's internal security problems had external linkages, the IB, which was responsible for internal intelligence, should also be in a position to collect independently intelligence about the external linkages- —either through its own source operations or through liaison with foreign security agencies. They felt that the IB should not be solely dependent on the R&AW for this purpose.

To start with, the IB was keen to have its own officers posted in the Indian High Commission in London and in the Indian Embassy in Washington DC to monitor the activities of the Khalistani elements in the UK and the US and to liaise with the local security agencies on this subject. The R&AW agreed to this when Saxena was the chief.

Since then, the IB has been raising from time to time the question of their having their own officers in all our neighbouring countries to collect intelligence having a bearing on our internal security. This is in addition to the posts in our important diplomatic missions abroad, which have been created for looking after the physical security of the missions and which have been filled up either by IPS officers from the IB or by IPS officers taken directly from the States. Thus, two parallel set-ups have come up abroad defeating the ideas and intentions of Indira Gandhi—the R&AW set-up and the IB set-up. Can the Indian tax-payer afford this luxury? Has this resulted in an improvement in the intelligence flow? Has this reduced the threats to our internal security? These are questions, which need to be objectively considered.

For the IB, which is responsible for counter-intelligence, the ISI and its officers posted under diplomatic cover in the Pakistani High Commission in New Delhi, are the most important targets. For the ISI, the R&AW and its officers posted in the Indian High Commission in Islamabad and before 1994 in the Indian Consulate-General in Karachi under diplomatic cover are the most important targets. This was so even before 1968 when IB officers used to be posted in Karachi and Islamabad under diplomatic cover. The intelligence agencies of all countries post their officers under diplomatic cover in foreign countries to collect intelligence. There is nothing unusual about this. The counter-intelligence agencies keep a careful eye on them and if they find that they are trying to penetrate the host Government, its intelligence agencies and security forces, they catch them and quietly expel them without ill-treating them. A certain civility is observed even in counter-intelligence. The same is the case in India and Pakistan also in respect of all intelligence officers except those of each other. On many occasions, the IB had caught intelligence agencies of the US and other Western countries trying to penetrate us through their officers in Delhi. It asked the MEA to quietly expel them without sensationalizing their activities.

However, these ground rules do not apply to the intelligence officers of India and Pakistan. The ISI does not allow suspected

Indian intelligence officers to function and lead a normal life. It keeps them under permanent surveillance and taps their telephones all the time. There is nothing secret about the surveillance. I used to call it bumper-to-bumper surveillance. If the ISI caught any R&AW officer under suspicious circumstances, it beat him up and even administered electric shocks to him before expelling him from Pakistan despite the fact that he enjoyed diplomatic immunity from arrest and ill-treatment. If criminals are subjected to third degree methods, they can at least approach a court or a human rights organization for justice. When intelligence officers are subjected to third degree methods, they have to grin and bear it.

The IB is not a saint. It does almost the same thing to suspected ISI officers posted in New Delhi. The only difference is that the IB does not administer electric shock. At least, it never used to when I was in service. Considering the brutal manner in which the IB and the ISI treat the suspected intelligence officers when caught, it is a wonder how R&AW officers volunteer for posting in Pakistan and those of the ISI volunteer for posting in India. It is equally a wonder how they manage to collect intelligence when posted to each other's country.

When I joined the IB in 1967, a senior officer of the Ministry of Home affairs (MHA) narrated to me a funny incident (he swore it was true) which illustrated the way the IB and the ISI treated each other. The IB used to maintain a permanent bumper-to-bumper surveillance on a suspected ISI officer posted in the Pakistani High Commission in New Delhi. Once, in winter, there was a heavy fog reducing visibility. The suspected ISI officer was returning home after a dinner outside. The IB's surveillance car followed him very closely. After he had driven for some time, the suspected ISI officer stopped his car. The IB's car also stopped. The ISI officer got out, walked to the IB's car and asked the head of the IB's surveillance team: "Care to come in for tea?" Only then, the IB team realised that while following the ISI officer's car bumper-to-bumper in poor visibility, they had entered his house without noticing it. The embarrassed IB team apologized, declined the invitation and drove back.

One can write a humorous book on the way IB/R&AW and ISI officers operate in each other's country and try to discourage the local people from interacting with the intelligence officers of the adversary. Once (before 1968) the source of an IB officer in the Pakistan Army headquarters told him he had managed to get hold of a classified document of the Army, but said he would not be able to let him take it to the mission for photostating. He said he would have to return it to him on the spot after perusal. The officer fixed his meeting with the source in a public park. He took with him his Personal Assistant along with a portable type-writer. He took the document from his source and his PA started typing it. The ISI surveillance team caught the officer and his PA and expelled them. Shocking, but true.

When Narasimha Rao was the Prime Minister, there were rumours in Pakistan that Nawaz Sharif, the then Prime Minister, had developed a romantic relationship with the sister of a well-known Bollywood actor. Worried over this, the ISI issued a secret circular to all public servants warning that the R&AW had started using attractive women for honey traps and asking them to report to it if any Indian woman approached them. It also said that about 50 attractive Indian women had been infiltrated by the R&AW into Punjab to organize honey traps. The news of this circular leaked out. The "Frontier Post" of Peshawar came out with a humorous editorial which made the following appeal to the R&AW: " Why this partiality to the Punjabis? Why send your attractive women only to them? We Pashtuns also like attractive women. Send us at least 10. Many of us are dying to be honey-trapped by attractive Indian women."

Sharad Pawar, who was then the Defence Minister, told a woman journalist working for a Delhi paper that the R&AW was tapping the telephone conversations of Nawaz Sharif with the sister of the actor and that it had secret recordings of Nawaz sharif singing love songs to her over telephone. Greatly excited that she got a scoop, she promptly carried it in her paper. A couple of days later, she got a defamation notice from the sister of the actor. She rushed to Sharad Pawar and sought his assistance for challenging the defamation notice. She wanted somebody in the Government of India to give her a letter that what she reported was correct. Sharad Pawar totally denied ever having told her anything about the relationship of this woman with Nawaz Sharif. " I don't even know who she is. Where is the question of my talking to you about her?"

In utter panic, she approached the late Amitabha Chakravarthi of the Indian Information Service, who was then on deputation to the R&AW, and sought our help to enable her to reply to the defamation notice. I asked Amitabha to tell her that the question did not arise since we were not aware of any relationship between the sister of the actor and Nawaz Sharif.

Such lighter moments were more an exception than the rule. Most of the time, the Indian and Pakistani agencies were brutal towards each other. Very often, it was the R&AW officers posted in Pakistan, who had to bear the brunt of the ISI's brutality in retaliation for what they alleged was the IB's brutality towards their diplomats in New Delhi. Such instances of mutual brutality increased under Zia-ul-Haq in Pakistan and Rajiv Gandhi in India.In 1988, the IB trapped Brig.Zaheer-ul-Islam Abbasi, a suspected ISI officer posted as Military Attache in the Pakistani High Commission in New Delhi, and had him thoroughly beaten up. The ISI retaliated in their usual manner against an Indian diplomat in Islamabad whom they suspected to be from the R&AW. The R&AW strongly protested to the IB against such actions being taken in New Delhi without even alerting it beforehand. The IB rejected the protest. The practice of ill-treatment of suspected intelligence officers posted in the capital of each other has continued till today. This needs to be stopped since it serves no purpose. It only adds to the mutual bitterness.

The R&AW played an important role in the normalization of relations between India and China for which it received high praise from Rajiv Gandhi. Before the assassination of Indira Gandhi, the Yugoslav intelligence, with which the R&AW had an excellent liaison relationship, had organized an invitation for Kao from China's external intelligence agency, known as the Ministry of State Security (MSS). Kao flew to Beijing via Tokyo. He was accompanied by

G.S.Mishra, one of the R&AW's leading experts on China who had served in Beijing for some years, Dr.S.K.Chaturvedi, who used to be the head of the Economic Intelligence Division of the R&AW, and B.K.Ratnakar Rao, an IPS officer from the Tamil Nadu cadre, who had served for many years as the Staff Officer of Kao.

The visit had two objectives— to lay the foundation for a liaison relationship between the R&AW and the MSS and to test the waters in China for a possible visit by Indira Gandhi to mark the normalization of the relations between the two countries. Two days after their arrival, as his talks with the Chinese political leaders as an emissary of Indira Gandhi and with senior Chinese intelligence officials were proceeding smoothly, Indira Gandhi was assassinated. He had to cut short the visit and return to Delhi via Hong Kong.

After Rajiv Gandhi took over as the Prime Minister, the R&AW briefed him on the visit of Kao to Beijing and its purpose. He was appreciative of the initiative taken by Kao and the R&AW and wanted the R&AW to pursue its efforts to set up a liaison relationship with the MSS and to pave the way for a visit by him to Beijing. The R&AW succeeded in establishing a liaison relationship with its Chinese counterpart. Not only that. Even a hotline was established between the chiefs of the two services so that not only the two chiefs, but also the Prime Ministers of the two countries could use this for the exchange of sensitive communications for which they wanted to avoid using the normal diplomatic channel between the Foreign Offices of the two countries.

Rajiv Gandhi accepted an invitation from the Chinese leadership to visit China in 1988. Much of the preparatory work for this visit, including the mutual consultations on the joint statement on the border dispute between the two countries to be issued at the end of the visit, was done through this hotline. Rajiv Gandhi also sent A.K.Verma on a top secret visit to China to ensure that his own visit and talks with the Chinese leaders would be successful. Rajiv Gandhi prepared himself thoroughly for the visit. He read diligently all the background notes on Sino-Indian relations prepared by the MEA and the R&AW. He also had discussions with some of the Indian experts on China. At his request, the R&AW arranged a secret visit to New Delhi by two China experts of the UK's Secret Intelligence Service (SIS) to brief Rajiv Gandhi on the Chinese negotiating techniques and other matters of relevance.

The visit of Rajiv Gandhi to China in December,1988, was highly successful and marked the culmination of the process of normalization of the diplomatic relations between the two countries. The high point of his visit was his very warm meeting with Deng Xiao-ping, which sent a significant message across to the people of the two countries and to the international community regarding the determination of the two countries to strengthen their mutual friendship and co-operation. On his return to India, Rajiv Gandhi had nothing but the highest praise for the role of the R&AW and Verma in contributing to the success of his visit.

When Narasimha Rao visited China as the Prime Minister in September,1993, his programme as drawn up by the Chinese was almost a carbon copy of the programme for the visit of Rajiv Gandhi except for one difference. It did not provide for a meeting with Deng. Rao felt disappointed and was very keen to have a meeting, however brief, with Deng. The Chinese authorities expressed their inability to accommodate his request on the ground that Deng was not well. Rao, who was aware of the role of the R&AW in connection with the visit of Rajiv Gandhi to China, sought its help in arranging a courtesy call by him on Deng. The R&AW took up the matter with the MSS through the hotline. It replied that Deng had not received Russian President Boris Yeltsin due to indisposition and that if they made an exception in the case of Rao, their action could be misunderstood by Moscow. It was apparent that the Chinese treated the meeting between Rajiv Gandhi and Deng as a special gesture to the son of Indira Gandhi. They were not prepared to extend the same gesture to Rao.

In a gesture to India at the time of the first Gulf war of 1991, when Chandra Shekhar was the Prime Minister with the support of the Rajiv Gandhi-led Congress (I), Chinese intelligence officials through the R&AW's liaison representative in Beijing offered to

recommend to their leadership the supply of oil to India to enable it
to meet any shortages it might face due to the war. The Government
of India did not avail of the offer. During the periodic meetings of
the officers of the R&AW and the MSS in New Delhi and Beijing,
R&AW officers used to raise without fail China's nuclear, missile and
military supply relationship with Pakistan and point out how this was
standing in the way of the full flowering of the bilateral relations,
but their standard reply was that they were supplying only defensive
equipment to Pakistan which would not pose a threat to India and
that they would be happy to consider any request from India for
the supply of defensive equipment, which would not pose a threat
to Pakistan.

Developments in South-East and East Asia, the US relations with
Japan and China's relations with Pakistan used to figure on the
agenda of all these discussions. In addition, they would invariably
ask for a briefing on the activities of the Dalai Lama and his followers
from the Indian territory. Despite our repeated assurances that the
Tibetans living in the Indian territory would not be allowed to pose a
threat to China and to Chinese leaders visiting India, they continued
to express concern over their presence and activities in the Indian
territory. However, they did not allow this to come in the way of the
development of the bilateral relations.

While the liaison relationship between the R&AW and the MSS
thus continued to develop satisfactorily and made an important
contribution to the success of Rajiv Gandhi's visit to China, the
R&AW's reporting on China—particularly in respect of military
intelligence— was frequently criticized by the Indian Army. The
R&AW had only two main sources of military intelligence about
China—its Western liaison contacts and the trans-border sources
from Tibet. Both these sources tended to exaggerate the over-all
Chinese military capability and military deployments in Tibet. The
Military Intelligence repeatedly challenged the R&AW's estimate of
the Chinese military deployments in Tibet as inflated. After having
refuted the MI's challenge for a long time, the R&AW had to admit
that its estimate needed to be revised downwards.

There was similar criticism from the MEA of its political coverage as based largely, if not totally, on open information. Not only the MEA, but even some liaison agencies expressed the view that the weekly reports of the R&AW were nothing but a collation of open information from the Chinese media. Some of the liaison agencies even asked the R&AW to discontinue sharing such open information since it was of no use to them. The analytical reports and assessments prepared by the R&AW also came in for criticism that they lacked depth and insights. Only the R&AW's reports on the state of the Chinese economy came in for high praise from the Ministry of Finance and the Planning Commission. Though these were also based largely on open information, they found the reports more analytical. Moreover, in the 1980s, when the Chinese leadership had started opening up its economy, the R&AW was the only agency or department of the Government of India, which was systematically monitoring economic developments in China.

The sizable increase in investments for improving the intelligence collection capabilities of the R&AW under Rajiv Gandhi did not produce the same beneficial results in respect of China as they did in respect of Pakistan. The R&AW's post-1968 renowned experts on China such as G.S.Mishra, S.N.Warty, Deepankar Sanyal, N.Narasimhan, etc were all of IB vintage hand-picked and got trained by Mallik. He also got trained a number of excellent linguists in India itself, Hong Kong and China. They served the organization with great distinction. The last of the IB-trained experts retired in January,2003. The China experts produced by the R&AW after its formation in 1968 were good, but the general impression was that they were not comparable to those of the IB vintage.

Unfortunately, human and material resources provided for strengthening the China expertise of the R&AW were not on par with those provided for the Pakistan division. The R&AW has had 16 chiefs since its formation in 1968. Of these, only one (N.Narasimhan—1991 to 93) could be described as a real China expert. This deficiency in respect of China continues. The Special Task Force for the Revamping of the Intelligence Apparatus set

up by the Government of India in 2000 on the recommendation
of the Kargil Review Committee (KRC) focused essentially on our
intelligence capabilities relating to Pakistan and counter-terrorism.
It also briefly dealt with economic intelligence and the security
implications of the Internet. But, it paid inadequate attention to an
examination of our intelligence collection and analysis capabilities
with regard to China. It is time to have a comprehensive examination
of our China-related inadequacies.

Continuity with innovative change was Rajiv Gandhi's contribution
to the operational policies of the R&AW relating to Pakistan,
Afghanistan and China. These policies had been laid down by Indira
Gandhi. After inheriting them, he imparted to them a vigour,a
laser-sharp focus and a new dynamism, which they lacked before his
taking-over as the Prime Minister. The biting power of the R&AW,
which had weakened between 1977 and 1980, was restored. It once
again became—as it was before 1977— an agency not only for the
collection and analysis of intelligence, but also for the defence and
enforcement of India's national interests in its neighbourhood
through covert non-diplomatic means, where diplomatic means were
found inadequate or ineffective. While the covert action capability
thus improved tremendously under Rajiv Gandhi, the improvement
in its intelligence collection and analysis capability did not keep pace
with the requirements of the nation and the time.

Rajiv Gandhi's operational policy with regard to Sri Lanka was
marked not by innovative change, but by bewildering confusion
ultimately leading inexorably to his brutal assassination in May,1991,
when he was the Leader of the Opposition. I call it his operational
policy and not the R&AW's policy because many of the twists and
turns in the policy could not be attributed to a single agency of the
Government of India. He was the source of much of the confusion,
which came to charactetrize our operational policy. The way our
operational policy with regard to Sri Lanka was mishandled by Rajiv
Gandhi and his successor V.P.Singh has not been the subject of a
detailed study in India. It was a typical example of how not to handle
a sensitive operation.

As I had mentioned earlier, when Rajiv Gandhi took over as the Prime Minister, he was immediately convinced of the wisdom of the operational policies laid down by his mother in respect of Pakistan and Afghanistan. However, he was not clear in his mind about the policy of activism in support of the Sri Lankan Tamils laid down by her. This activism, which had initially remained secret, became public knowledge even when she was the Prime Minister when a well-known weekly of New Delhi came out with some of the alleged details of this covert activism. Some of these details were correct, but many wrong. Whatever might have been the merits of the policy of covert activism laid down by her, it must be said to her credit that she instinctively understood the importance of having a single nodal agency to pursue this covert option. And she had laid down two clear-cut objectives for this policy— to make the Government of Sri Lanka responsive to the security concerns of India and to give the Sri Lankan Tamils a strong voice and a capability to find a negotiated political solution to their problems without the Government of India unduly getting involved in the process of finding a political solution.

Rajiv Gandhi, who was initially hesitant to pursue the policy of his mother, subsequently became— for reasons which I was never able to understand—an over-enthusiastic follower of the policy.In his pursuit of the policy, he brought about changes which proved counter-productive and ultimately led to confusion and disaster. For the implementation of her operational policy, Indira Gandhi almost totally relied on the R&AW and on a triumvirate consisting of Kao, Saxena and the late G.Parthasarathi. While carrying out her instructions, they sought to exercise some caution and moderation in her thinking and actions. She valued their advice and listened to them.

Under Rajiv Gandhi, there was not a single nodal agency. In his over-enthusiasm to implement his policy, he inducted a multiplicity of agencies and dramatis personae into the scene— the R&AW, the IB, the Tamil Nadu Police, the Directorate-General of Military Intelligence (DGMI), the Army and the MEA. These agencies kept stepping on each other's toes. There was an awful lack of co-ordination. The chiefs and senior officers of these agencies—instead of exercising caution and moderation in his thinking and actions—vied with one another in egging him on into more and more unwise actions. There was a total lack of coherence in policy-making. The Joint Intelligence Committee (JIC), which was supposed to bring about such coherence in thinking and actions, failed in its duty to do so.

The plethora of Sri Lankan Tamil organizations, which came into being with the benediction of the Government of India, pursued their own narrow partisan interests rather than the over-all interests of the Sri Lankan Tamils as a whole. They took full advantage of the lack of coherence and co-ordination in New Delhi to take assistance from a variety of sources inside and outside India in order to strengthen themselves not only against the Sinhalese, but also against each other.

They took money from the R&AW without the IB and the DGMI being aware of it. They took money from the IB without the R&AW and the DGMI being aware of it. They took money from the DGMI without the IB and the R&AW being aware of it. They took money from the discretionary grant of the MEA without any of the intelligence agencies being aware of it. They took money from the Tamil Nadu Police without the Government of India being aware of it. They took assistance from the Indian intelligence agencies. At the same time, they had no qualms over seeking and accepting assistance from foreign terrorist organizations such as Pakistan's Harkat-ul-Mujahideen with the blessings of the ISI, the Hezbollah, the Palestine Liberation Organization (PLO) of Yasser Arafat and the Popular Front for the Liberation of Palestine (PFLP) of George Habash.

When Prabakaran, the leader of the Liberation Tigers of Tamil Eelam (LTTE), was disinclined to accept the Indo-Sri Lankan Agreement of 1987, which led to the induction of the Indian Peace-Keeping Force (IPKF) into the Tamil areas of Sri Lanka, Arafat sent a message to Rajiv Gandhi offering his good offices for making Prabakaran accept the agreement. After politely declining his offer,

Rajiv Gandhi asked the intelligence agencies to check up how Arafat claimed to have some influence over Prabakaran. Their enquiries brought out that the LTTE was in secret touch with the PLO's so-called diplomatic mission in Delhi without the knowledge of the Government of India and that senior PLO representatives used to visit Chennai secretly to meet LTTE leaders.

There was not only a multiplicity of agencies and Departments of the Government maintaining contacts with the different Sri Lankan Tamil groups, but there was also a multiplicity of privileged interlocutors holding secret talks with Prabakaran and other Tamil leaders on behalf of Rajiv Gandhi—with one not knowing what the other was doing. The decision to induct the IPKF into Sri Lanka to restore normalcy and to make the LTTE amenable to accepting what it viewed as a dictated peace seemed to have been taken without a proper assessment of the ground realities in the Tamil areas of Sri Lanka and the likely difficulties in carrying out counter-insurgency tasks in a foreign territory.

The Indian Army seemed to have imagined that since it was familiar with counter-insurgency operations in different areas of the Indian territory, the operations in the Tamil areas of Sri Lanka should be no different. One was told that an over-confident and over-enthusiastic Gen.Sunderji, the then Chief of the Army Staff, told Rajiv Gandhi that the IPKF would be able to accomplish its mission within a month. When this did not happen and the IPKF got involved in a quagmire, he put the blame on the intelligence agencies—particularly on the R&AW— for not warning him in advance of the capabilities, strength and motivation of the LTTE. As a Lt.Gen., he did the same thing in 1984 when he was put in charge of the military operation against the Khalistani terrorists, who had occupied the Golden Temple in Amritsar. When the operation took a longer time than expected and became messy due to a fierce resistance put up by the terrorists, he blamed the intelligence agencies for not providing adequate intelligence about the capability of the terrorists inside the Temple.

While not a single agency or department of the Government of India had a complete picture of what was being done by various

agencies and departments in relation to Sri Lanka, there was one
agency outside India, which must have had a complete picture. That
was the US Central Intelligence Agency (CIA). It was getting from the
French external intelligence agency copies of all reports being sent
to the PMO by the IB and the R&AW which the French agency was
getting from its source in the office of the then Principal Secretary
to the PM. It was also getting a large number of sensitive documents
and information from the office of the R&AW in Chennai through its
head, who was allegedly being run as a source by a CIA officer posted
in the US Consulate at Chennai. The IB's surveillance team, which
used to take video-recordings of the movements and meetings of this
CIA officer, once reportedly noticed in one of its video clips the local
R&AW chief jogging along with the CIA officer on the Marina beach.
Further enquiries gave cause for suspicion that this officer had been
won over and recruited by the CIA. He was called to Delhi ostensibly
to attend a meeting with the head of the R&AW without making
him aware that he was under suspicion. On his arrival, he was taken
into custody and interrogated by a joint team of counter-intelligence
experts from the IB and the R&AW. He reportedly confessed and
was detained in the Tihar jail in Delhi for a year under the National
Security Act. One was told that Rajiv Gandhi was against jailing him,
but Joshi, the then chief of the R&AW (1986-87), insisted on his
being sent to jail in order to convey a firm warning to other officers
not to fall a prey to the temptations offered by foreign intelligence
agencies.

When Indira Gandhi was the Prime Minister, an IPS officer of the
R&AW, who used to deal with Sri Lanka and who had made a name
as an upright and religious-minded officer, approached Kao and
requested him to have his name recommended by the R&AW for
the Indian Police Medal. At Kao's request, the R&AW did so. The
procedure was that the R&AW used to send the recommendation to
the MHA, which would put it up to the Prime Minister along with the
personal file on the officer kept in the MHA. This personal file used
to contain all papers on the work and conduct of the officer ever
since he joined the IPS. The MHA did so.

After some days, the file came back from Indira Gandhi with the following note: "Please see the report in his personal file at Flag X. I am surprised that an officer with such a background should have been recommended for the Police Medal." In the personal file was a report sent 20 years earlier by the Chief Secretary of the State of the officer to the Home Secretary of the Government of India.

In his report, the Chief Secretary had stated as follows: After joining the State, the officer had got engaged to a girl and taken a dowry of Rs.one lakh from her parents. Before the marriage, his parents started demanding more money as dowry.When the girl's parents expressed their inability to pay more, the officer cancelled his engagement to the girl and refused to return the amount paid initially. In fact, he and his parents denied having taken any amount. The girl's parents sent a written complaint to the Chief Secretary, who ordered an enquiry. The enquiry could not find provable evidence against the officer. The Chief Secretary personally interviewed the girl and her parents. While forwarding the enquiry report to the Home Secretary, the Chief Secretary had remarked that while no evidence could be found against the officer, he had no reason to disbelieve the allegations of the girl and her parents.It was this officer who was subsequently recruited by the CIA. The inherent defect in his character, which was unnoticed by the R&AW, had apparently been noticed by the CIA and he was targeted for recruitment.

Possibly by unintended coincidence, even as the penetration of the R&AW's office by the CIA through this IPS officer was detected after he had caused some damage, another officer joined the R&AW's headquarters when Rajiv Gandhi was the Prime Minister and managed to ingratiate himself with the senior officers to such an extent that he was considered a blue-eyed operative of the organization. He claimed to have access to the documents of a division of the US State Department, which dealt with external economic assistance, through his sister, who was a US Government servant working in that Division. He managed to get from her copies of a number of classified reports of her Division relating to South Asia.

The R&AW was priding itself on the fact that it had succeeded in penetrating the US State Department through a mole. Years later, in 2004, it came out that this officer was a mole of the CIA in the R&AW. He must have been of even a greater value to the CIA than the head of the R&AW office in Chennai because it had him whisked out of India and gave him shelter in the US after he came under suspicion. To enable him to escape from India without being caught, it reportedly issued to him and his wife US passports under different names. This extraordinary action of the CIA, which amounted to its admitting that he was its mole, gave an idea of what should have been his value to the CIA. It apparently wanted to prevent at any cost his interrogation by the Indian counter-intelligence experts. Even at the risk of a serious misunderstanding with the Government of India, it helped him to flee to the US and settle down there. His name is Major Rabinder Singh.

Shortly after the exit of Rajiv Gandhi as the Prime Minister, there was another worrisome incident in the R&AW headquarters. A conference of the Directors-General of Police and the heads of the central police organizations on security-related issues was held in the conference hall of the R&AW. Among those, who attended the conference was K.P.S.Gill. Shortly before his arrival, a dummy improvised explosive device (IED) was found in a corner of the Control Room of the organization. It was dummy in the sense that it had been properly assembled, but there was no explosive charge in the cavity meant for it. The person, who planted it, apparently did not want to cause any explosion. At the same time, he wanted to show that he had access to the Control Room. Who was he—an insider or an outsider? What was his identity? It could not be established.

In 1996, the IB was reported to have detected a penetration of their organization at the headquarters by the CIA at a very senior level. In 2006, there were reports of the penetration of the National Security Council Secretariat (NSCS), which is part of the PMO, by the CIA. These detections show serious weaknesses in the counter-intelligence and internal security set-ups of the IB and the R&AW. The IB and the R&AW act as watch-dogs of the internal security set-ups in other Government departments—the IB internally and the R&AW externally— but who is to act as an independent watch-dog of the counter-intelligence and internal security set-ups of the IB and the R&AW so that our policy-makers are assured that they are competent enough to prevent a penetration of their own offices by foreign intelligence agencies. It is time to pay attention to this, if this has not already been done.

There are two options. The first is to appoint an IB officer as the head of the Counter-intelligence and internal security set-up of the R&AW and vice versa. The second option is to emulate the CIA and some other foreign agencies and create a post of Inspector-General in the intelligence agencies to act as an independent watch-dog of the performance of the intelligence agencies and the state of their internal security and counter-intelligence. In the US, only officers known for their independence, objectivity and personal integrity are considered for appointment to this post. Their reports go directly to the Congressional Oversight Committees with copies to the head of the agency. In India, till we set up the system of parliamentary oversight of the intelligence agencies, his reports can go directly to the Prime Minister, with copies to the head of the agency.

Rajiv Gandhi enthusiastically shared his mother's interest in Africa and ensured that the requests from the African countries for training and other assistance and from the ANC and the SWAPO for any assistance were met. By the time apartheid came to an end in South Africa and Namibia became independent, Rajiv Gandhi had lost the elections. After his release from decades of detention, one of the first countries visited by Nelson Mandela, the ANC leader, was India when V.P.Singh was the Prime Minister. At the celebrations to mark the independence of Namibia—again when V.P.Singh was the Prime Minister— the Congress (I) delegation led by Rajiv Gandhi as the Leader of the Opposition was accorded greater honours by the Namibian authorities than the delegation of the Government of India. It was their way of expressing their gratitude to India, the Congress (I), Indira Gandhi and Rajiv Gandhi for what they did to help the anti-apartheid movement and for the independence of

Nambia. Future generations of R&AW officers should know and should be proud of the role of the R&AW in this. It shows what good the R&AW can do for the country if it gets the right guidance and encouragement from the political leadership of the country. The R&AW has immense potential for promoting the national interests of the country.It is for the political leadership to be aware of this potential, to nurse it and make full use of it. Indira Gandhi and Rajiv Gandhi did. The other Prime Ministers didn't.

No other Prime Minister of India—not even Indira Gandhi— took such an active interest as Rajiv Gandhi did in the IB and the R&AW and its officers and in encouraging initiatives to improve their working. Rajiv Gandhi computerized the working of the R&AW, made the officers at all levels become computer-literate and made the level of computer-literacy of an officer an important quality to be reflected in his Annual Confidential Reports. He initiated proposals for improving the conditions of service of intelligence officers while in service and their quality of life after their retirement, keeping in view the harsh and almost anonymous life led by them. Despite his being an active and powerful Prime Minister, he could not push his proposals through due to opposition from the IAS officers. One understands that some of these proposals for serving officers have since been implemented by Dr.Manmohan Singh, the present Prime Minister, on the advice of M.K.Narayanan, the National Security Adviser.

CHAPTER XVI

Under V.P.Singh & Chandra Shekhar

There were two chiefs of the R&AW under V.P.Singh—Verma and G.S.Bajpai. Verma, who had been appointed as the chief by Rajiv Gandhi in June,1987, continued without being disturbed by V.P.Singh till his superannuation on May 30,1990. Immediately after taking over as the Prime Minister in December,1989, V.P.Singh removed the chiefs of the IB and the CBI appointed by Rajiv Gandhi and replaced them with his own nominees. These changes were attributed to his suspicion that the heads of these two organizations had let themselves be misused by Rajiv Gandhi for partisan political purposes as well as in connection with the Bofors cover-up. Fears that he might similarly replace Verma, who enjoyed the total trust of Rajiv Gandhi, were belied.

However, in the beginning, he did have some misgivings about the R&AW. This became evident when he did not associate the organization actively with the crisis management following the kidnapping on December 8,1989, of Rubaiya Sayeed, the daughter of Mufti Mohammad Sayeed, his Home Minister, by terrorists of the Jammu and Kashmir Liberation Front (JKLF). The terrorists demanded the release of some of their associates from jail. The Government succumbed to the pressure and released them in order to rescue the daughter of the Home Minister. The meek surrender of the Government to the demands of the terrorists created a weak image of the Government and led to an outpouring of euphoria in the Valley. This marked the beginning of widespread terrorism in the State, which has continued for nearly 18 years with the support of the ISI.

This incident was followed in April, 1990, by another in which some terrorists kidnapped Mushir-ul-Haq, the Vice-Chancellor of the Srinagar University, and Abdul Ghani, his Secretary, and demanded the release of some of their associates, who were in jail. The V.P.Singh Government, which had been rattled by public criticism of its action in conceding the demands of the terrorists involved in the earlier kidnapping, took up a firm line now and refused to release the prisoners. The kidnappers retaliated by killing both of them.

There was considerable public anger over what was perceived as the double standards followed by the Government— it released some terrorists in order to save the life of the daughter of the Home Minister, but let two ordinary citizens be brutally killed by refusing to meet the demands of the terrorists involved in their kidnapping. The dead bodies of these two persons were brought to Delhi for burial. When Inder Gujral, the then Minister for External Affairs, and George Fernandes, the then Minister for Railways, went to the burial ground to pay homage to the deceased, their relatives and others, who had gathered there, abused them and refused to let them attend the burial ceremony. Worried by the hostile attitude of the mourners, the police advised the two Ministers to leave.

In a way, it was a blessing in disguise for the R&AW that V.P.Singh did not associate it with the crisis management drill after the two kidnapping incidents. There was a tremendous public criticism of the differing yard-sticks adopted by the Government while dealing with the two incidents. The R&AW escaped this criticism.

V.P.Singh curried cheap popularity with the extremists and terrorists not only in J&K, but also in Punjab. He was soft to people like Simranjit Singh Mann, who were suspected to be sympathetic to the Khalistani terrorists. There was considerable demoralization in the police administration as a result of his populist actions and his reluctance to back in public police officers, who were valiantly fighting against the Khalistani terrorists.

The ISI took full advantage of the situation in J&K by stepping up the training and arming of a large number of extremists from the

Valley, who had gone across to Pakistan-Occupied Kashmir (POK), and infiltrating them back into the Valley. Pakistan's radio and TV stations stepped up their broadcasts and telecasts to the Muslims of J&K. The widespread outbreak of terrorism in J&K coincided with mass public demonstrations in Sofia, the capital of Bulgaria, and in Bucharest, the capital of Romania, against the dictatorial communist Governments in those countries. The Pakistani TV repeatedly telecast video clips of these mass demonstrations and appealed to the Muslims of the State to emulate the demonstrators of Sofia and Bucharest. Thousands of recorded cassettes with appeals to the Kashmiri Muslims to rise in revolt against the Government of India were smuggled into the State and disseminated. There were attacks on Hindu Pandits, the original inhabitants of the valley, and they were forced to flee to Jammu and Delhi.

Alarmed by these developments, the Bharatiya Janata Party (BJP), on whose support V.P.Singh was dependent for his survival in power, stepped up its criticism of his weak handling of terrorism in J&K and Punjab. He took some corrective measures in J&K. In May,1990, he appointed G.C.Saxena, former chief of the R&AW, who was already working as an Adviser to Vinod Pandey, the Cabinet Secretary, as the Governor of J&K in the place of Jagmohan. He started associating the R&AW actively with counter-measures against the ISI.He asked it to step up its covert actions against Pakistan. He set up a PSYWAR Committee consisting of officers from the R&AW, the IB, the MHA, the MEA, the Ministry of Defence (MOD) and the Ministry of Information and Broadcasting to counter the ISI's PSYWAR directed towards the Muslims of the State. An officer of the Indian Information Service on deputation to the R&AW was appointed as the convenor of this committee.

This Committee recommended that the R&AW should procure urgently from its operational funds a large number of jammers to jam Pakistani broadcasts and telecasts and the Border Security Force (BSF) was asked to operate these jammers. At the request of the Committee, the R&AW set up mobile broadcasting stations in the State to broadcast to the people of Pakistan-Occupied Kashmir (POK) and the Northern Areas (Gilgit and Baltistan). When the terrorists tried to prevent the holding of college examinations in the Valley, this Committee had the students flown to Jammu at the Government's cost to take the examination. When the terrorists tried to prevent traders from other parts of India from going to the State in order to buy dry fruits, saffron and products of the local cottage industries, this committee had the producers with their products flown to Delhi at the Government's cost to sell their products at special Kashmiri trade Fairs organized for this purpose. Vinod Pandey made the R&AW responsible for implementing all these schemes. Highly impressed by the operational capability of the R&AW, the new Government started associating it with all counter-measures. The various steps taken gave a breathing time for Saxena, the new Governor, to work out his strategy for revamping the intelligence and counter-terrorism apparatus and start implementing it. The appointment of Saxena as the Governor was a shrewd move since he enjoyed the trust of all parties—and particularly of the Congress (I) and Rajiv Gandhi, who had a very high regard for his professionalism.

In a potentially controversial move, Vinod Pandey wanted the R&AW to organize clandestine arms training for the cadres of the Rashtriya Swayam Sevak Sangh (RSS) in the Jammu area so that they could be used for countering the Pakistan-sponsored terrorists. One had the impression that this idea had originated from L.K. Advani, the BJP leader, who was exercising pressure on the Government to start this training quickly. The R&AW felt very uncomfortable about this idea. Under sustained pressure from Pandey, it held two secret meetings with a representative of the Jammu branch of the RSS to discuss the modalities of this training. The first meeting was held in a Jammu hotel and the second in Hotel Ambassador in Delhi. By then, serious differences had cropped up between V.P.Singh and the BJP over Advani's plan to take a rath yatra to Ayodhya to seek public support to its demand for the construction of a Ram temple in the place then occupied by the Babri Masjid. Pandey directed the R&AW not to take any further action on the project, which remained a non-starter.

V.P.Singh came to office with a single-point agenda —to exploit the Bofors issue to discredit Rajiv Gandhi and end his political career once and for all. The sudden outbreak of widespread terrorism in J&K came in the way of his single-minded pursuit of this agenda, but despite his preoccupation with the crisis management in J&K, he managed to find time to orchestrate the campaign against Rajiv Gandhi and the Congress (I) on the Bofors issue, with Vinod Pandey acting as the co-ordinator of this orchestration. The services of the IB, the R&AW, the CBI, a private detective in Europe and many journalists willing to co-operate were used in this orchestration. When nothing seemed to be coming out of all this, he tried to divert attention from his failure to keep up his electoral promise to find out the truth in the Bofors scandal by raising the issue of the implementation of the report of the Mandal Commission for the reservation of seats for the backward classes in higher educational institutions. This led to widespread protests by young students, some of whom tried to indulge in self-immolation. At a time when the entire concentration of the nation was required to be focused on countering the activities of the ISI in J&K and Punjab, the violence unleashed by the Mandal Commission issue came in the way of such concentration.

Immediately after V.P.Singh took over as the Prime Minister, Arun Nehru, a close associate of Rajiv Gandhi during the Prime Ministership of Indira Gandhi, who subsequently fell out with him after he had succeeded his mother, and Ram Jethmalani, the lawyer and a close associate of the late Ramnath Goenka, the proprietor of the "Indian Express" group of newspapers, complained to V.P.Singh that under Rajiv Gandhi's orders, the R&AW had kept them under secret surveillance during their travels abroad. Arun Nehru made the complaint in writing through a demi-official letter addressed to the Prime Minister. Jethmalani complained orally.

On the orders of V.P.Singh, Vinod Pandey asked the R&AW for a report on both the complaints. The R&AW told Pandey that Arun Nehru's complaint was incorrect. Subsequently, it was found that once when he had gone to the UK, an IB officer posted in the

Indian High Commission in London had been asked to report on
his activities. This officer had served for some years in the R&AW
before going back to the IB. At the time he was asked by the Ministry
of Home Affairs to report on the activities of Arun Nehru in the UK,
he was no longer in the R&AW.

The R&AW also told Pandey that it was correct that the MHA had
asked it to report on the activities of Jethmalani when he had visited
the USA on a couple of occasions when Rajiv Gandhi was the Prime
Minister. The reports sent by it to the MHA were largely based on
reports carried by the ethnic Indian media in the US, which had
covered his programme in detail and reported on his statements and
speeches. The R&AW sent to Pandey a summary of the various reports
sent by it to the MHA on his activities in the US along with photocopies
of the office copies of the reports. The R&AW also told Pandey that it
was not correct that it had kept Jethmalani under surveillance or had
enquiries about him made through secret sources.

After going through its reply, Pandey asked for the file of the
R&AW, which contained the papers about Jethmalani's visits to the
US. He apparently wanted to satisfy himself that in its reply, the
R&AW had covered all relevant facts and had not concealed any
other fact from him. The R&AW took up the stand that only the
Prime Minister was entitled to see its files. This was the convention
since it was formed in 1968, but there were no written orders on
the subject. Pandey referred the matter to V.P. Singh for orders. He
directed that an officer of the R&AW should take the file to Pandey,
who should immediately return it to him after going through it. This
was done. Pandey was satisfied with the reply sent by the R&AW on
the complaint of Jethmalani. There the matter ended.

The issue of the right of the Principal Secretary to the Prime
Minister and the Cabinet Secretary to see the administrative and
operational files of the R&AW had kept coming up from time to
time. There was a time when the R&AW was taking up the stand that
only the Prime Minister could see any of its files—administrative or
operational. Once a Cabinet Secretary refused to pass orders on a
recommendation of the head of the organization for promotions to

certain senior posts unless he was shown the relevant administrative files. Ultimately,it had to agree to it.

When R&AW officers are posted in the Indian diplomatic missions abroad, their performance as diplomats is reviewed by the heads of the mission and their contribution as intelligence officers is reviewed by their controlling officers in the R&AW headquarters. The evaluation of their conduct and behaviour by the heads of missions used to be ignored by it while considering them for promotion. Their suitability for promotion was assessed purely on the basis of the evaluation by their controlling officers in the headquarters. The evaluations done by the heads of missions were not taken into consideration. In fact, these were kept in a separate file which was not shown to the Cabinet Secretary while making recommendations for promotions. A Cabinet Secretary made a big issue of it and declined to pass orders on the recommendations for promotions unless he was shown all the evaluations on the conduct and performance of the officers recommended—whether done by the officers of the MEA posted as heads of missions or by the controlling officers of the R&AW in the headquarters. Ultimately, the R&AW had to give in and show to him the folders containing the evaluations done by the heads of missions too. In the case of Jethmalani, Pandey insisted on his right to see even an operational file of the R&AW. His right in this particular case was upheld by V.P.Singh,but he did not pass any general orders on the subject.

When Narasimha Rao became the Prime Minister, the heads of the organization, on their own, started the practice of marking to the Principal Secretary to the PM and the Cabinet Secretary copies of all their top secret reports to the Prime Minister on operational matters. They had a valid ground for starting to do so. They felt that by doing so they would create a greater awareness in the minds of these two officers about the operational performance of the organization. Once Yevgeny Primakov, the then head of the Russian external intelligence agency, had made a top secret visit to Delhi as a special emissary of Boris Yeltsin, the then Russian President, for talks with the head of the organization. He had also made a courtesy call on Narasimha Rao. The then head of the organization had marked to the Principal Secretary to the PM copies of all his reports to the PM regarding Primakov's visit. A leading national daily of New Delhi had referred to the top secret visit in a report on India's relations with Russia. Enquiries gave cause for suspicion that the Principal Secretary to the PM had spoken about the visit to the correspondent of the paper, who wrote the report. On coming to know of this, Rao directed the organization to stop marking to the Principal Secretary and the Cabinet Secretary copies of sensitive operational reports.

One understands that this due care and caution was once again diluted when A.B.Vajpayee was the Prime Minister. It was said that he preferred to leave even sensitive operational matters to Brajesh Mishra, his Principal Secretary and National Security Adviser, to handle. One was also given to understand that no other head of the PMO had as much access to information about sensitive operational matters as Mishra had during his tenure. It must be said to his credit that there was no leakage. He carefully protected the operational secrecy of the R&AW.

During the tenure of V.P. Singh, for the first time since 1947, an exercise was undertaken to examine whether the time had come to set up a Parliamentary Oversight Committee to monitor the functioning of the intelligence agencies. The suggestion for setting up such a committee came from Jaswant Singh of the BJP. The enquiry into the Watergate scandal in the US brought to light serious instances of the misuse of the intelligence machinery by President Richard Nixon for partisan political purposes and for covering up his illegal acts. This led to comprehensive reforms for giving the two Houses of the Congress certain powers to oversee the functioning of the intelligence agencies. These powers were meant to enable the Congress not only to prevent the misuse of the agencies by the chief executive for partisan political purposes, but also to scrutinize their performance on a continuous basis in order to see whether they were fulfilling the national security purposes for which they were set up.

Many other countries, including Israel —where, initially, there was considerable resistance to the idea—have since emulated the

US model of intelligence oversight by the Parliament. In certain countries such as the US, the Congress or the Parliament itself sets up such oversight committees without the chief executive having any say in their constitution. In certain other countries such as the UK, the chief executive nominates the oversight committee in consultation with the leaders of the parties represented in the Parliament.

Today, India is one of the very few democratic countries in the world where the chief executive continues to be exclusively responsible for the functioning of the intelligence agencies, with the two Houses of the Parliament having no powers of oversight. In the case of the other Ministries and Departments of the Government of India, there are parliamentary committees with limited powers of oversight, but not in the case of the intelligence agencies. The general impression in the public is that the Indian intelligence officers resist the idea of parliamentary oversight lest their operational secrecy be affected. This is not so. At least not in the R&AW, when I was in service. Many of us were opposed to parliamentary oversight in operational matters, but were in favour of oversight in administrative matters such as recruitment, training, promotions, non-operational expenditure, travel etc. Some of us also favoured a limited parliamentary monitoring of the performance of the agencies in order to subject their intelligence production and analysis capabilities to a limited external audit.

Such an oversight has many advantages. It removes wrong impressions in the minds of the parliamentarians and the public about the agencies. It prevents instances of favouritism, nepotism and corruption in the agencies. It deters any temptation on the part of the chief executive to misuse the agencies for partisan political purposes. It ensures that the agencies effectively perform the national security tasks for which they were set up.

Unfortunately, in India, the resistance to any move towards parliamentary oversight has often come more from the political leadership than from the intelligence officers. This is due to a fear in the minds of the political leaders that parliamentary oversight would dilute their control over the intelligence agencies and come in the way of their misusing the agencies for partisan political purposes.

When V.P.Singh asked Vinod Pandey to examine the advisability of setting up a parliamentary intelligence oversight committee as suggested by Jaswant Singh, Pandey called for the views of the IB and the R&AW. G.S.Bajpai, who was then the chief of the R&AW, called a meeting of his senior officers to discuss this. All the officers without exception favoured the idea. I do not know what recommendation was ultimately made by Bajpai to Pandey. Nor do I know what was the view of the IB. However, the end result of this exercise was zilch. V.P.Singh started facing difficulties from his partners in the National Front coalition and lost his interest in any reform in the system of intelligence oversight.

The time has come to revive this issue once again. Public opinion should force the political leadership to set up an intelligence oversight mechanism.In the absence of such an oversight, the intelligence agencies continue to be judges of their own performance and probity. Gaps in their performance as was alleged to be the case by the Army during the Kargil conflict with Pakistan in 1999 or shortcomings in their probity as seen from the case of Rabinder Singh, the CIA's mole, come to notice only when   a major national security set-back takes place. How indifferent is the political leadership to the vital task of improving the performance and probity of the agencies would be evident from the fact that the Parliament has not so far found the time or energy to debate the lessons of the Kargil conflict and the Rabindra Singh case. It is a crying shame. There is an old cliché— every country gets the intelligence agencies it deserves. It is very true of India.

Under V.P.Singh, the Army once again raised the issue of allowing it to run clandestine source operations from the Indian diplomatic missions abroad. After carefully examining the matter, he reiterated the original decision of Indira Gandhi that the Army should collect only tactical military intelligence through trans-border sources and should not run any clandestine operation outside the country. However, he removed the restrictions imposed by his predecessors on the depth upto which it could run trans-border source operations from the Indian territory.

A.K.Verma retired as the chief of the R&AW on May 31,1990, after a very successful three-year tenure, which saw the R&AW regain the operational élan, which it used to have under Kao after it was formed in 1968. He encouraged young officers with original ideas. To quote a famous phrase of the CIA, Verma was a risk taker, but not a risk seeker. He liked officers who showed initiative and original thinking and had the courage to take risks without being adventuristic. He could not stand mediocre officers in the R&AW and had a healthy contempt for the officers of the MEA, which often earned him their enemity.He was not bothered so long as he was able to produce results and enjoyed the confidence of the Prime Minister. Unfortunately, under him, the relations with the IB and the DGMI were not as cordial as they should have been. This came in the way of effective co-ordination in the functioning of the agencies. Rajiv Gandhi, who apparently sensed this, suggested a novel idea to improve co-ordination. He wanted that an officer of the R&AW should function as one of the staff officers of the DIB and vice versa. He wanted a similar arrangement with the DGMI. Verma agreed to give it a try, but there was opposition from the IB and the DGMI. It was, therefore, a non-starter.

Verma was succeeded by G.S.Bajpai, an IPS officer of the Uttar Pradesh cadre, who had served in the IB before moving over to the R&AW after it was formed in 1968. He had a distinguished service in Geneva and New York as the head of the R&AW stations there. He had also served for many years in the Ministry of External Affairs as the head of the set-up, which was responsible, inter alia, for physical security in the Ministry as well as in the Indian diplomatic missions abroad. He played a very important role, along with Romesh Bhandari, then Secretary dealing with West Asia in the MEA, in persuading the Government of the United Arab Emirates, to deport to India a group of Khalistani hijackers and in bringing them to India.

Before his appointment as the head of the R&AW, he had also served as the Chairman of the Joint Intelligence Committee (JIC) of the Government of India and as Secretary (Security). As Secretary (Security), he was responsible for co-ordinating security

arrangements for V.P.Singh. He served as the head of the R&AW
under V.P.Singh as well as his successor Chandra Shekhar for 14
months before his superannuation on July 31,1991. He managed
to establish an excellent relationship with both of them and enjoyed
their confidence.

There was a tremendous improvement in man management when
he was the chief. Man management was one of the weak links in
the R&AW ever since its formation in 1968. All the chiefs before
Bajpai, including Kao, created an elitist culture. They tended to live
in an ivory tower of their own, with their interactions confined to
the officer class. They hardly interacted personally with the junior
staff in the various cadres. They remained distant figures for them.
While I was in service, Bajpai was the first and last chief, who broke
this elitist culture, came out of the ivory tower and made himself
easily accessible to all members of the staff from the bottom to the
top. The deteriorating situation in J&K and other crisis spots such
as Pakistan and Afghanistan kept him extremely busy. Despite this,
he managed to find the time to attend to the grievances and day-
to-day problems of the staff. Under him, for the first time in the
history of the organization, the staff morale was quite high. After
my retirement, I had heard serving officers say that after Bajpai,
the only other chief, who took equal interest in the problems of the
staff and made himself easily accessible to them was A.S.Dulat, an
officer of the IB, who headed the R&AW from the end of 1999 to the
beginning of 2001.

The staff in an intelligence organization—whatever be their cadre
or juniority or seniority—function in a very difficult atmosphere, with
very little contact with the public and with no access to organizations
such as the Union Public Service Commission, the Central Vigilance
Commission etc for ventilating their grievances. If the head of the
organization does not seek them out,listen to their problems and help
them out, nobody else would. It is unfortunate that in the nearly 40
years of the existence of the organization, only two chiefs succeeded
in creating in the minds of all the members of the staff a feeling
of being wanted and valued. During the tenure of Bajpai, instances

of anonymous complaints and ventilation of grievances and anger through the columns of the media, which have become the bane of the organization, sharply came down. Another positive contribution of Bajpai was the improvement in the relations with the IB and the DGMI as well as with the MEA, the MOD and the MHA, which are the main consumers of the products of the R&AW.

When Bajpai took over, the relations of Benazir Bhutto, the then Prime Minister of Pakistan, with her Army and the ISI had started deteriorating. The Army and the ISI had started a hush-hush campaign against her, alleging that she was an agent of the R&AW and had betrayed the Khalistan movement by stopping assistance to it. There were serious tensions between her and Nawaz Sharif, the then Chief Minister of Punjab, who had become the blue-eyed boy of the Army and the ISI. The allegations against her by Gen.Mirza Aslam Beg, the then Chief of the Army Staff (COAS), and Hamid Gul put her in a defensive position. To get over the resulting embarrassment, she stepped up the ISI's assistance to the jihadi terrorists in J&K and adopted a highly combative stance against the Government of India on the Kashmir issue.However, her actions could not help her and she was sacked as the Prime Minister by Ghulam Ishaq Khan, the then President, in August,1990, at the behest of Gen.Beg and Hamid Gul. Nawaz Sharif, who took over as the Prime Minister after the elections that followed her dismissal, gave the ISI a free hand in J&K for intensifying its proxy war against India.

As a result, the initial months of Bajpai as the chief kept him almost totally preoccupied with improving the collection of intelligence regarding the activities of the ISI in J&K and other parts of India and maintaining the tempo of the activities of the covert action division of the R&AW. He strengthened the R&AW's network with various segments of Pakistan's political class as well as civil society, which were well disposed towards India. However, the deteriorating situation in J&K did not receive the full-time attention of V.P.Singh, who became more preoccupied with countering internal threats to his position in his National Front Coalition than with dealing with the increased threat from Pakistan and its ISI in J&K. The kind of attention, which he paid to the situation in J&K during his initial months as the Prime Minister when there was no major internal political challenge to him, was lacking in the second half of his tenure. If despite this, the situation in J&K did not get out of control, the credit for this should largely go to the security forces and the intelligence agencies. They had to deal with the situation largely on their own without much of a guidance and leadership from the Prime Minister of the day.

Leadership and guidance improved considerably under Chandra Shekhar, who succeeded V.P.Singh as the Prime Minister on November 10,1990, with the support of the Congress (I). Very soon after taking over, he became the darling of the bureaucracy––particularly in the intelligence agencies. He was very accessible to the heads of the intelligence agencies and the security forces and very clear-minded with no confusion in his mind as to how to deal with national security issues. He valued the advice of the intelligence chiefs and was quick and bold in taking decisions. He held Bajpai in very great esteem and sought his advice without hesitation on all important national security issues.

As Chandra Shekhar took over as the Prime Minister, the events in the Gulf, in the wake of the August,1990, Iraqi occupation of Kuwait, moved towards a war.The R&AW did not have much of a role to play in the evacuation of the Indian citizens affected by the Iraqi invasion of Kuwait. This was creditably handled by Rattan Sehgal of the IB, who was then posted as Joint Secretary in the MEA.

The R&AW did come into the picture in an exercise to examine the implications of a Gulf war on India's energy security. Various stand-by options were examined. The R&AW remained in touch with its counterparts in the Chinese intelligence community for an exchange of ideas on this subject. A Minister in the Cabinet of Chandra Shekhar, who claimed to have access to the Saddam Hussein Government in Iraq, reported an offer by Saddam Hussein to meet India's energy requirements. As suggested by this Minister, Chandra Shekhar deputed a senior official of the R&AW for preliminary talks with a personal emissary of Saddam. This proved to be an embarrassing non-starter. There were reasons to doubt the credibility of the claims made by this Minister regarding his access to the Iraqi leadership.

As preparations for the liberation of Kuwait by an American-led coalition gathered momentum and as the war broke out, the Government of India secretly agreed to provide re-fuelling facilities for American planes from its Pacific Command flying to the Gulf with logistics-related supplies. This was called off after an Indian newspaper broke the story with a photograph of an American plane in an Indian airfield. During the course of the war, Chandra Shekhar visited the R&AW headquarters for the first time and addressed the senior officers extempore on India's foreign policy, with special reference to the Gulf war. He made a tremendous impression on the officers by the lucidity of his presentation and command of facts and by the forthrightness with which he answered questions from the officers.

Just before the outbreak of the Gulf war, a delegation of the Chinese external intelligence headed by its No.2 had visited India at the invitation of the R&AW for one of the periodic discussions between the two agencies on the regional situation. Chandra Shekhar had lunch with the members of the delegation and their interlocutors from the R&AW in a guest house of the R&AW. Before his meeting with them, he had been briefed by the R&AW on the origin and evolution of this liaison relationship. Chandra Shekhar appeared to have been highly impressed by the initiative taken by Kao for establishing this relationship and by the way it had been taken forward by Saxena and his successors.

After the Gulf war was over, Bajpai visited China at the invitation of the chief of the Chinese external intelligence. His wife had accompanied him. He also took me along as his staff officer. Apart from talks with the chief and other senior officials of the Chinese intelligence, Bajpai's engagements in China also included a courtesy call on Li Peng, the then Chinese Prime Minister. Bajpai and his wife made a tremendous impact on the Chinese leaders and officials.Both of them had a cordial, open and warm-hearted way of interacting with people. Bajpai's natural cordiality and personal warmth stood the R&AW in good stead in its liaison relationships with foreign agencies as well as in its relationships with other departments of the Government of India. He was a bridge-builder and not a bridge-breaker. The R&AW needs more such officers.

In Afghanistan, despite the withdrawal of the Soviet troops, the Government of President Najibullah, which was very friendly to India, proved surprisingly stable. In fact, in the beginning of 1989, Najibullah's troops beat back an attempt by a combined force of the Afghan Mujahideen, the Arab followers of Osama bin Laden and Pakistani ex-servicemen to capture an Afghan Army post at Jalalabad. Despite being outnumbered and outgunned, the Afghan Army post repulsed the invaders after inflicting heavy casualties on them.

Even before this fiasco, there were reports of differences in the camp of the Mujahideen and growing resentment over the way the ISI tried to manipulate them to promote Pakistan's agenda in Afghanistan. These differences deepened after this fiasco. One of the highly respected Mujahideen leaders, who was a well-wisher of India, sought a meeting with the head of the R&AW in London. After taking Chandra Shekhar's permission, Bajpai flew to London, met him and immediately returned to Delhi. This was the beginning of our contacts with those Mujahideen leaders, who were unhappy with what they looked upon as the insidious role of the ISI in Afghanistan.

The British intelligence, which had apparently kept the Afghan Mujahideen leader under surveillance, came to know of Bajpai's secret meeting with him. After he had retired, they strongly expressed their unhappiness over this meeting without mentioning Bajpai by name. Their unhappiness was not over the meeting itself, but over their not being informed in advance about it. This is an example of the double standards followed by the Western intelligence agencies. Their officers in New Delhi used to hold secret meetings with critics of Najibullah in Indian territory without informing the R&AW about it. In fact, they once secretly contacted Rashid Dostum, the Afghan Uzbeck leader, when he had come to Delhi for a medical check-up in a hospital of the Indian Army and persuaded him to desert with his troops from Najibullah's army. It was this desertion which brought down Najibullah in April,1992 They never used to inform the IB or the R&AW about their secret meetings with the critics of Najibullah in order to bring him down, but the British made a song and dance when Bajpai met an anti-Pakistan Mujahideen leader in London. We replied to them suitably and there the matter ended.

Rajiv Gandhi had been closely monitoring the handling of the foreign policy by the Chandra Shekhar Government. Vidya Charan Shukla, the Foreign Minister in the new Government, was previously in the Congress (I). Reportedly through Shukla, Rajiv Gandhi had sent a message to Chandra Shekhar regarding the previous dialogue between the R&AW and the ISI organized by former Crown Prince Hassan of Jordan and the progress made during the discussions on the Siachen issue. He suggested that this dialogue should be resumed to carry forward the discussions on terrorism and the Siachen issue. Chandra Shekhar accepted his suggestion and had a message sent to Nawaz Sharif, the then Prime Minister of Pakistan, whom he had met during the SAARC summit at Male in the Maldives in December,1990. Nawaz Sharif replied through one of the officers in the Pakistani High Commission in New Delhi that there were no papers on the subject in the ISI and that, on being contacted, Hamid Gul denied having met Verma to discuss any issue. From its files, the R&AW prepared a summary of the discussions at the two meetings held by Verma with Gul. Chandra Shekhar sent this to Nawaz Sharif. He also wrote that if the latter had any doubts in his mind because of Gul's denial, he could check up with Hassan, who had organized the dialogue.

Nawaz Sharif agreed to the proposal and Bajpai and Lt.Gen.Assad Durrani, the then DG of the ISI, met in a hotel in Singapore in the beginning of 1991 to resume the dialogue. Durrani insisted that the meeting should be held in a hotel to be selected by the Pakistani authorities and that the two chiefs should stay in the same hotel. He also insisted that the discussions would be held in his room and not in Bajpai's room. It was apparent that he wanted to prevent the

R&AW from secretly recording the discussions while, at the same time, recording them himself. Despite this, the R&AW agreed to both the suggestions. There was hardly any useful discussion. He kept alleging that the R&AW was trying to instigate the Sindhi nationalists. At the same time, he denied that Pakistan was helping the Khalistani terrorists in Punjab and the jihadi terrorists in J&K. Unlike Gul, he was avoiding any substantive discussions on the Siachen issue. It was a dialogue of the deaf. Thereafter, this exercise was called off. The impression one had was that whereas Gul was highly professional and self-confident, Durrani was hardly professional and lacked self-confidence.

In September,2006, Prime Minister Manmohan Singh and President Pervez Musharraf of Pakistan had discussed the possibility of bilateral co-operation in counter-terrorism during their meeting in the margin of the summit of Non-aligned nations at Havana. They agreed to set up a Joint Counter-Terrorism Mechanism to facilitate exchange of intelligence to prevent acts of terrorism and mutual legal assistance to facilitate investigation into acts of terrorism. The first meeting of this mechanism was held at Islamabad on March 6 and 7,2007.

I have been strongly critical of this mechanism for various reasons. Its basic premise that India and Pakistan are common victims of jihadi terrorism is wrong. India has been a victim of jihadi organizations sponsored by the ISI to achieve its strategic objective of changing the status quo in J&K and damaging the Indian economy. Pakistan has been a victim of anti-Shia sectarian terrorism by organizations which want the Shias to be declared non-Muslims and Pakistan to be proclaimed a Sunni State. These organizations are not sponsored by the ISI and they are not active in India. Pakistan has also been a victim of Al Qaeda because of its perceived pro-US policies. The pan-Islamic objective of Al Qaeda of creating an Islamic Caliphate has no support so far in the Indian Muslim community.

Pakistan is not going to sincerely co-operate with us in dealing with terrorist organizations, which are of its own creation. A charade of co-operation will be counter-productive and in the long run will create more bitterness in the bilateral relations. What Pakistan has been using against us is old or classical terrorism, which is often used by States as a political and strategic weapon against adversaries. There is always a certain degree of politicization in respect of classical terrorism, which stands in the way of bilateral co-operation. The Western intelligence agencies were not co-operating with us against Khalistani terrorism till the Kanishka tragedy of June,1985. They were disinclined to co-operate with us against jihadi terrorism till the kidnapping of some Western tourists by the Al Faran in J&K in 1995. If co-operation against classical terrorism is so difficult even among friendly nations, one could imagine the kind of difficulties that would arise between adversaries.

But there are certain post-9/11 mutations of terrorism, where there is no question of politicization. Terrorism experts refer to them as New Terrorism. There are three of them—maritime terrorism, terrorism directed at energy security and terrorism involving Weapons of Mass Destruction (WMD). If one of these acts of new terrorism takes place in India or Pakistan, both of them will equally suffer the consequences. There could be large human casualties, economic and environmental damage. Organizations such as Al Qaeda, which presently advocate new terrorism and are trying to acquire the required capability, pose a common threat to India as well as Pakistan. Any co-operation between India and Pakistan, to be meaningful, has to start with joint action against new terrorism, which could be made to work, and not against old terrorism, which would not work — at least in the short term.

After my retirement, I have been writing off and on on the need for a liaison networking between the R&AW and the ISI. This is different from a Joint Counter-Terrorism Mechanism. A liaison networking enables the chiefs and senior officers of intelligence agencies of two countries—whether friend or foe— to get to know and measure each other in flesh and blood over a drink or a meal instead of knowing of each other only through the media. This itself is a confidence-building measure. They meet each other periodically without a formal agenda and without anybody else being present and compare notes on developments of common interest. Once a reasonable mutual comfort level is established they start slowly moving into specifics.

Since 1947, we have been having such a liaison relationship with the intelligence agencies of all Commonwealth countries, but not with those of Pakistan. We have maintained a liaison relationship with the intelligence agencies of China, at the best of times as well as at the worst of times. When Rajiv Gandhi was the Prime Minister, he even directed the R&AW to set up, with the prior approval of the leadership of the African National Congress, a liaison relationship with the intelligence agencies of the apartheid regime in South Africa in order to enable India to play a role in bringing about an early and smooth end to apartheid. Though it is almost 60 years since India and Pakistan became independent, neither country has thought in terms of setting up an intelligence liaison relationship. It is time to start thinking of it. In the long term, it will be more meaningful than a Joint Counter-Terrorism Mechanism.

CHAPTER XVII

The Assassination Of Rajiv Gandhi

A few months after I had retired and settled down in Chennai, the late S.A.Subbiah, who had succeeded me in Geneva and subsequently became the head of the Sri Lanka division in the headquarters, rang me up from Delhi to say that he was coming to Chennai specially to meet me to discuss about the LTTE. I told him I would meet him in the R&AW guest house where he had planned to stay.

After his arrival, I went to the guest house. He told me: "Sir, I have come to meet you for two reasons. First, I wanted to thank you for saving the reputation of the organization. The R&AW has come out largely unscathed from the enquiry held by the one-man enquiry commission of retired Chief Justice J.S.Verma on the security failures, which enabled the LTTE to kill Rajiv Gandhi. There has been all-round appreciation of your assessment sent to Vinod Pandey after V.P.Singh took over as the Prime Minister on likely threats to Rajiv Gandhi's security. In your assessment, you had said that there was a greater threat to the security of Rajiv Gandhi as the Leader of the Opposition than to the security of V.P.Singh as the Prime Minister. You had also stated that the main threats to Rajiv Gandhi would be from the Khalistani terrorists in the North and from the Sri Lankan Tamil terrorist organizations in the South. Subsequently, at inter-departmental meetings to discuss the security arrangements for Rajiv Gandhi as the Leader of the Opposition, you had strongly pleaded for the continuance of the security cover of the Special Protection Group (SPG) to him. Sir, the second reason I wanted to meet you was to find out who was the source who told you that there was a threat to Rajiv Gandhi's security from the Sri Lankan Tamil terrorist organizations. We notice that you had been saying this even when Rajiv Gandhi was the Prime Minister. We wanted to re-establish contact with your source, who seems to be very well-informed, but I could not find in the files left by you any source report on this subject"

I told Subbiah that my repeated cautions on the likelihood of a threat to the life of Rajiv Gandhi from the Sri Lankan Tamil terrorist organizations were not based on any source report. It was my assessment based on what I had heard after I returned from Geneva in 1988 about the deep feelings of humiliation and anger entertained by some of these organizations—particularly by the LTTE and its leader Prabakaran—over the way they were treated by Rajiv Gandhi and his advisers after the conclusion of the Indo-Sri Lanka Peace Accord of 1987. They also nursed strong grievances over the alleged violations of the human rights of the Sri Lankan Tamils by the Indian Peace-Keeping Force sent to Sri Lanka to restore peace in the Tamil areas.

I also told Subbiah that my foreboading was also influenced by the warnings which I was getting repeatedly from the Chennai office of the R&AW regarding the likelihood of a threat to Rajiv Gandhi, even when he was the Prime Minster, from the Sri Lankan Tamils. The Chennai office of the R&AW was then headed by an outstanding and low-profile IPS officer of the Karnataka cadre. Every time Rajiv Gandhi as the Prime Minister went to the South, this officer used to ring me up to say that the SPG should be alert to the possibility of a threat to his life from the Sri Lankan Tamils.

I told Subbiah that my problem was that everybody in Delhi—in the intelligence community, in the JIC, in the MHA, in the Army headquarters, in the MEA and in the PMO—had convinced themselves that the Sri Lankan Tamils would never harm Rajiv Gandhi because he and his mother had done more to help them than any other Indian leader. All my cautions—based on my own assessment and on that of the then head of the R&AW's Chennai office— were treated with skepticism.

Even shortly after the assassination of Rajiv Gandhi, at a meeting of concerned officers, I was asked for my views as to who might have killed him. Without a moment's hesitation, I replied "LTTE". My view was dismissed. The prevailing view was that he had fallen a tragic victim to the factional politics in the Tamil Nadu Congress (I) or that he must have been killed by extremist elements of Tamil Nadu. It was only after a video-recording showing the suicide bomber and the blast recorded by a photographer, hired by the LTTE that was recovered, everybody accepted that it was the LTTE which had assassinated him.

The Government of India had appointed two enquiry commissions in the wake of the assassination of Rajiv Gandhi. The first Commission constituted by retired Chief Justice J.S.Verma was asked to go into the intelligence and physical security lapses which were responsible for the assassination. The second, constituted by retired Justice M.C.Jain, was asked to go into the conspiracy aspect. The Verma Commission kept itself strictly confined to its terms of reference and carried out a thorough enquiry with a laser-sharp focus into the acts of commission and omission of the intelligence and security agencies, which contributed to the assassination.

The Jain Commission lost focus and sought to go into matters, which had little relevance to the issue of an LTTE conspiracy. As a result, it took a very long time to complete its enquiries and the Government had to give it one extension after another. It even sought to go into the wisdom of the entire Sri Lanka policy of the Government, the operational policies of the R&AW and the IB etc. This caused considerable embarrassment to the Narasimha Rao Government at various stages.

It had to face a dilemma— if it agreed to the course of action of the Commission and placed before it all the operational files demanded by it, the operational security of the intelligence agencies would have been diluted. If it did not agree to it, there might have been allegations of a cover-up by the Government and its intelligence agencies. Ultimately, the intelligence agencies let him have access to whatever files he wanted to see and whatever information he wanted, even if, in their view, those were not relevant to his terms of reference. They did this in order not to give room for any suspicion. Despite all the time taken and all the access given to him, the Commission's report left much to be desired. As had happened during the enquiry into the assassination of Indira Gandhi, the enquiry into the assassination of Rajiv Gandhi too planted many needles of suspicion, without being able to remove any of the suspicions. Without throwing light to remove the areas of darkness surrounding the two tragic assassinations, the two enquiries only added to the darkness.

The CBI itself, under the brilliant leadership of Vijay Karan, S.K. Dutta and D.R.Karthikeyan and with the equally brilliant co-operation of the late Subbiah, carried out a thorough investigation of the LTTE's plot to kill Rajiv Gandhi, its successful execution , the identities of those involved—whether in Sri Lanka or India or elsewhere— and their respective roles. Many of those involved—the principal killers— committed suicide after the assassination through a suicide bomber and thereby evaded arrest and prosecution. Many others, who did not or could not commit suicide, were identified, arrested and prosecuted. The case ended in their conviction. Prabakaran and others, who conceived and orchestrated the conspiracy from their headquarters in the Northern Province of Sri Lanka, have managed to escape the reach of the law so far.

Apart from the investigation of the assassination and the related conspiracy, another important aspect was the identification of the acts of commission and omission by the political leadership of the day, the intelligence agencies and those responsible for physical security which resulted in the assassination of Rajiv Gandhi. Any objective examination of the circumstances, which led to his assassination, would have clearly brought out that Rajiv Gandhi was a tragic victim of the politicization of his physical security by the Government of V.P.Singh and its senior officers, the failure of the Chandra Shekhar Government to rectify the situation, the failure of the intelligence agencies to closely monitor the activities of the LTTE from the point of view of his security, the shocking negligence of the Tamil Nadu Police and the total lack of co-ordination among the agencies responsible for his protection.

So long as he was the Prime Minister, the SPG, which was set up after the assassination of Indira Gandhi, was responsible for the protection of Rajiv Gandhi and his family. It was patterned after the US Secret Service, which is responsible for the protection of the US President and his family. The US Secret Service also exercises some responsibilities for the protection of all past Presidents and their families. When the SPG Act was passed by the Parliament, it was given the responsibility only for the protection of the Prime Minister and his family. Since it was created, it had developed expertise in all matters relating to the PM's security— close proximity protection, access control, anti-explosives checks, advance examination of the places to be visited by the Prime Minister etc. It had also developed a well-tested drill for co-ordination with other agencies at the Centre and with the Police of the State to be visited by the Prime Minister. The SPG was in a position to neutralize any threat arising as a result of acts of possible negligence by the State Police. The Prime Minister virtually enjoyed two layers of protection—one by the State Police and the other by the SPG. There was thus an in-built fail-safe mechanism. Its work was supervised continuously by a senior officer of the rank of Secretary designated as Secretary (Security).

Once Rajiv Gandhi ceased to be the Prime Minister after his party lost the elections in November, 1989, and became the Leader of the Opposition, he was no longer entitled to protection by the SPG. However, he continued to be the most threatened political leader of the country and the threat to his security was much higher than that to even V.P.Singh, the new Prime Minister. Even though Rajiv Gandhi himself, who was a proud man, never raised the issue of his security, his party was greatly concerned over it and repeatedly took it up with the PMO and the Cabinet Secretary as well as with V.P.Singh himself. The Government made the pretense of doing everything necessary and possible for the protection of Rajiv Gandhi—keeping in view the suggestions of the Congress (I)— without taking the one step that would have assured his protection—namely, amending the SPG Act to make the SPG responsible for the protection of past Prime

Ministers too. Congress (I) would have definitely supported such an amendment. For reasons, which were not clear to me, the V.P.Singh Government avoided doing this. The SPG Act was amended after the assassination of Rajiv Gandhi to make the SPG responsible for the protection of all past Prime Ministers too and their families. Had this been done before his assassination, this great tragedy could have been averted.

It was my view that even if there was any political difficulty in having the SPG Act amended, ways could be found to continue to extend the SPG protection to him through an executive decision of the Prime Minister. The only problem that would have arisen was with the Finance, which might not have approved the expenditure incurred on his protection by the SPG since he was legally not entitled to it. This difficulty could have been got over by meeting the expenditure out of the operational funds of the intelligence agencies. I knew of instances where special physical security had been provided to even private persons, who were not in the Government, by meeting the expenditure out of the operational funds of the intelligence agencies. The Government could have easily extended this gesture to Rajiv Gandhi.

At every stage, attempts were made to embarrass Rajiv Gandhi and the Congress (I). When his party urged that the SPG protection be extended to him, it was told that while this would not be possible, the Government could transfer to the Delhi Police SPG officers in whom he had personal confidence so that they could continue to provide close-proximity protection to him. The whole thing was mischievously made to appear by the V.P.Singh Government as a question of personal loyalty to Rajiv Gandhi and not of institutional competence. The Congress (I) wanted SPG protection for Rajiv Gandhi not because he liked some SPG officers, but because it had better expertise and competence than the Police.

Since he was no longer entitled to the use of Government aircraft, he started traveling by the flights of the Indian Airlines, but attempts were made to deny him even the courtesy of traveling upto the tarmac in his car and directly getting into the aircraft. At the meetings of

the co-ordination committee, which I used to attend on behalf of
the R&AW, the requests and concerns of the Congress (I) regarding
his security were treated more with sarcasm than seriousness.
Surprisingly, matters were not set right when Chandra Shekhar
succeeded V.P.Singh as the Prime Minister. He was dependent on
the parliamentary support of the Congress (I) for remaining in
office and would have done whatever the Congress (I) wanted him
to do. But, the Congress (I) did not raise with him the question of
the inadequacy of the security provided to Rajiv Gandhi with the
same persistence with which it took up the issue with V.P.Singh.

The intelligence agencies knew that Rajiv Gandhi was top on the
hit list of the Khalistani terrorists. Even when Rajiv Gandhi was the
Prime Minister, the R&AW had drawn attention to the likelihood
of a threat to his security from the Sri Lankan Tamil extremist
organizations. It repeated this warning after he became the Leader
of the Opposition. These warnings did not receive the attention
they deserved because they were based on assessments and not on
specific intelligence. When there is such an assessment indicating
the likelihood of a threat to a VVIP, the intelligence agencies are
expected to initiate specific operations through their sources and
through technical means to look for concrete indicators of such
a threat. No such action was taken because everybody presumed-
disastrously as it turned out— that, while the LTTE and other Sri
Lankan Tamil organizations might indulge in acts of terrorism
against each other in Indian territory, they would not indulge in acts
of terrorism against any Indian leader. The only human intelligence
report of some relevance came from the German intelligence a few
months before the assassination stating that a Sri Lankan Tamil living
in Germany had been visiting Chennai and that he was reputed
to be an expert in explosives. Unfortunately, this was not properly
enquired into by the IB. They maintained that their enquiries did
not indicate that he was an explosives expert. The entire focus of the
intelligence coverage of the LTTE was on its activities in Sri Lanka,
its gun-running etc. There was no specific focus on likely threats to
Rajiv Gandhi's security from it.

After the assassination, the Monitoring Division of the R&AW, energized by Subbiah, did outstanding work in tracking down the movements of those involved in the conspiracy to kill Rajiv Gandhi on an hour-to-hour basis, but the Monitoring Division too had failed to detect the conspiracy to kill Rajiv Gandhi before the tragedy took place. The interceptions made after the assassination and the repeated breaking of the LTTE's code by the code-breakers of the R&AW indicated that the LTTE's communications security was poor. If it was poor after the assassination, it was most likely that it was poor before it too. The monitoring was not as systematic before the assassination as it was after it.

After my retirement, while I was going through the report of the Jain Commission, it was evident that the IB had better interception capability with regard to the LTTE than the R&AW, which had a better code-breaking capability than the IB. The two would not tell each other of their respective capabilities and would not pool their capabilities to produce results. It was evident from the incident of clandestine air-dropping of arms and ammunition by an unidentified organization at Purulia in 1995 and from the Kargil military conflict with Pakistan in 1999 that the intelligence agencies continue to keep each other in the dark about their respective capabilities and avoid pooling them.

In the case of the Purulia air-drop by unidentified elements, the R&AW did not tell the IB that the information about the planned air-drop came from the MI-5, which, in turn, got it from the pilot of the plane hired by the extremists. He was a retired pilot of the British Air Force and had reportedly alerted the MI-5 through the British Defence Ministry the moment the extremists tried to hire him as a pilot. The R&AW could have shared all the details with the IB and the two could have mounted a joint operation in collaboration with the pilot to lay a trap on the ground. This was apparently not done.

In the case of the Kargil conflict, the moment the DIB reported about unusual happenings in Pakistan's Northern Areas, the R&AW could have taken the initiative for proposing a joint operation by the Aviation Research Centre (ARC), the IB and the Directorate-

General of Military Intelligence (DGMI) for an aerial surveillance of the areas indicated by the IB. This does not seem to have been done.Sharing of knowledge of each other's capabilities—particularly in respect of intelligence collection— and joint or co-ordinated exploitation of these capabilities should be the norm if we have to avoid such surprises.

The LTTE succeeded in blowing up Rajiv Gandhi by taking advantage of the negligence and weak supervision of the IB and the Tamil Nadu Police. This would show that those responsible for physical security for our leaders had failed to learn the right lessons from the assassination of Indira Gandhi. The same casualness, the same lack of attention to detail, the same inadequate supervision, which cost Indira Gandhi her life, cost the life of her son too. Since 1947, no other Prime Minister had taken more interest in improving our intelligence and security agencies and done more to improve their conditions of service than Indira Gandhi and Rajiv Gandhi. What a shocking tragedy that these agencies, which owed them so much, so miserably failed to protect them. Every officer, who had served in our agencies at that time—in whatever capacity— should hang his or her head in shame. We failed them.

After the assassination of Rajiv Gandhi, Chandra Shekhar took up the stand that it was almost impossible to protect a VIP from suicide terrorists. This is totally wrong. It is very difficult to protect a soft target such as a shopping area or the crowd in a public place from a suicide terrorist or, for that matter, even from a terrorist, who does not indulge in suicide terrorism. But a hard target such as a VVIP or a VIP can be protected from a suicide terrorist through effective ant-explosive check and access control. Rajiv Gandhi was killed because the IB and the Tamil Nadu Police had failed to ensure an effective anti-explosive check and access control.

It was reported that Justice J.S.Verma, who had enquired into the failures of the intelligence and security agencies, felt that the officers of these agencies, who testified before him, were not very forthcoming. While forwarding his report to the Government, he, therefore, suggested that the officers, who had anything to do with

Rajiv Gandhi's physical security, should hold an introspection session in order to identify their own deficiencies and take action to correct them.The IB convened such an introspection session. All serving senior officers, who were responsible for the physical security of Rajiv Gandhi, and even those, who had retired after his assassination, attended it. I too.Nothing useful came of it. No one was prepared to admit that there were any deficiencies. I suggested that we should look into the way in which the report from the German intelligence about the visit of an LTTE sympathizer, reputed to be an explosive expert, to Chennai was verified before it was rejected. My suggestion was not accepted by the IB officers. It turned out to be more a self-justification than an introspection session. Our intelligence and security agencies rarely admit their faults and deficiencies. That is why we keep moving from one tragedy to another, from one disaster to another.

CHAPTER XVIII

Terrorism And Karma

The attitude of the Ministry of External Affairs (MEA) towards the R&AW was always marked by a mix of suspicion, jealousy and skepticism. The suspicion was particularly strong during the days when Kao was the head of the organization under Indira Gandhi. Many MEA officers, except T.N.Kaul, former Foreign Secretary, who was a close personal friend of Kao, suspected that the organization was seeking to become an alternative or a covert foreign service. This suspicion increased when the organization's overseas set-up expanded fast between 1972 and 1977. The exit of Kao in 1977 and the action taken by Morarji Desai to cut down its strength in the headquarters as well as abroad brought down this suspicion to a considerable extent, but it was never totally removed.

The jealousy was attributable to the access which the heads of the R&AW always enjoyed to the heads of Government or State of many countries through its extensive liaison network. In all countries of the world, the intelligence chiefs always enjoy the closest and the easiest access to their heads of government or State. The heads of the agencies having a liaison network among themselves are, therefore, able to provide to each other access to their respective heads of government or State. Over the years, the heads of the R&AW had close access to the heads of State or Government of the USSR/Russia, France,Iran, Egypt, the pre-1992 Afghanistan, Mauritius,Sri Lanka, the Maldives, Nepal, Bangladesh, Singapore and China.

As the Senior Adviser to Indira Gandhi in the Cabinet Secretariat, Kao had access even to the then US President Ronald Reagan through his Vice-President George Bush, whom he had known when the latter was the Director of the CIA for a short period in the 1970s. Other chiefs of the R&AW did not, however, have access to any US President, but they had access to the heads of State or Government of other countries. This access enabled the heads of the organization to play the role of the intermediaries of our Prime Minister on many occasions. The heads of many foreign Governments felt more comfortable dealing with their counterparts in India through the head of the R&AW than through the head of the Indian diplomatic missions in their countries or through the Foreign Secretary of the Government of India.

The skepticism related to the capability of the R&AW officers to collect sensitive human intelligence (HUMINT) of real value in foreign policy making and implementation. The heads of many Indian missions abroad—except in the neighbouring countries-– tended to remain unimpressed about the intelligence-collection capabilities of the R&AW officers posted in their missions. Often, many of them nursed doubts even about the intellectual honesty of some of the R&AW operatives. They thought they deceived the Government by feeding open source information as secret source information. The late R.D.Sathe, former Foreign Secretary, under whom I worked in Paris, used to say that many of the field operatives of the R&AW were nothing but glorified plagiarists.

However, in the case of the neighbouring countries, the Foreign Service officers admitted that the R&AW operatives had access to secret intelligence, but even in those countries, the R&AW's capability to provide advance warnings of looming critical situations was rated low. This was particularly so in Bangladesh. The organization's reputation in respect of that country took a nose-dive after the assassination of Sheikh Mujibur Rehman in 1975. The organization was also caught napping in Afghanistan when the Soviet troops intervened in 1979. In 1991, despite its close relations with the KGB, the Soviet intelligence agency, the R&AW failed to detect or sense the feeling of unease in the KGB over the direction in which Mikhail Gorbachev was taking the country.

Narasimha Rao, who had served as the Minister for External Affairs under Indira Gandhi and Rajiv Gandhi, shared some of these negative feelings —typical of the MEA— towards the R&AW. He had also served as the Home Minister under Indira Gandhi during her second tenure as the Prime Minister. He came to share some of the mixed feelings of the IB too towards the R&AW. He graded the professionalism of the IB higher than that of the R&AW. He was aware of the contribution of the R&AW to the successful outcome of Rajiv Gandhi's visit to China in 1988. Despite this, he came to office with some skepticism about the real capabilities of the R&AW. He was a born skeptic. He had become incorrigibly so as he grew up in life. He took not only the entire world, but often himself with a pinch of salt. It was, therefore, no wonder that his initial perceptions of the organization were far from positive.

When a new Prime Minister takes over, the head of the R&AW sends him detailed notes on the on-going sensitive operations of the organization, its capabilities and accomplishments. A few days after the submission of these notes to him, the chief meets the new Prime Minister to brief him personally on all the points covered in these notes and to answer any questions he may have. As it had happened with Rajiv Gandhi, V.P.Singh and Chandra Shekhar, in the case of Rao also, these notes and the personal briefings for the first time made him aware of what exactly was the role of the R&AW and how did it differ from the roles of the IB, the DGMI and the MEA. His attitude started changing in a direction more favourable to the organization.

This change was further facilitated by the developments in the USSR, which was on the verge of disintegration after the failure of the August,1991,anti-Gorbachev coup by the KGB. During the interregnum, when Boris Yetsin was moving to the top leadership of Russia, but had not yet replaced Gorbachev de jure, the head of the R&AW had visited Moscow at the invitation of Yevgeny Primakov, a good friend of India and the R&AW. He was appointed as the head of the KGB after the collapse of the coup. The KGB, like the IB of pre-1968 days, used to be responsible for internal and external intelligence. The Russian authorities decided to bifurcate it and create two separate agencies—one for internal intelligence and security and another for external intelligence. Primakov was appointed as the Director of the Foreign Intelligence Service.

Primakov arranged courtesy calls by the head of the R&AW on Gorbachev, who was already on the way out, and Boris Yeltsin, who was well set to take over as the President of Russia. The two leaders received him very warmly and asked him to convey to Rao that there would be no change in Moscow's close relations with India whatever be the changes in the political dispensation in Moscow. The R&AW chief cut short his stay in Russia, flew back to Delhi and reported personally to Rao the details of his warm meetings with Gorbachev and Yeltsin and their messages to Rao. No such message had come to Rao from the Russian leadership through the channels of the MEA. He was highly impressed.

This good impression was further strengthened in the subsequent months by two other developments. J.N.Dixit, the then Foreign Secretary, visited Moscow to meet officials and leaders of the new dispensation headed by President Yeltsin. He felt that his proposed visit was not being given the importance it deserved by the Russian authorities. He had heard of the good equation of the R&AW with Primakov. At his request, the R&AW sought the assistance of Primakov for arranging meetings for Dixit with important political leaders too. This was got done immediately by him. As the Indian High Commissioner in Colombo, Dixit used to be critical of the R&AW. This was because of his unconcealed jealousy over the ready access enjoyed by the then head of the R&AW to President Jayewardene. As the Foreign Secretary, he realized that the R&AW could be a valuable asset in the pursuit of our foreign policy if only the MEA knew how to use it.

The second development was the first visit of Yeltsin to India in January,1993, after taking over as the President of Russia. His visit was preceded by a secret visit to Delhi by Primakov as the guest of the R&AW. He also called on Rao for discussions. Primakov's discussions paved the way for the successful outcome of Yeltsin's visit.

Among other factors, which brought about a positive change in the attitude of Rao towards the R&AW was its role in internal security. Its liaison co-operation with the Western intelligence agencies brought in some excellent intelligence about the activities of the Khalistani terrorists. The Monitoring Division of the R&AW did excellent work in intercepting the telephone conversations of the Khalistani terrorists, who had kidnapped Liviu Radu, a Romanian diplomat posted in Delhi, with their counterparts in Lahore and Frankfurt, and of the terrorists, who had unsuccessfully tried to kill Mahenderjit Singh Bitta, the leader of the Youth Congress, through a remote-controlled car bomb, at New Delhi in August,1993. Their telephone conversations with their associates in Canada after the attempt were systematically intercepted by the Division.

Subbiah did outstanding work in detecting—through the interception of the LTTE's communications— an attempt by the LTTE to smuggle a consignment of arms and ammunition from Karachi to the LTTE-controlled areas in the Northern Province of Sri Lanka. These arms and ammunition had been given to the LTTE by Pakistan's Harkat-ul-Mujahideen (HUM), with the complicity of the ISI. The movement of the LTTE ship carrying this consignment was continuously monitored and it was ultimately intercepted by the Indian Coast Guard. However, before the ship could be captured, its crew set fire to it as a result of which it sank. While the arms and ammunition carried by it could not be seized, some of the crew members were captured alive. Their interrogation revealed the links between the LTTE and Pakistan. Kittu, a close confidant of Prabakaran, who was traveling by the ship, chose to commit suicide by going down the sea with the burning ship.

The contribution of the R&AW in this operation was highly appreciated by the then Cabinet Secretary and Rao. The Cabinet Secretary put up a detailed note on the operation to Rao with the following remark: "What a pity the details of this operation could not be revealed to the media!"

This is an operational dilemma faced by the intelligence agencies all over the world. For every instance of intelligence failure, which becomes public knowledge, there are innumerable instances of intelligence successes. Such successes help in preventing acts of terrorism and other threats to national security. They also often help in advancing the cause of the national interest—typical examples being the R&AW's role in the successful visit of Rajiv Gandhi to China in 1988 and in strengthening India's relations with Russia post-1991. These successes had to be kept a secret—at least during the time they were achieved. This was necessary to preserve the future effectiveness of the intelligence agencies' operational capabilities.

Without an adequate knowledge of such successes, the public, the media and the parliamentarians tend to judge the agencies only on the basis of their failures. In other countries, where there is the system of congressional or parliamentary oversight, the intelligence agencies are able to share at least some knowledge of their successes with the oversight committees. In India, there is no scope for this due to the absence of a system of parliamentary oversight.

As a result, the knowledge of the successes of the agencies—whether the R&AW or the IB— is confined to the Prime Minister, the Home Minister too in the case of the IB, the National Security Adviser, the Principal Secretary to the Prime Minister and the Cabinet Secretary. Thus, one often finds the Prime Minister of the day strongly defending the intelligence agencies against allegations of incompetence levelled by the media, other sections of the public and the parliamentarians. Unfortunately, their defence does not carry conviction in the absence of knowledge. After the Kargil conflict, Vajpayee strongly asserted on many occasions that there was no intelligence failure as alleged by the Army and the opposition. Others were not convinced by his assertions. This is an occupational hazard with which intelligence agencies have to live.

Many issues relating to the pros and cons of intelligence co-operation came up during the Prime Ministership of Rao. While encouraging clandestine intelligence co-operation with other countries in India's national interest, Indira Gandhi was more aware than any other political leader of India – before or after her – that such co-operation was a multi-edged sword. She realized that if not handled properly, it could damage our national security by facilitating the penetration efforts of foreign agencies in our territory. It could confuse our political leadership and induce it into wrong decisions or actions by the planting of disinformation on them through intelligence and other officers enjoying the confidence of the political leadership. If not effectively controlled and monitored, intelligence liaison could enable foreign agencies to play different government departments and agencies against one another.

She was particularly concerned over the dangers of US intelligence agencies taking advantage of their co-operation with their Indian counterparts to penetrate our setup. She was afraid that such penetration could soften our government servants occupying sensitive positions and make them amenable to US influence and favourable to US interests, thereby damaging our national security. She viewed intelligence co-operation with foreign countries as a sword that should be under the personal control and supervision of the Prime Minister.

She had laid down strict *Do's and Don'ts* in regard to intelligence liaison. These were done both orally and through orders written in her own hand, without even dictating them to her personal assistants. Examples:

- Each and every instance of intelligence co-operation with a foreign country should be with her personal clearance and she should be kept informed of the action taken.

- All intelligence co-operation would be only through the R&AW, which would act as the nodal agency, maintain written records of all contacts with foreign intelligence agencies, and operate as the interface between foreign intelligence agencies and Indian agencies needing their assistance.

- Foreign intelligence agencies should not be allowed to interact directly with any government department, agency or individual officer bypassing the R&AW under the pretext of facilitating co-operation.

In pursuance of these instructions, the R&AW used to maintain detailed records of all interactions with foreign intelligence agencies in one place, periodically review the usefulness of the intelligence co-operation, and keep the Prime Minister informed. Every time a new Prime Minister assumed office, the head of the R&AW would prepare a detailed note on the history of all intelligence co-operation for his/her information and brief him/her personally on the liaison network.

Like Indira Gandhi, Rajiv Gandhi and Narasimha Rao also had a good understanding of the need for a strict control through a single nodal agency over all contacts with foreign intelligence agencies, particularly those of the US, which have immense financial and other resources and are aggressive in their penetration efforts.

When Rao was the Prime Minister, a determined effort was made by the intelligence agencies of the UK and the US to weaken the security architecture as laid down by Indira Gandhi and Rajiv Gandhi. They started demanding that their intelligence officers posted in their diplomatic missions in New Delhi should be allowed to interact directly with the officers of the IB, the CBI and the Delhi Police, without having to go through the R&AW. They started socializing directly with the officers of these organizations, without the knowledge of the R&AW, by taking advantage of the friendships made during liaison meetings. Such meetings were often attended by officers of the IB under the chairmanship of an officer of the R&AW.

The R&AW, with the prior approval of the Prime Minister, repeatedly turned down their requests for direct contacts with the IB and other organizations. It also conveyed its unhappiness over their officers socializing with the officers of the IB without its knowledge. Despite this, such breaches of the *Do's and Don'ts* for liaison relationships continued to take place. When Douglas Hurd, the British Foreign Secretary under the then Prime Minister John Major, visited New Delhi in 1992, he took up this matter directly with Rao. He told him that co-operation in counter-terrorism between the two countries could be improved further if the British intelligence agencies—

and particularly, the MI-5, their Security Service— were allowed to liaise directly with the IB in matters relating to counter-terrorism. He claimed that no such restrictions existed in the relations of the British intelligence agencies with their counterparts in other Commonwealth countries and in the NATO countries. Rao, who had been briefed on the subject by the head of the R&AW, firmly rejected Hurd's request.

The CIA too kept raising this issue of direct liaison with the IB from time to time. However, it must be said to their credit that the US never raised this at the political level.The MI-6 and the CIA also started pressing the R&AW and, through it, the IB for joint operations for the collection of intelligence about Iran and North Korea. Their repeated requests in this regard were rejected by the R&AW with the prior approval of Rao. It was the policy of the R&AW since its inception in 1968 that the liaison relationships should be confined to an exchange of intelligence and assessments and that there should be no joint operations. However, before 1968, the IB had co-operated with the CIA in some joint operations for the collection of intelligence about China's nuclear programme.

One of the problems faced by the R&AW arose from the fact that the IB itself was in favour of being allowed to have direct liaison with foreign intelligence agencies in matters concerning counter-terrorism. Successive heads of the IB felt that the procedure laid down by Indira Gandhi for all liaison to be routed through the R&AW and to be controlled by it was outdated and needed to be changed. They took up this issue with the PMO on many occasions, but their requests for a change in the procedure were rejected.

The R&AW knew that, despite this, the IB was encouraging the British and American intelligence officers posted in New Delhi to come to them directly. It also did not discourage the practice of its officers socializing with the intelligence officers of these countries. Whenever the R&AW took up this matter, they denied doing so.

The IB is responsible for counter-intelligence. Prevention of penetration of the Government by foreign intelligence officers is an important aspect of counter-intelligence. To ensure this, they issue from time to time instructions regarding contacts of Government servants with foreign diplomats and other foreigners. These instructions were often violated by the IB officers themselves in the name of co-operation in counter-terrorism.

It was this habit which enabled the CIA in the 1990s to penetrate the IB at a very high level through a woman officer posted in the US Embassy in New Delhi for purposes of liaison with the R&AW. This officer headed the IB's counter-intelligence division and, in that capacity, was responsible for keeping a watch on the foreign intelligence officers posted in New Delhi. He allegedly put himself in a position where he was recruited by her as her agent.

When this case was detected two years after my retirement through joint surveillance by the IB and the R&AW, this officer was sent out of the IB on premature retirement and the woman CIA officer was asked to leave the country. I was told that Frank Wisner, the then US Ambassador, avoided complying with the order of the MEA for sending her back to the US. He reportedly contended that the IB officer was not her agent, but her liaison contact for the sharing of intelligence.

Despite this incident, the issue of a change of procedure in liaison matters was again raised by the IB before the Special Task Force for the Revamping of the Intelligence Apparatus, headed by G.C.Saxena, which was set up by the Vajpayee Government in 2000. I was a member of this Task Force. After upholding the principle laid down by Indira Gandhi that the R&AW should be the nodal agency in all liaison matters, the Task Force recommended that in certain special cases the IB could be allowed to interact directly with foreign intelligence officers with the prior approval of Secretary (R).

One understands that in recent years, the increase in acts of terrorism and the understandable emphasis on the need for strengthening international intelligence co-operation have led to a dilution of the effectiveness of the counter-penetration measures laid down in the past. As a result, innumerable contact points are believed to have emerged, with no centralised system of control, supervision and record-keeping.Many, who are not professional intelligence officers and who have not had the benefit of counter-intelligence and counter-penetration training, have been jumping into the game of intelligence co-operation. Nothing would gladden the hearts of the trained penetration experts of foreign intelligence agencies, particularly the CIA, more than the perceived loosening of control. Unless this dangerous trend is checked and reversed, we might find one day that the sensitive establishments of this country have been badly penetrated under the guise of intelligence cooperation.

In the US, during the Clinton Administration, two serious instances of the penetration of the CIA and the FBI by the Soviet/Russian intelligence agencies were detected. Apart from the secret, in-house enquiries in the agencies, there were detailed open enquiries by the Congressional oversight committees, which led to major reforms in the counter-intelligence set-up. The findings of the Congressional committees were released to the public through the media.

In India, we have not had even a detailed debate in the Parliament--not to talk of parliamentary enquiries— about one instance of the penetration of the PMO by the French intelligence detected after Rajiv Gandhi became the Prime Minister, two instances of the penetration of the R&AW by the CIA during the tenure of Rajiv Gandhi and Vajpayee, one instance of the penetration of the IB again by the CIA during the Prime Ministership of Rao and one instance of the penetration of the National Security Council Secretariat (NSCS) again by the CIA detected during the Prime Ministership of Dr.Manmohan Singh.The NSCS is part of the PMO.

Before the death of Indira Gandhi in 1984, there were many instances of penetration of other Government departments, including the Armed Forces, by foreign intelligence agencies, including the ISI, but not of the intelligence agencies. After her death, there have been disturbing instances of penetration of even the intelligence agencies. Till now, all the detected instances were by the CIA. This does not mean that there have not been instances of successful penetrations or unsuccessful attempts to penetrate our intelligence agencies by other agencies, including the ISI. This is an indicator of the weakening of our security and counter-penetration architecture since the death of Indira Gandhi . In the name of co-operation in counter-terrorism, a more permissive atmosphere has been unwittingly encouraged.

After Narasimha Rao took over as the Prime Minister in 1991, the situation in J&K deteriorated further. The terrorists, who were previously indulging mostly in attacks with hand-held weapons, started using improvised explosive devices (IEDs) in a big way. They almost succeeded in carrying out a decapitation strike in the police headquarters in Srinagar. J.N.Saxena, the then DG of Police, and some of his senior officers narrowly escaped with only injuries. There were instances of kidnapping, either for ransom or for securing the release of detained terrorists. Some terrorists occupied the Hazratbal, the Muslim holy shrine in Srinagar in which the hair of the Holy Prophet is kept. After a game of patience lasting several days, they were persuaded to vacate the shrine without any incident. However, there was criticism of what was perceived as the soft approach of Rao towards the terrorists, who were allowed to escape after vacating the shrine.

Rao had three bilateral meetings with Nawaz Sharif, the then Pakistani Prime Minister, in the margins of international conferences at Davos in Switzerland, Jakarta and Harare. These did not produce any results. There was hardly any flow of worthwhile intelligence from the local population. The flow of intelligence from Khad, the Afghan intelligence agency, stopped after the collapse of the Najibullah Government in Kabul in April,1992. The Mujahideen, who seized control of Kabul, arrested Najibullah, disbanded his army and the Khad and set up their own intelligence agency, largely staffed by serving and retired officers of the ISI. They allowed the pro-Pakistan terrorist organizations of J&K such as the Hizbul Mujahideen and Pakistani jihadi organizations such as the Harkat-ul-Ansar (later re-named Harkat-ul-Mujahideen) to set up training camps in Afghan territory.

The R&AW continued with its policy of establishing contacts with the more moderate elements among the Afghan Mujahideen in the hope of persuading them not to allow the terrorist organizations to set up training camps in their territory.Meetings were held with these leaders in Switzerland and Italy. The moderate Afghan leaders expressed their friendship for India despite what they perceived as its support to the USSR and the troops of Najibullah in the past, but they were not in a position to help us or even to supply intelligence to us. For all practical purposes, under the façade of the rule by the Mujahideen, it was the ISI, which was controlling the country.

The Western intelligence agencies, which were helping India in its counter-terrorism operations against the Khalistani terrorists, were disinclined to similarly assist us against the terrorists in J&K. They agreed with the Pakistani contention that it was a disputed territory. They were not prepared even to admit that there was terrorism in J&K. There was no flow of intelligence from them despite the active role played by the Mirpuri community in Europe—particularly in the UK— in funding the terrorists. The Mirpuris are the Punjabi-speaking residents of Kashmir, who had migrated to Europe from the Pakistan-Occupied Kashmir (POK) due to the poor economic conditions there. Many of them had been displaced from their land by the construction of the Mangla dam in the Mirpur area. The Pakistan Government, which had constructed the dam, for the benefit of the Punjabi farmers, had done nothing for the rehabilitation of the displaced persons. One would have expected these persons in Europe to be against the Pakistan Government. Unfortunately, over the years, the R&AW had totally failed to actively interact with these persons and win them over. It had kept a distance from them. The ISI took advantage of this and managed to turn them against India and make them support the terrorist organizations in J&K.

The US attitude on this question was particularly unco-operative and unhelpful. It even refused to have any discussions with the officers of the R&AW and the IB on terrorism in J&K. The CIA took up the stand that there was no terrorism in that State. In this context, it would be necessary to trace the consistently unhelpful attitude of the CIA in matters concerning Pakistan right from the day the IB established a liaison relationship with the CIA after India became independent in 1947. While the CIA was helpful in matters concerning China, it was even hostile in matters concerning Pakistan. Protection of Pakistan from the consequences of its wrong-doing against India has been a consistent element in US policy-making towards India and Pakistan ever since 1947 – whichever party was in power in Washington, DC.

The Sino-Indian war of 1962 brought out the serious inadequacies in the IB's capability for the collection of technical intelligence about China. After obtaining the approval of the then Prime Minister Jawaharlal Nehru,the IB sought the assistance of the US intelligence for strengthening its TECHINT capability. The US intelligence, with the approval of John F Kennedy, the then US President, agreed to supply the required equipment and train IB officers who would be using this equipment. However, it imposed a condition that this equipment would be used only for the collection of TECHINT from China and not from Pakistan.

When the R&AW was formed in September 1968, the division handling this equipment was transferred to it. In the 1970s, Kao visited Washington, DC at the invitation of the then Director of the CIA to discuss Indo-US intelligence cooperation. Some years later, he mentioned to me that during his discussions in Washington DC, the CIA chief told him as follows: "Ramji, we all cheat in this profession. I know R&AW will cheat and use the equipment given by us for the collection of TECHINT about Pakistan. Make sure our State Department does not come to know of it. If it does, it will demand that we cancel our cooperation with you and withdraw from you the equipment given by us. I will have to do this."

Under the instructions of Rao, the IB, the R&AW and the Ministry of Home Affairs mounted a coordinated campaign to make the international community and US political and public opinion aware of the Pakistani sponsorship of terrorism against India. The IB and the R&AW prepared a detailed dossier giving details of all the evidence collected by them against the ISI. A team consisting of two officers of the Home Ministry and one from the IB was sent to Washington to hand over copies of this dossier to the US authorities and request them to declare Pakistan as a State sponsor of terrorism. After doing so, they also presented the dossier at a press conference at the Washington Press Club. The State Department summarily rejected the dossier.

In 1991, terrorists belonging to the Jammu & Kashmir Liberation Front (JKLF) attacked a group of young Israeli tourists, who had gone to J&K and tried to kidnap them. Many of the young Israeli tourists had just then completed their compulsory military service before coming to India for tourism. They snatched the weapons from the terrorists and fought them back. The terrorists managed to kill one of the Israelis and kidnap another, who was subsequently released. Following this incident, Jewish circles in the world—and particularly in the US— started criticising the unsympathetic attitude of the US towards India's complaints against Pakistan.

Just before the Presidential elections of November 1992, President George H W Bush, the father of the present President, reportedly ordered a second look at the dossier against Pakistan submitted by India. The officials, who did so, reportedly recommended that instead of declaring Pakistan a State sponsor of terrorism, it could be placed in a list of suspected State sponsors of terrorism. Bush, who lost the election to Bill Clinton, did not act on the recommendation. He left the decision to his successor.

After assuming office in January 1993, Clinton placed Pakistan on a list of suspected State sponsors of terrorism. The weighty nature of the Indian dossier played a role in this decision, but there was a more important reason. The CIA had developed a strong dislike of Lt.Gen Javed Nasir, the then DG of the ISI, for not cooperating with a drive launched by it to persuade the Afghan Mujahideen to sell back to the US their unused stock of Stinger missiles, given to them for use against the Soviet troops. The US used the Indian dossier to force the then Prime Minister Nawaz Sharif to remove Javed Nasir and some other ISI officers, whom it looked upon as uncooperative in its efforts to buy back the Stinger missiles, from the ISI. Nawaz Sharif complied with the US demand.

Benazir Bhutto, who was then the Leader of the Opposition, rang up Peter Galbraith, son of the former US Ambassador to India J K

Galbraith, and some other university mates of hers, who were close friends of Clinton, to request them to see that Pakistan was not declared a State sponsor of terrorism. She told them she expected elections to be held in Pakistan later that year and that she was confident of coming back to power. She assured them that if she came back as the Prime Minister, she would stop the ISI's use of terrorism against India.

In July 1993, Warren Christopher, the then Secretary of State, announced that the US had decided to remove Pakistan from the list of suspected State sponsors of terrorism for want of adequate evidence. Benazir Bhutto won the elections in October 1993, and returned as the Prime Minister. But she did not ask the ISI to stop the use of terrorism against India. The R&AW used to have in its archives the transcripts of Benazir Bhutto's telephonic conversations with Peter Galbraith and others, which led to the removal of Pakistan from the list of suspected State-sponsors of terrorism.

The situation became worse in J&K after she returned to power. Even though she had tried to stop the ISI's assistance to the Khalistani terrorists during her first tenure as the Prime Minister between 1988 and 1990, it was under her that the ISI started helping the Kashmiri terrorist organizations in a big way in 1989. She was the most virulent towards India so far as J&K was concerned and gave the ISI total freedom and the required funds to do whatever it wanted in J&K. Her virulence and the ISI's assistance to the jihadi terrorists operating in J&K increased after she returned to power in 1993.

Between 1988 and 1993, the ISI was trying to achieve its aims in J&K mainly with the help of indigenous Kashmiri terrorist organizations such as the JKLF and the Hizbul Mujahideen. In 1993, after finding that the indigenous Kashmiri organizations were unable to make headway against the Indian security forces, the ISI started infiltrating into J&K and other parts of India Pakistani jihadi organizations such as the Harkat-ul-Ansar (later renamed the Harkat-ul-Mujahideen), which had fought against the Soviet troops in Afghanistan in the 1980s. This infiltration of Pakistani jihadis of Afghan vintage picked up momentum after she returned to office as the Prime Minister. The ISI's policy of using Pakistani jihadi veterans from Afghanistan in the proxy war against India had her total backing.

She strongly disliked Narasimha Rao because she nursed a grievance that when she came to India on a private visit in 1991 to attend the cremation of Rajiv Gandhi, she was not given the importance she deserved as the Leader of the Opposition in Pakistan by the Congress (I). She expected to meet important Congress (I) leaders. She could not. Her visit was mostly handled by a Joint Secretary in the MEA. Her dislike of Rao was reflected in her policies towards India. The only Indian leaders for whom she had some regard were Indira Gandhi and Rajiv Gandhi.

She not only stepped up the ISI's assistance to the Kashmiri and Pakistani terrorists, but she also asked the ISI to step up its Psychological Warfare (PSYWAR) against India. She repeatedly spurned the efforts of Rao and his Foreign Secretary, J.N.Dixit, to resume the dialogue between the two countries. A number of so-called non-papers sent by India to Pakistan on this subject were rejected by her with contempt. She imposed pre-conditions for any dialogue with India such as the reduction in the number of Indian troops deployed in J&K on counter-terrorism and counter-infiltration duties and an improvement in the human rights situation in the State. At least Rao had three meetings with Nawaz Sharif in the margins of international conferences. There were no meetings with her. She avoided coming to India for the SAARC summit held at New Delhi in May,1995. She sent Farooq Leghari, the figurehead President of Pakistan, to attend the summit.

She levelled wild allegations of violations of the human rights of the Kashmiris by the Indian security forces and mounted a vicious campaign to have India condemned on this issue before the European Parliament and the UN Human Rights Commission in Geneva in 1994. Her efforts were successfully countered by Rao with the help of Salman Khurshid and Farooq Abdullah, former Chief Minister of J&K. At tremendous risk to his life, Farooq Abdullah responded immediately to Rao's request to go to Europe to counter the Pakistani propaganda at international conferences on Kashmir got organized by the ISI at Brussels and Vienna and during the annual session of the UN Human Rights Commission at Geneva. Benazir's efforts to have a resolution condemning India adopted by the Commission miserably failed partly because Iran declined to support the resolution and partly thanks to the determined opposition to the resolution put up by Salman Khurshid and Abdullah. Vajpayee, who led the Indian delegation to the Commission meeting at the request of Rao, claimed credit for the failure of the Pakistani efforts, but the real credit should go to Salman Khurshid and Abdullah. Benazir and the ISI officers abused them as Muslims working on contract for the Government of India. They ignored this abusive campaign with the contempt it deserved.

The R&AW ought to be proud of having played an active, behind-the-scene role in frustrating the ISI's PSYWAR campaign against India. Its PSYWAR Division, which was then ably headed by the late Amitabha Chakravarthi of the Indian Information Service, mobilized the support of the anti-Pakistan elements in J&K and in the Muslim community in the rest of India as well as the sub-continental Muslim diaspora in Europe to defeat the ISI-sponsored PSYWAR campaign against India. This was a glorious chapter in the use of the techniques of counter-PSYWAR by the R&AW. The entire credit for this should go to the late Amitabha Chakravarthi. Unfortunately, more details of the techniques used by him cannot be revealed.

Even while stepping up assistance to the terrorists in J&K and other parts of India, Benazir and, before her, Nawaz Sharif had to constantly keep looking over their shoulder to see what was happening in Sindh, which was boiling. Initially, beginning from 1988, the Sindhi nationalists rose in revolt demanding an independent Sindhudesh. Subsequently, the Mohajirs (the migrants from India) and the Seraikis of southern Punjab also rose in revolt. The Mohajirs wanted independence for Karachi, where they are in a majority, under the name Jinnahpur. The Seraikis called for a partition of Punjab in order to create a separate Seraiki State. The Shias too started demanding a separate province for the Shias consisting of the Shia majority Northern Areas (Gilgit and Baltistan) and some adjoining areas of the North-West Frontier Province.

The intensity of the struggles launched by the Sindhis and the Mohajirs led to a serious situation in Sindh—particularly in Karachi. The ISI tried to bring the situation under control through the ruthless use of force, by creating differences between the Sindhis and the Mohajirs, and by creating a split in the Mohajir Qaumi Movement led by Altaf Hussain, which was spearheading the struggle of the Mohajirs. The Shias in the Northern Areas too took to a violent resistance movement against the occupation of their territory by the Pakistanis and against the ISI's policy of re-settling Sunni ex-servicemen in Gilgit and Baltistan in order to reduce the Shias to a minority. A similar policy of re-settling Punjabi ex-servicemen in Sindh and Balochistan was followed in order to reduce the Sindhis and Balochs to a minority in their traditional homeland.

Unable to control the situation, Nawaz and after him, Benazir blamed India for the deteriorating situation. The ISI mounted a campaign to have India condemned for interfering in Pakistan's internal affairs in retaliation for its assistance to the people of J&K. When Nawaz was still the Prime Minister, the ISI sent Hussain Haqqani, a Pakistani journalist close to it, to New Delhi with a detailed dossier purporting to give details of the training camps allegedly run by the R&AW for the Sindhi nationalists and the Mohajirs. He contacted a journalist of "India Today", handed over to him a copy of the so-called dossier and wanted him to have it published in his journal. He promised to get more details for him if his journal so desired. The "India Today" journalist showed the so-called dossier to Amitabha Chakravarthi and sought his comments. Amitabha, after consulting me, told him that the so-called dossier was totally fabricated. He pointed out that it was an apparent attempt by the ISI to have the Sindhi nationalists and the Mohajirs discredited by projecting them as the agents of the R&AW. Ultimately, the "India Today" decided not to publish it.

Haqqani also contacted some old friends of Benazir, who had known her from her student days in the UK and the US, and made enquiries about her personal life and her Indian contacts. The Pakistan People's Party (PPP) of Benazir came to know of this through a contact in the Pakistani High Commission in New Delhi. Its Central Committee met in Islamabad and passed a resolution condemning his enquiries. Haqqani, who also served for a short while as the Pakistani High Commissioner in Colombo and tried to develop contacts for the ISI in the Muslim communities of Sri Lanka's Eastern Province and in South India, is now working as an academic in the US.

Ever since the days of Zia-ul-Haq, the ISI had been trying to create feelings of alienation among the Muslims of not only J&K, but also in other parts of India in order to foment acts of terrorism in the Indian territory outside J&K too. While it succeeded in J&K, it could not succeed in other parts of India. At the invitation of the Jamaat-e-Islami (JEI) of Pakistan, some members of the Students' Islamic Movement of India (SIMI) had clandestinely visited Pakistan in the late 1980s. The arrest and interrogation of one of them in the early 1990s revealed that they had received arms training in a camp set up by the JEI. The arrested person also revealed that their instructor was a Sudanese national . When the trained persons did not take to terrorism after their return to India, he visited India secretly along with a member of the JEI and contacted those trained in Pakistan. He urged upon them to help their co-religionists in J&K by organizing acts of terrorism in the Indian territory outside J&K. Even after his visit, they were reluctant to take to terrorism.

However, the situation changed after the demolition of the Babri Masjid in Ayodhya in Uttar Pradesh by a group of Hindutva agitators. The demolition marked an important watershed in the attitude of sections of the Muslim youth towards Pakistan and towards the pan-Islamic ideology sought to be propagated from there by the Pakistani jihadi organizations.

The use of jihad as a weapon against non-Muslims was not the brain-child of Osama bin Laden and his Al Qaeda. It was the brain-child of the religious leaders and military officers of Pakistan ever since the day Pakistan became independent on August 14,1947. Pakistan's jihad against India did not start in 1989. It started in 1947. Even Jawaharlal Nehru—despite his strong secular credentials— had repeatedly been drawing attention to the jihad based on hatred for India being waged by Pakistan since 1947. His warning even found mention in the address delivered by Dr.Rajendra Prasad, the first President of India, while inaugurating the budget session of the Indian Parliament on March 18,1957. He said, "There has been no abatement in Pakistan of the campaigns of hatred and jihad (against India). The policy of the Government of India and the general approach of our people have been that we shall not respond to these with hatred, but shall continue our endeavours to promote friendly relations while defending our land and our legitimate interests." (Quotation taken from the column of "The Hindu" of March 19,2007, titled "This Day That Age")

Between 1947 and the 1980s, Pakistan was waging this jihad mainly with the help of its nationals infiltrated into India. It could not find many supporters in the Indian Muslim community. From the 1980s onwards, it started getting the support of some Muslim youth in J&K. Since the demolition of the Babri Masjid in December, 1992, it has been getting the support of sections of the Muslim youth in other parts of India too.

Before December,1992, there were frequent outbreaks of Hindu-Muslim riots in different parts of India, but no acts of jihadi terrorism in the Indian territory outside J&K. Since the demolition of the Babri Masjid, the ISI and the Pakistani jihadi organizations sponsored by it such as the LET, the Harkat-ul-Mujahideen (HUM), the Harkat-ul-Jihad-al-Islami (HUJI) and the Jaish-e-Mohammad (JEM—formed in 2000 due to a split in the HUM) have been taking advantage of the pockets of anger in some sections of the Muslim youth. They have been finding a fertile soil in pockets of the Indian Muslim community outside J&K for their pan-Islamic ideology. Some of the blame for the spread of jihadi terrorism to other parts of India as a result of the demolition of the Babri Masjid could be attributed to Narasimha Rao.

It must be said to the credit of India's national security bureaucracy-
— in the IB, the R&AW and the MHA— that they kept urging him
to prevent the assembling of the Hindutva volunteers in Ayodhya,
dismiss the UP Government, impose the President's rule in UP and
deploy the central para-military forces to prevent any law and order
situation. L.K.Advani, the Bharatiya Janata Party (BJP) leader, who
kept meeting Rao at the latter's request for discussions, was assuring
him that there would be no damage to the Masjid. A Hindu religious
leader, who had some friends at the senior levels of the R&AW,
repeatedly cautioned that Rao should not trust any assurances given
by Advani. He expressed his fear that the Hindutva volunteers might
demolish the Masjid. What he stated was conveyed to Rao orally.

One got the impression that Rao was in two minds. Sometimes, he
felt he could trust the assurances of Advani. Sometimes, he felt he
could not. Once he told the R&AW that he did not like Advani coming
to his house for discussions, lest there be mischievous speculation in
the media. He asked whether the R&AW had a secret guest house
in which he could meet Advani without the media coming to know
about it. The R&AW told him that it had such a guest house, which
was being used by Rajiv Gandhi for secret discussions with the Akali
leaders before Operation Blue Star in 1984. He developed second
thoughts and gave up the idea. He then asked the R&AW to give him
a secret recording device and explain to him how to use it. He wanted
to use it for recording his discussions with Advani in his house. It was
given to him. After the demolition of the Masjid, he returned the
device to the R&AW. He did not say whether he had used it and, if so,
what happened to the recording. Nor did the R&AW ask him.

The demolition of the Babri Masjid could have been prevented if
Narasimha Rao had imposed the President's rule in UP and banned
the congregation of the Hindutva volunteers at Ayodhya. It might
have caused some violence, but much of the violence would have
been directed against the Government of India and the security
forces. There would have been no serious Hindu-Muslim clashes.
No feelings of hurt in the hearts of the members of the Muslim
community. But he did not do so. Why did he fail to intervene?

There was much speculation among the bureaucrats, but no clear-cut answers. Some described him as a Hindutva sympathizer behind a secular façade. Others said he trusted Advani's assurances that there would be no damage to the Masjid. Some even saw his Chanakyan acumen in action, According to them, his perceived inaction was tactical and had a strategic objective, namely, to deprive the BJP of an exploitable electoral issue in future. They believed that he did anticipate serious Hindu-Muslim clashes, but once that was brought under control, the BJP would no longer be able to whip up the emotions of the Hindus by exploiting the Babri Masjid issue.

Whatever be the answer, there was widespread unease in senior bureaucratic circles over his failure to prevent the demolition. There was no doubt it was a political failure and not merely a bureaucratic or administrative failure. Sensing this unease, Rao invited to his house all officers of the rank of Additional Secretary and above in the Government of India in order to address them on the state of the nation in the wake of the demolition. It was a remarkable initiative, the like of which no other Prime Minister had ever undertaken. He delivered a somewhat confusing and rambling speech. It didn't make sense to many of us. As I left the meeting, I could not help nursing a feeling that in his own highly elliptical manner, he was trying to convey a message to the bureaucrats that the demolition was in the karma of the nation and that there was no need to feel disturbed over the Government's perceived inaction.

The demolition was followed by acts of violence by angry Muslims, which led to the use of force by the Police against the rioting Muslims. As it always happens during and after communal riots, members of the Muslim community accused the police—particularly in Mumbai— of excessive use of force against the Muslims and of failing to protect them. The acts of violence by the Muslims in protest against the demolition were expected. The police were not taken by surprise.

What took the police and the intelligence agencies by surprise was the 12 well-orchestrated explosions in Mumbai on March 12, 1993, in which 235 innocent civilians were killed. It was the first act of mass casualty terrorism on the ground in India. The mass casualty terrorism by the Khalistani terrorists in June,1985, which brought down the Kanishka aircraft, was in the air. It was also the first act of reprisal terrorism by jihadi terrorists in Indian territory outside J&K. It was the first act of terrorism in which the ISI brought about a nexus between the jihadi terrorists and the organized crime mafia.

It was also the first major act of terrorism directed against important economic targets. Since 1981, the ISI had been asking the Khalistanis to attack economic targets. The jihadi terrorism in J&K, which started in 1989, also disrupted the tourist economy of the State. On March 12,1993, it used the mafia group headed by Dawood Ibrahim, then living in Dubai, and a group of Muslims angry over the demolition of the Babri Masjid and the perceived failure of the police to protect the Muslims during the subsequent communal riots in Mumbai to organize attacks on important economic targets as an act of reprisal. Since then, we have been having periodic attacks of jihadi terrorism in different parts of India carried out by Pakistani jihadi terrorist organizations, with the help of the members of the SIMI and some Indian Muslims recruited in India and the Gulf.

Since 1947, Pakistan could not succeed in its efforts to instigate the Muslim youth of India outside J&K to take to jihad to assert the rights of the Muslim community and to protect themselves from the Hindus and what was perceived as the pro-Hindu police. Whereas Muslims from many countries of the world went to Pakistan in the 1980s to participate in the jihad against the Soviet troops in Afghanistan, Indian Muslims kept away from it. They also refrained from being influenced by Wahabism and its pan-Islamic ideas. Despite their anger and grievances over many issues, they did not identify themselves with the jihadi organizations of Pakistan and did not subscribe to their pernicious ideas.

All this changed after the demolition of the Babri Masjid. Sections of the Muslim youth outside J&K started gravitating towards the ISI, the Pakistani jihadi organizations and their pernicious ideas. Thus began the pan-Islamic radicalization of sections of the Indian Muslim youth. For 45 years, Pakistan could not succeed in making them take to arms and improvised explosive devices (IEDs). The anger caused by the demolition of the Babri Masjid did it. The Congress (I) of Narasimha Rao and the BJP of L.K.Advani should equally share the blame for unwittingly facilitating the spread of the ISI-sponsored jihad to other parts of India from J&K.

The serial blasts of March 12,1993, took everybody by surprise. Neither the Mumbai Police nor the IB nor the R&AW had the least inkling of it. They had misread the post-demolition Muslim riots as one of those disturbances, which kept taking place in India from time to time and subsided without leaving any after-effects. They were not prepared for the jihadi aftermath of the Babri Masjid demolition. There was total confusion and even panic as the news of the blasts reached New Delhi. The connection to the Babri Masjid demolition and the ISI was immediately made in the minds of the national security managers, but they had no idea who could have been responsible for it.

Many in the intelligence community connected the modus operandi of the terrorists in Mumbai to that of the Irish Republican Army (IRA) in the UK. That night, there was a   dinner organized by the officers of the R&AW to bid farewell to N.Narasimhan, who had retired as chief of the R&AW on February 28,1993. The talk at the dinner was about the similarities between the MO used in Mumbai and that often used by the IRA in the UK. In February, 1993, there was an attempt by a group of jihadi terrorists of Pakistani and Arab origin to blow up the New York World Trade Centre with the help of a truck loaded with ammonium nitrate, which was used as an explosive material. It was a spectacular act of reprisal terrorism, but it could not achieve the terrorists' intended objective of bringing down the towers. A few days before the Mumbai blasts, I had prepared a detailed assessment of the New York explosion and its ominous significance.

Among those who had carefully read it and remembered it on March 12,1993, were Narasimha Rao and S.Rajgopal, the then Cabinet Secretary. Among those, who had seen, but not read it—or read it without realizing the significance of the New York explosion-— were the senior officers of the R&AW and the IB. As the news of the explosions in Mumbai were being received in New Delhi, there were hardly half a dozen people among the policy-makers in Delhi, who made the connection in their mind between the MO of the Mumbai blasts and that of the New York explosion. Amongst them were Rao himself, S.Rajgopal, Naresh Chandra, who after retiring as the Cabinet Secretary, was assisting Rao in handling the aftermath of the Babri Masjid demolition, and myself.

At the time the Mumbai explosions took place, Maharashtra was fortunate in having Sharad Pawar as its Chief Minister. In the wake of the communal riots in Mumbai earlier that year, Rao had persuaded Sharad Pawar, the then Defence Minister in the Government of India, to go back to Mumbai once again and take over as the Chief Minister of Maharsashtra for a second tenure in order to restore law and order. The Government of India was fortunate in having Rao as the Prime Minister and Rajesh Pilot as the Minister of State for Internal Security. Rao, Pilot and Sharad Pawar exhibited leadership qualities of the highest order in the management of the crisis created by the blasts.

Disregarding possible dangers to his life, Pawar immediately went round the scenes of the explosions in order to assess the situation for himself. He set up a crisis management group under his chairmanship to prevent any communal backlash and any more acts of terrorism and to direct the investigation into the blasts. Rao asked Pilot to fly to Mumbai immediately with a team of senior intelligence and security officials and scientists to assess the situation for himself and report to him and to extend to the Maharashtra Government whatever help it needed. Rao set up a crisis management group in Delhi chaired by the Cabinet Secretary to monitor the situation in the whole of India and to assist the Maharashtra Government in its crisis management.

S.Rajgopal,the then Cabinet Secretary, M.D.Godbole, the then Home Secretary in the Government of India, and N.Raghunathan, who had just then taken over as the Chief Secretary of Maharashtra, worked as a team in handling the crisis. I had not seen such team work for many years before. The fact that all the three of them belonged to the IAS cadre of Maharashtra helped. They had known each other quite well. Sharad Pawar knew them well and had total confidence in them.

Rao requested A.P.Abdul Kalam and Dr.K.Santanam, then working in the Defence Research and Development Organization (DRDO), to fly to Mumbai and assist the crisis management group there in the forensic investigation. At the request of Sharad Pawar, Rao also asked J.S.Bedi, who had taken over as the chief of the R&AW from N.Narasimhan on February 28,1993, to fly to Mumbai and assist Sharad Pawar. The Cabinet Secretary suggested to Bedi that since I had been dealing with international terrorism for some years and made a detailed study of the New York World Trade Centre explosion, he should take me also with him. Bedi flew to Mumbai in a special aircraft in the morning of March 14, 1993. I accompanied him.

It is important to digress here for a while to discuss about a change in the perception of Rao about the R&AW from positive to once again negative that had come about in the months before the Mumbai blasts. This change occurred in 1992 when the Dalai Lama sought an appointment from Rao to make a courtesy call on him. After consulting the R&AW, Rao agreed to receive the Dalai Lama for an unpublicized courtesy call. All previous Prime Ministers had done it, but kept it a secret from the Indian public as well as the Chinese lest there be undesirable speculation about any political significance of the courtesy call.

The R&AW advised Rao that unlike his predecessors, he should take the initiative to inform the Chinese beforehand about the intended courtesy call. The R&AW told him that the Chinese would greatly appreciate such transparency. Rao accepted the advice. The R&AW drafted a personal message from Rao to Li Peng, the then Chinese Prime Minister, informing the latter that he would be receiving the Dalai Lama purely as a respected leader of the Buddhists and that there was no political significance to the meeting. The message was sent to Li Peng through the hotline between the R&AW and its Chinese counterpart—the Ministry of State Security.

Within a few hours, a strong reply came from Li Peng protesting against Rao's decision to receive the Dalai Lama. It described the Dalai Lama as Tibet's chief splittist and rejected Rao's contention that there was no political significance to it. Rao was taken aback by the strong Chinese reply. The R&AW told him that the Chinese reply reflected the traditional Chinese position on the Dalai Lama and that it had expected the Chinese to protest. The R&AW advised Rao that he should not worry about the Chinese protest and that he should go ahead with the appointment.

Rao was upset by the stand taken by the R&AW. He said: "If you had expected that the Chinese would protest as you now claim, you should have told me about it and should not have advised me to send that message, which has provoked this reply." I do not know whether he went ahead with the appointment. Most probably, he did not. Thereafter, he was hesitant to accept the R&AW's advice in important matters of state having a bearing on India's relations with other countries.

In the months preceding the Mumbai blasts, the inter-personal relationships among senior officers of the R&AW had become bad. They had started planting stories against each other in the media and carrying tales against each other to the Prime Minister's Office (PMO). A senior officer posted in the headquarters fell ill with a severe attack of malaria after a tour of the R&AW's border posts in Mizoram and passed away. His wife complained that her husband would have resisted the attack of malaria and survived but for the fact that he had been demoralized due to humiliating treatment by the organization. Some officers instigated her to carry her complaint to the PMO.

Rao started receiving anonymous complaints about the alleged misuse of ARC aircraft by senior officers for personal travel along with their wives and about the recruitment to the Research & Analysis Service (RAS) of the sons of two senior officers of the organization. Rao was particularly upset that while putting up to him the list of the proposed new recruits for approval, the organization had not mentioned that two of the recommended recruits were sons of senior

R&AW officers. On receiving anonymous complaints about the recruitment, he asked the Cabinet Secretary to go into the procedure followed by the organization while making direct recruitment. This led to a suspension of all direct recruitment to the RAS for some months till the examination by the Cabinet Secretary was completed. Following the examination, a decision was taken to take more IPS officers on long-term deputation—directly from the States as well as through the IB The past exemption of the organization from the purview of the Union Public Service Commission (UPSC) was diluted.

The media carried reports of a succession struggle in the organization, which was found to have been planted by a senior officer. There were allegations of a "Tamil mafia" having taken control of the organization. Relations with the IB became strained once again when a CIA officer complained that some senior officers of the IB,who had gone to Washington to attend a training course, had not settled the bills of their wives, who had accompanied them. The IB was unhappy that the R&AW put this down in writing instead of informally bringing this to its notice for having the bills settled. The practice of senior officers taking their wives with them during their foreign travels increased and there were allegations that they were not re-imbursing to the Government the proportionate expenditure incurred on their wives. These complaints and allegations led to the creation of a negative perception about the organization in the mind of Rao.

Fortunately, these negative perceptions did not last long. The R&AW managed to have its reputation rehabilitated by its contribution to the successful investigation of the Mumbai blasts. It managed to procure photocopies of the manifests of the flights of the Pakistan International Airlines (PIA) by which the perpetrators of the blasts had traveled from Dubai to Karachi for being trained by the ISI and then returned from there. It collected evidence that the Pakistani Consulate in Dubai had issued visas on plain papers to them so that there were no entries in their passports regarding their travel to Pakistan. It also collected evidence, which showed that on their arrival in Karachi the perpetrators were received by ISI officers at the tarmac and driven out of the airport without their having to pass through immigration formalities. It gathered evidence of the travel of some of the perpetrators to Dubai via Kathmandu after having carried out the explosions. Rao said that the wealth of evidence collected by the R&AW was worth its weight in gold. The IB forgot their temporary unhappiness with the R&AW and the two organizations co-operated brilliantly once again.

Sharad Pawar's habit of talking freely to the media about the evidence collected by the R&AW led to some of its sources, who had provided valuable documentary evidence, being exposed and sacked from their jobs by their employers. Some of the sacked sources even feared a risk to their lives. The R&AW protested to the Cabinet Secretary over Sharad Pawar's action in sharing with the media some of the evidence gathered by the R&AW. It was decided that thereafter all evidence collected by the R&AW should be sent to the IB, the PM and the Cabinet Secretary only. The IB was asked to take appropriate follow-up action without creating problems for the sources of the R&AW.

The Monitoring Division of the R&AW too did excellent work in intercepting communications originating from Dubai, Karachi and Kathmandu regarding the escape of the perpetrators after carrying out the explosions. There were reasons to believe that some of the intercepted conversations of the perpetrators were with Dawood Ibrahim himself in Karachi. Those talking over phone were not only discussing about the escape of the perpetrators, but were also indulging in general gossip about their activities in India. A prominent name which figured in these gossips was that of the late Kalpanath Rai, who was a Minister in Rao's Cabinet. There was a reference to a member of Dawood Ibrahim's gang staying in the servants' quarters of Rai in Delhi. There was another reference to a member of the gang once being helped to stay in a guest house of a public sector enterprise by the office of Rai. These intercepts were brought to the notice of Rao.

Immediately after the Mumbai explosions, the US State Department, as it usually does, issued an advisory asking its citizens not to travel to India and its diplomats posted in India to call off all their tours. Thomas Pickering, who was the US Ambassador to India, had been transferred to Moscow. When the explosions took place, he had already handed over charge as Ambassador in New Delhi, but had not yet taken off for Moscow. Because of the advisory, he got stuck in New Delhi for days. He was impatient to start functioning from Moscow. He started pestering the State Department to let him fly in disregard of its advisory. It told him to consult the Indian security officials and follow their advice.

An official of the US Embassy called on me and sought my advice. I told him: "Who am I to give advice to your Ambassador? Your State Department never consulted us before issuing the advisory, which is totally unwarranted. You tell your Ambassador to seek the advice of his department." He said the State Department wanted him to follow our advice. I persisted in my refusal to give any advice. Those were the days when we were not afraid of ticking off the Americans and we had full confidence that the political leadership would totally back us. Not like today, when we bend backwards to curry favour with the Americans. Some days later, Pickering did take off for Moscow.

The then Canadian Foreign Minister also got stuck in New Delhi where he had stopped for a day on his way to Beijing. The Canadians usually followed US advisories in security matters. The Foreign Minister was getting impatient. The Canadian High Commission in New Delhi was then advised by their Foreign Office to consult Indian security officials. A High Commission official met me. I told him: "Since you follow US advice, better ask them. Why do you ask me?" After a few hours, he came back to me again and said his Foreign Minister was insisting they should get the clearance of Indian security officials.

I told him I would not give any advice to his Foreign Minister, but I would tell him what advice I would give to my own Prime Minister if he asked me. I added I would tell my Prime Minister as follows: "Sir, our security agencies have taken all possible security precautions. Despite this, nobody can give a 100 per cent guarantee that the terrorists cannot strike if they are determined to. You should not allow this to come in the way of your normal functioning. The moment you do so we would lose half the battle against them."

The Canadian official asked: "Won't your Prime Minister misunderstand if you spoke like that?" "No," I replied. "On the contrary, he would appreciate it." He asked me whether he could mention this to his Foreign Minister. I told him he could. That night, he took off for Beijing.

Immediately after the explosions, Rao accepted the advice of the R&AW that we should invite the counter-terrorism experts of the US, the UK and other Western countries to visit the spot and see the weapons and other evidence gathered by the police during the initial investigation. The timers were of American origin, the hand-grenades of Austrian design and some AK-47 rifles of Chinese-make. The evidence indicated that the terrorists had got all this from the ISI.

The idea was that if the Western counter-terrorism experts saw the evidence immediately after the explosions, they might go back and tell their political leadership they were convinced that the ISI was behind the explosions, even though they might not share their findings with us.

The police recovered from the blast site some hand grenades of Austrian design and a timer. Austrian experts flew to New Delhi, examined the hand-grenades and certified in writing that these grenades were of Austrian design and had been manufactured in a Pakistani government ordnance factory with technology and machine tools sold by an Austrian company to the Pakistan Government. They said the Government of India could use their report for any purpose it desired.

American counter-terrorism experts, who visited Mumbai at our invitation, saw the timer and said that it looked like timers manufactured in the US. They wanted to take it to the US for forensic examination. They promised they would return it after the examination. I agreed to it. After some days, they sent me an unsigned report on a plain piece of paper that the timer had been manufactured in the US and was part of a consignment given by the US to Pakistan in the 1980s.

I pointed out that this was the smoking gun which they had been asking for and said they should now be able to declare Pakistan a State sponsor of terrorism. They said this was not sufficient evidence against the Government of Pakistan. They claimed that there were instances of leakage of arms and ammunition from Pakistan Government stocks into the hands of arms smugglers and contended that the terrorists could have procured it in the smugglers' market. They also said that their report could not be used by us in a court of law.

When I asked them to return the timer, they claimed that their forensic laboratory had destroyed it by mistake and that they were taking action against the lab for negligence. After my retirement, I used to narrate to Kao and others how the Americans cheated me by destroying the timer. Once, Kao asked: "How were you so naive in trusting them and handing over the timer to them? One should never trust the US in matters concerning Pakistan. The US will never act against Pakistan for anything it does to India." This is as valid today as it was in the past.

When the US experts were visiting Mumbai, a British journalist posted in New Delhi came to know from a source in the Mumbai police about their visit and the name of the hotel where they were staying. He rang them up and wanted to interview them. They strongly denied they were counter-terrorism experts, cut short their stay in India and went back to the US. They were apparently afraid that if the terrorists came to suspect that the US was helping India, they might target US nationals.

The British experts, who visited Mumbai, helped the R&AW in establishing that the AK-47 rifles and their ammunition, which were recovered by the Mumbai Police, had been manufactured in China. They even gave us the location of the factories in China where they were manufactured and the year of manufacture. We then gave to the

Chinese the details of the AK-47 rifles of Chinese-make recovered in Mumbai and asked them whether they had sold them to Pakistan. They claimed that in the Chinese arms factories record-keeping was in a mess and as such they had no record as to whom they had sold them. They pointed out that in the past they had sold AK-47 rifles to a number of countries in Asia and Africa and added that the recovery of the rifles in Mumbai did not necessarily mean the terrorists got them from Pakistan.

While clearly exhibiting their disinclination to hold Pakistan accountable for the blasts and the death of the civilians, the CIA and the Chinese external intelligence, independently of each other and without each knowing of the suggestion made by the other, offered to organize a dialogue between the R&AW and the ISI so that the heads of the two organizations could discuss the matter away from the glare of publicity and co-operate in the investigation of the blasts. What the US was suggesting was a joint counter-terrorism mechanism similar to what Prime Minister Manmohan Singh had agreed to during his talks with President Pervez Musharraf in Havana in September, 2006. The US offer was made after a visit by James Woolsey, the then Director of the CIA, to Islamabad for talks with Nawaz Sharif. The Chinese offer was made through the liaison channel in response to the R&AW's taking up with them the question of the AK-47 rifles and ammunition of Chinese manufacture recovered after the blasts.

Narasimha Rao rejected both these offers. He said: "The R&AW has been having a relationship with the CIA for 25 years. It has not been able to get its co-operation in counter-terrorism. Before suggesting to us counter-terrorism co-operation with Pakistan, let the US first co-operate sincerely with us in counter-terrorism. We know how Zulfiqar Ali Bhutto deceived Indira Gandhi at Shimla. He made an oral promise to work for the conversion of the Line of Control into the international border. After getting his soldiers back, he totally denied making any such promise to her. Now Hamid Gul is even denying meeting and discussing Siachen with Verma. It will be a dangerous illusion to think anything will come out of co-operation between the ISI and the R&AW. Let us not commit the same mistake

again and again." Narasimha Rao said no formal reply need be sent
to the US and China on their offer. "Let them guess from our silence
that we are not in favour of it."

One had an impression that Rao's rejection of the two offers was
also strongly influenced by the advice of J.N.Dixit, the then Foreign
Secretary, who reportedly felt that Verma had exceeded his brief by
discussing the Siachen issue with Hamid Gul, whereas he was asked
to meet Gul only to discuss Pakistani support to terrorism. It was
true that Rajiv Gandhi had agreed to the Verma-Gul dialogue only to
discuss Pakistani sponsorship of terrorism against India. But, when
it was found at the first meeting that Gul was more interested in
discussing Siachen than terrorism, Rajiv Gandhi himself encouraged
Verma to discuss Siachen.

Even after Rao's rejection of the offers from the US and China, the
question of the advisability of an informal dialogue—if not a formal
liaison relationship— between the intelligence agencies of India and
Pakistan kept cropping up. Dixit's views were clear: There was no
need for such a dialogue or a liaison relationship. If, however, at any
stage, the Prime Minister felt it necessary to have it, the IB should
handle it and not the R&AW. Dixit's mind had been influenced by his
reported unhappiness over his being kept in the dark regarding the
R&AW's operations when he was the High Commissioner in Pakistan
and Sri Lanka. He felt that the IB officers and their chiefs were more
transparent with him than their R&AW counterparts.

Within a few days of the explosions, the Mumbai Police, the IB
and the R&AW had identified the terrorists responsible, procured
documentary evidence of their travel to Pakistan for training and
details of the arms and ammunition got by them from Pakistan and
recovered the unutilized ones.

We are so good in investigating an act of terrorism after it
has taken place, but our record of prevention leaves much to
be desired. It is not that we do not get preventive intelligence.
For every successful act of terrorism there are many which were
prevented by timely and precise intelligence, but the public will

always judge the intelligence agencies by what they could not prevent and not by what they did.

For months after the explosions, there was an intense debate among officials in New Delhi whether the Mumbai explosions were due to an intelligence failure. Intelligence officials strongly contested this and pointed out that the investigations had revealed that there were persons, including public servants, posted in Maharashtra, who were apparently aware that there had been clandestine landings of arms and ammunition on the coast though they did not know these were meant for use in Mumbai. They chose not to alert the intelligence agencies and the police about it. Intelligence officials, therefore, contended that this showed that it was not a case of failure of intelligence, but a case of failure of integrity. The Government decided not to order an enquiry as to whether there was an intelligence failure.

Nawaz Sharif was the Prime Minister of Pakistan at the time of the Mumbai blasts. He strongly denied Indian charges regarding the involvement of the ISI. Benazir, who succeeded him as the Prime Minister following the elections held in October, 1993, was different from the Benazir of 1988-90. During her first tenure, she had given the ISI a free hand in J&K, but tried to control its activities in Punjab. After she returned to office towards the end of 1993, she removed even this control. The ISI had a free hand to organize acts of terrorism anywhere in India it liked. In December 1993, coinciding with the first anniversary of the demolition of the Babri Masjid, there were explosions on trains in North India organized by the SIMI at the instigation of the ISI.

Even as the ISI was stepping up the activities of the terrorists supported by it in different parts of India, Pakistan found itself unable to bring the deteriorating situation in Sindh—particularly in Karachi—under control. Serious differences cropped up in the pro-Pakistan Government set up by the Afghan Mujahideen in Kabul after the fall of Najibullah in April, 1992. Afghan Mujahideen groups, which were unhappy with the efforts of the ISI to strengthen Pakistan's control in Kabul, sought Indian assistance for resisting the ISI and the pro-Pakistan Mujahideen groups led by Gulbuddin Heckmatyar of the Hizbe-Islami.

Unable to control the situation in Karachi, Benazir complained to her friends in the US State Department that the R&AW was behind the unabated violence, which was showing signs of spreading from Sindh to Pakistani Punjab. India strongly denied her allegations. In July,1994, the Indian authorities, on the basis of precise intelligence, arrested one of the perpetrators of the Mumbai explosions, who had taken shelter in Karachi after the explosions. His interrogation brought out a wealth of details regarding the recruitment, training and arming of the perpetrators by the ISI, the role of the ISI in the selection of the economic targets to be attacked and the role played by Dawood Ibrahim in the entire conspiracy. It also brought out how the ISI had shifted the perpetrators to Bangkok and kept them in a hotel for some time in order to prevent detection of their presence in Karachi by the US authorities. The R&AW also separately learnt from its sources that under pressure from the Dubai authorities to quit Dubai, Dawood Ibrahim had shifted his office and residence to Karachi. He was living there as a Pakistani citizen.

The Government of India brought all this to the notice of the US authorities, but they were still reluctant to hold Pakistan responsible for acts of terrorism taking place in Indian territory and to declare it a State-sponsor of terrorism. Instead, when Benazir made baseless allegations to her friends in the State Department that the R&AW was behind the violence taking place in Sindh, without being able to produce any evidence in support of her allegations, they took her seriously and threatened to act against India as mentioned in the first Chapter. This highlighted once again the extent to which the State Department was prepared to go in order to protect Pakistan.

It was this protection extended to Pakistan by the State Department ever since the days of the anti-Soviet jihad in Afghanistan and it was their practice of closing their eyes to the spawning of jihadi terrorists in Pakistani territory, that led to the emergence of the Pakistan-Afghanistan region as a breeding ground of Al Qaeda, the Taliban and numerous other jihadi terrorist organizations. So long as these

organizations were killing only innocent Indians, the US State
Department took the stand that Pakistan could do no wrong. It was
only after the 9/11 terrorist strikes in the US homeland that their
eyes opened—that too partially.

An over-anxiety to protect Pakistan from the consequences of its
misdeeds still continues to be the defining characteristic of policy-
making in the State Department. I do not wish ill of the US, but I am
convinced in my mind that if there is an act of terrorism in the US
homeland involving the use of weapons of mass destruction (WMD)
one day, it would have originated from the Pakistani territory. Only
then the eyes of the State Department would open fully. That would
be a bit too late—after the horrible deaths of thousands of innocent
civilians in the US.If that is the karma of the US, how can one help
it?

CHAPTER XIX

Looking To The Future

So, I retired on August 31,1994. After 27 years in the intelligence profession.

Nobody knew I existed till then. How many aliases I had!

As I was driven home that evening, I was determined that would be the end of my 27 years of anonymity. I will read. I will write. I will speak. I will let others see the world through the eyes of an ex-intelligence professional.

My first article was carried by the "Hindustan Times" on September 1,1994. It was titled "Human Rights & Human Wrongs."

I wrote initially two articles a week. Then four. It is almost one a day now. I have lost count of the articles I have written since I retired. A Pakistani reader keeps count of them.

Who is going to read all this? I am often asked.

I don't care. Let nobody read. Those who don't read are the losers. Not me.

How can you openly say you were in the R&AW?

Yes. I do. It is better people get to know it from the horse's mouth. Otherwise, if I conceal my R&AW background, people will anyhow guess it. They will start wondering why I am concealing my past identity.

Aren't you worried about your security? You go around abusing the terrorists of various hues?

Why should I be?

Haven't you asked for physical security? Many other senior officers have, even though there is no threat to their security.

I have never felt the need for it.

And so on and so on.

In the first few months after my retirement, there was a plethora of such questions. No more.

A retiring Government servant is allowed to live in his government accommodation in Delhi for four months after his retirement.

Everybody does it. And keeps trying for a post-retirement job.

I didn't. I even refused the jobs, which were offered to me.

I packed and left Delhi for Chennai on September 20,1994.

Why is he in such a hurry to leave?

There were speculations galore.

A journal of Mumbai came out with a story that I had fled to Paris with many Top Secret files of the R&AW and that I was living there with a lovely, sexy French girl with whom I had developed a relationship when I was posted there.

I wrote to the Editor: "How I wish what you wrote was true. I would have loved nothing better than having a lovely, sexy French woman in my bed every night. How sad, it is not true! Am living in a small Tamil Nadu Housing Board flat in Chennai."

He never apologized. Never published a correction.

Did my career as an intelligence officer give me satisfaction?

Of course, it did. Anonymity comes to me naturally. I loved the anonymity of the profession.

Analysis comes to me naturally. Nothing excited me more than the many years I spent as an intelligence analyst.

Quick thinking and the ability to improvise come to me naturally. Without those qualitites, I would not have been able to achieve whatever I did as an intelligence operative.

Risk-taking comes to me naturally. Without it, I would have been nowhere in this profession.

There are many things I learnt in this profession.

Never make a tall claim. Tall claims have a nasty way of coming back home to haunt you.

Don't fight shy of admitting your inadequacies and failures. Admitting them is the best way of correcting your inadequacies and preventing future failures.

Avoid jargonization. Nothing bores people more than jargon.

Be strict with yourself and generous with others. You will be admired and respected.

Give credit to where it is due. Avoid credit-grabbing. Nothing makes you look cheaper than credit-grabbing.

What wonderful superiors I had the privilege of working under. They gave the organization its vision, its élan. They made it stand taller than the tallest bureaucracy of Delhi.

What wonderful junior colleagues I had the pleasure of working with. Without them, the vision of the superiors would have vanished in thin air. They gave it a palpable shape. A reality. They made its élan its motivating force.

The R&AW is a living organization. It never ceases to grow. It never stops learning.

Like all living organizations, it has had the best of times and it has had the worst of times.

It has had its spells of glory, it has had its spells of utter failures.

Is the R&AW the organization, we need or is it the organization, we deserve?

Partly both.

It is like the proverbial curate's egg. Good in parts.

An emerging power such as India, which is aspiring to take its place by 2020 among the leading powers of the world, has to have an external intelligence agency, which has the ability to see, hear, smell and feel far and near.

An agency, which has the ability to operate imaginatively and daringly, analyse lucidly, anticipate unfailingly and manage unanticipated crises effectively.

An agency, which has the courage to tell the truth as it needs to be told without worrying about the consequences.

An agency, whose officers take pride in working for the national interests and resist the temptation to work for the partisan political interests of the party in power or their own personal interests.

An agency, whose officers look upon themselves as missionaries of knowledge—open and secret— and not as cheap careerists interested in the chair they want to occupy and not in the mission the nation has entrusted to them.

Is the R&AW such an organization?

Not yet.

Has it fulfilled the purposes for which its was set up by Indira Gandhi and Kao?

Only partly.

How would I grade the organization one year before its 40th anniversary.

- Strong in its capability for covert action, weak in its capability for intelligence collection, analysis and assessment.

- Strong in low and medium-grade intelligence , weak in high-grade intelligence.

- Strong in TECHINT, weak in HUMINT.

- Strong in collation, weak in analysis.

- Strong in its ability to network with foreign agencies, weak in its networking with other agencies in India.

- Strong in investigation, weak in prevention.

- Strong in crisis management, weak in crisis prevention.

- Obsessive in its secrecy, fearful of transparency.

What needs to be done to remove the deficiencies?

- A recruitment policy, which is able to attract to the organization the best that the open market has to offer.

- Emphasis on merit in promotions and not on seniority.

- The constant weeding-out of the unfit.

- Encouragement of professionalism and discouragement of careerism.

- A readiness to accept external auditing of its management and performance in order to constantly identify and eliminate inadequacies and bad practices.

- Elimination of service parochialism and cultivation of an esprit-de-corps.

The removal of these deficiencies depends largely on the organization itself—but not totally. It also depends on the political leadership and other sections of the bureaucracy. They have to realize that a well-performing intelligence agency is a necessary tool and asset in policy-making. They must help it evolve.

If the task of building-up a well-performing intelligence agency does not get the attention it deserves, we will have an agency that we deserve and not the agency that we need as one of the two rising powers of Asia.

The Indian intelligence community is steadily expanding—like the communities of other countries.

It had two agencies in 1947—the IB and the military intelligence. Today, it has eight— the IB, the Directorate-General of Security, the R&AW, the Directorate-General of Military Intelligence, the Directorate-General of Air Intelligence, the Directorate-General of Naval Intelligence, the Defence Intelligence Agency and the National Technical Research Organization.

Their co-ordination is a full-time job. It is done presently by the National Security Adviser, in addition to his other responsibilities relating to strategic policy-making. It is time to think in terms of a National Intelligence Adviser, directly answerable to the Prime Minister.

The intelligence agencies and the security forces are the two main swords of the nation. If they are not properly maintained, they will get rusted. The good maintenance of the security forces receives adequate attention.The good maintenance of the intelligence agencies needs equal attention. We can neglect it only at our own peril.

INDEX